Contemporary Hospitality and Tourism Management Issues in China and India

Contemporary Hospitality and Tourism Management Issues in China and India

Today's Dragons and Tigers

Stephen Ball
Susan Horner
Kevin Nield

AMSTERDAM • BOSTON • HEIDELBERG • LONDON • NEW YORK • OXFORD
PARIS • SAN DIEGO • SAN FRANCISCO • SINGAPORE • SYDNEY • TOKYO
Butterworth-Heinemann is an imprint of Elsevier

ELSEVIER

Butterworth-Heinemann is an imprint of Elsevier
Linacre House, Jordan Hill, Oxford OX2 8DP, UK
30 Corporate Drive, Suite 400, Burlington, MA 01803, USA

First edition 2007

British Library Cataloguing in Publication Data
A catalogue record for this book is available from the British Library

Library of Congress Cataloging-in-Publication Data
A catalog record for this book is available from the Library of Congress

ISBN 978-0-7506-6856-9

For information on all Butterworth-Heinemann publications
visit our web site at books.elsevier.com

Printed and bound in Great Britain

07 08 09 10   10 9 8 7 6 5 4 3 2 1

Working together to grow
libraries in developing countries

www.elsevier.com | www.bookaid.org | www.sabre.org

ELSEVIER   BOOK AID
            International   Sabre Foundation

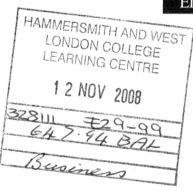

Author Biographies

Professor Stephen Ball EdD, MPhil, BSc (Hons), FIH, FHEA

Stephen Ball is Head of the Centre for International Hospitality Management Research (CIHMR) and Professor of Hospitality Management at Sheffield Hallam University. He is Chair of the Council for Hospitality Management Education (CHME), the subject body for hospitality management in the UK, and Visiting Fellow at two other UK universities.

Having graduated with a BSc in Geography from Manchester University Stephen went on to successfully complete an Advanced Postgraduate Diploma in Hotel and Catering Administration at Manchester Metropolitan University. He had previously worked in the brewing industry, retailing and pub retailing industries and the hotel industry. He has also worked in National Health Service Catering Management in two London hospitals.

He commenced lecturing in higher education in 1982. He has a wealth of experience in university school quality management, subject group leadership, course leadership, external examining, curriculum design and hospitality teaching from HND to postgraduate level both in the UK and abroad. In his career in higher education he has supervised and examined research students, authored or edited five books (including *Hospitality Operations: a Systems Approach, Food Supply Chain Management: Issues for the Hospitality and Retail Sectors and Fast Food Operations and Their Management*), written numerous articles, book chapters, reports and keynote presentations. He co-researched three editions of the British Hospitality Association's annual *British Hospitality: Trends and Statistics* and co-authored 'A Review of Hospitality Management Education in the UK' for CHME.

He has presented conference papers on many topics related to hospitality management, ranging from the use of humour in hospitality to branding in hotels, in the UK, Canada, Croatia, Iceland, Finland and Palestine and has taught in Hong Kong and Singapore on Hospitality and Tourism masters and undergraduate distance learning courses. He has also undertaken academic work in many other countries including China, New Zealand, Switzerland, Dubai, Germany and USA. He has produced distance learning materials for worldwide use and has acted as consultant, and designed and delivered executive development programmes, for a number of UK and international hospitality organisations including Holiday Inns, Bass Taverns and Sodexho. He has an MPhil on productivity management in fast-food chains which focussed upon a case study of Wimpy International. His Doctorate was based on research leadership in Universities. He has organised conferences and seminars including the 12th annual CHME research conference for which he also edited the proceedings.

He is a member of the Editorial Board for the journal *Tourism & Hospitality Research* and of the Editorial Advisory Board for the *Journal of Hospitality, Leisure, Sport and Tourism Education* (JoHLSTE). His current teaching, research and writing interests relate to hospitality and tourism business development and entrepreneurship, productivity and operations management, leadership and higher education.

Dr. Susan Horner EdD, MBA, BSc, FIH

Susan Horner is the Postgraduate Programme Leader for Hospitality and Tourism and International Co-ordinator with a special focus on India at Sheffield Hallam University. Her academic specialisms are Consumer Behaviour and Marketing in the Hospitality and Tourism sectors. She teaches marketing and marketing communications to undergraduate and postgraduate students and supervises doctoral level students both at the University and in Hong Kong.

Before entering academia Susan worked for Unilever both in the UK and abroad developing and marketing food and catering products across the world. Since joining the University Susan has completed a number of major consultancy projects in a wide variety of hospitality and tourism organisations in areas such as marketing, staff recruitment, development and training, and catering provision.

As part of her work Susan has travelled widely in both India and China. At present she spends a great deal of time travelling to India on behalf of the University. She has developed courses in India in collaboration with Indian Universities and carried out joint research and publication with academics in India. She has advised students, colleges and Universities in India on educational and employment issues and has worked extensively with a wide range of agencies. She has also given public lectures in both India and China on the hospitality and tourism industries.

Susan is an active researcher and has published articles, papers, books and conference presentations. She has published a wide range of books which have been translated into Chinese including *Consumer Behaviour in Tourism, Business Travel and Tourism, International Cases in Tourism Management and Leisure Marketing.*

Susan is also a visiting Professor at the University of Girona and Escola Universitaria De Turisme in Barcelona, Spain. She is a founder member of the Centre for International Hospitality Management Research at Sheffield Hallam University.

Dr. Kevin Nield EdD, MSc, BA, PGCE, FHEA, FIH

Kevin Nield is a Teaching Fellow and Faculty Learning, Teaching and Assessment Co-ordinator in the Faculty of Organisation and Management, Sheffield Hallam University. His teaching specialisms are International Hospitality Management and Quality Management.

Before entering academia Kevin had worked in a variety of positions and for a number of organisations within the retail and hospitality industries. Since joining the University he has carried out a number of consultancies for organisations within the hospitality and tourism industries on matters as diverse as tourism satisfaction on the Black Sea, staff development and catering provision.

As part of his work Kevin has travelled widely in both India and China. At present he spends more time in China, travelling to China at least four times a year. He has been responsible for setting up and providing degree courses for hospitality and tourism students in Hong Kong. Within China he has advised students, colleges and universities on educational and employment opportunities in the UK and China. He has given public lectures in China on the hospitality and tourism industries and employability.

Kevin is an active researcher and has published in excess of over 70 articles, papers, books and conference presentations. His main research interests are the Chinese learner (the subject of his doctoral thesis) and customer and tourist satisfaction. He is currently working with the Rhodes Hotel Association on a longitudinal study of tourism satisfaction on the island and is a co-director of two FDTL-funded projects concerned with graduate employability and staff support.

Kevin is the director of the Centre for Pedagogic Innovation and Research and is founder member of the Centre for International Hospitality Management Research.

Contents

Contents

Foreword

In 1979, at the age of 32, I dragged my family to Hong Kong in what turned out to be the best career move I ever made. Back in those days, friends and colleagues begged us not to go; some out of concern, but many because they knew then what I know now. "You'll never come back", they said. And they were right. Once you let Asia get under your skin, it is almost impossible to turn your back on the unlimited possibility and excitement that the region represents. It was like that then, and it will become incrementally more so in the years to come.

In many respects, India and China, home to half of the world's population, are the future. In these pages, you will begin to comprehend the dramatic forces that are at work in these two great nations; forces that are generated within a set of rich and intriguing cultural environments – the word "environments" is used quite deliberately because each country is host to a great diversity of micro-cultures.

India, where I spent the past six years of my career, boasts 415 living languages, although a mere 22 of them are officially recognised by the Indian government. The cultures of India are layered with religions, coloured by regional traditions and seasoned by rural and urban contrasts. Spend a few days trekking the Himalayan foothills around Shimla; then ride a camel through the deserts and palaces of Rajasthan. Fly south to sail the coastal backwaters of Kerala; then go shopping in the riotous markets of Kolkata. Visit state after state, and you will feel as if you are actually visiting different countries. There are many Indias, and yet there is only one India. No matter how often you eat from your local takeaway, nothing prepares you for the true tastes of India and its diverse cuisines. It is the same in China. No one who experiences China will ever confuse the subtlety of Cantonese food with the robustness of Pekingese; the richness of the food from Shanghai with the spiciness of Sichuan. Although everyone speaks one common language, Putonghua, every province has its own set of languages and dialects.

In China and India, powerful economic forces collide with these cultural elements to impact the social and demographic fabric of every state, region or province, challenging its people to produce their own unique solutions.

Into this rich and heady mix comes the traveller, with a myriad of purposes and needs, to move about the country, to stay in distinctive accommodation and to enjoy an array of products and services. What began as a trickle has grown into a flood, as tides of domestic travellers create new currents. As the forces of demand and supply explode, unlimited opportunities present themselves to young and not-so-young professionals who seek excitement, growth and texture in their lives and careers.

This book is therefore timely. I am not aware of another text that explores the economic, cultural, social and demographic dimensions of two great nations in such an accessible style. In its pages, you will be inspired by the case studies and the optimism, potential and promise that they illustrate. One such story is that of Mohan Singh Oberoi, a simple Punjabi who rose from being a humble clerk to become the founder of a dynasty. Along the way, he bought the hotel where he first worked, and employed the man who originally hired him as General Manager of the second Oberoi Hotel. His son, PRS Oberoi has made his family's name synonymous with quality and luxury. I feel fortunate to have been associated with the Oberoi Group since 2000 – another life-changing experience. I was entrusted with the Oberoi Centre of Learning and Development, a small powerhouse that grooms the young managers who, on a daily basis, deliver the highest standards of hotel service and a commitment to their guests, greater than any I have witnessed before or since. The stories that you will read here teach us that we should never again doubt that the Indians, or the Chinese, can run world-class hotels and compete with any other hotel company you could name.

Once you have dipped into this book, you are sure to want to know more. The snapshots of success presented in these pages can only hint at the scale of opportunity that lies in the twin powerhouses of China and India. You will be inspired to dig deeper, to learn more, and to experience these countries and these companies first hand – perhaps as a traveller, but perhaps, like me, as a great career move. Not for one second have I ever regretted that decision of almost three decades ago when some inner voice said, "Go East, young man".

As a postscript, let me share a personal connection to the title of this book, "Today's Dragons and Tigers". Like all expats, soon after arriving in Hong Kong, someone gave me a Chinese name to put on my business card. The three characters, when spoken in Cantonese, were meant to sound a little like my surname, Longworth. I was ridiculously proud to be known as *"Lung Wai Foo"*. When literally translated, *"Lung"* means Dragon, and now represents the first part of my love affair with Asia – China. *"Wai Foo"* means Powerful Tiger, representing the most recent stage of my Asian Odyssey – India. So, in these pages, please enjoy the authors' insights into "Today's Dragons and Tigers" and seek your own connections. If it is not too Zen to say so, may you become one with them.

David Longworth
Education and Training Consultant
formerly Vice President,
The Oberoi Centre of Learning and Development,
Delhi

Acknowledgements

We have endeavoured to write this book in a style that is easy to read and valuable for all readers in both the academic and commercial worlds in which we all operate. The research and experiences that underpin this book are far too numerous to mention and would take a lifetime and another book to explore, so here we can only mention and thank some of the key people and organisations that have been so influential in our professional and personal lives.

We would first of all like to thank all of our students, both past and present, who have challenged us constantly and given us the insiders' view to the Chinese and Indian market. We hope that this book gives all future students a deeper insight into their sector.

We would like to thank Sheffield Hallam University for giving us the opportunity to visit both China and India over the last decade to research, teach and build links. It is these visits that inspired us to write the book. We hope that this book will now add value to the international agenda of the University.

We would like to express our thanks to our many colleagues all over the world who have helped in so many ways with the writing of this book. Of particular note here are listed below:

Mr David Longworth previously of the Oberoi Group of India who helped us to gain an important insight into the hospitality industry in India.

Mr Leslie Bailey of McDonald's Hong Kong who progressed from being an excellent student to a senior manager in the industry.

Dalip K. Singha and Major General B.N. Kaul of the Welcomgroup Graduate School of Hotel Administration MAHE Manipal, India who both inspired joint developments in India.

N.G. Vinod, Head of International Development and Head of Tourism and Travel Christ College Bangalore, who inspired our joint research, publications and course collaboration.

Professor Jagmohan Negi Professor and Director of Hospitality and Tourism Amity University New Delhi India who inspired many ideas.

And finally it is important for us to express our thanks and gratitude to all the people who have helped us in our personal lives whose support and advice has helped us to achieve great things.

For now we wish you all happy reading and hope the book inspires you to visit China and India again and again.

Stephen Ball, Susan Horner and Kevin Nield

Organisation of the Book

The book is organised into three distinct parts.

Part One   Chinese and Indian Contexts

Part One is intended to acquaint the reader with the Chinese and Indian contexts. To achieve this Chapter 1 deals with the economic environments of China and India. It gives an analysis of the two countries' economies while considering economic policy and constraints upon economic growth. Chapter 2 considers cultural theory and the cultural backgrounds and immense cultural diversity of China and India. Chapter 3 examines the social and demographic perspectives of China and India. To achieve this it examines population structures, policy, language and government.

Chapter 4 is the final chapter in Part One. It analyses, generally, the Chinese and Indian contexts by surveying tourism trends in the two countries. The chapter gives an array of statistics and underpins this with an analysis of tourism policy and barriers to tourism.

Part Two   Hospitality and Tourism Development and Management in China (including Hong Kong and Macau)

Part Two is devoted to China. It gives an analysis and overview of hospitality and tourism development. It achieves these by considering the component parts of hospitality and tourism separately. Chapter 5 deals with hotels and resorts; it provides an historical overview of hotel and resort development in China and uses this as a base to review and evaluate present and future trends in the sector.

Chapter 6 appraises the restaurants, fast food and contract food-service sector in China. It discusses issues and trends and chronicles the development of Chinese cuisine. Chapter 7 concentrates upon tourism business in China. It further develops issues that were discussed in Chapter 4.

Part Three Hospitality and Tourism Development and Management in India

Part Three is essentially a mirror image of Part Two. It is solely devoted to hospitality and tourism development in India. Chapter 8 deals with hotels and resorts; it provides an historical overview of hotel and resort development in India and uses this to review and evaluate present and future trends in the sector.

Chapter 9 investigates the restaurants, fast food and contract food-service sector in India. It focuses upon issues and trends in Indian cuisine. Chapter 10 develops issues that were discussed in Chapter 4 while concentrating upon the tourism business in India.

A unique pedagogic feature of this book is that it uses case studies to illustrate or extend some of the points in the text. There is a short illustrative mini case study in each of the Chapters 5 to 10. While at the end of the book there is a series of case studies that have discussion questions/tasks attached; these generally longer case studies may be used for individual reflection and/or as the basis for classroom debate.

Introduction

The title of this book *Contemporary Hospitality and Tourism Management Issues in China and India: Today's Dragons and Tigers* was settled on after much deliberation. The tiger is a symbol of India while the dragon is a symbol of China. The Bengal tiger is the national animal of India and it exudes power and beauty while the dragon is often used in the West, but less so in China itself, as a national emblem of China. The Chinese dragon symbolises power and excellence and has long been a symbol of auspicious power in Chinese folklore and art. The Chinese use the term "Descendants of the Dragon" as a sign of ethnic identity and the dragon still commands much respect in Chinese culture.

These historical symbols of China and India were chosen not for their antiquity but because they are appropriate reflections of modern day China and India. These images neatly encapsulate the strengths and purposefulness of the two most populous nations that are rapidly developing into major world economic powers. They are also used here as metaphors representing the state of the contemporary hospitality and tourism industries of China and India.

This book is aimed at second and third-year undergraduate university students and postgraduate students who are registered within the fields of hospitality management, hospitality studies, tourism management and tourism studies and other related courses. It will be of particular value to those students studying international versions of courses in these fields.

In addition, it will be attractive to the wider management and business fields concerned with business development and management in China and India at both undergraduate and postgraduate levels. A rapidly increasing number of students are now entering UK universities from the region. They will find this book of particular interest. It would also be of interest and value to hospitality and tourism professionals who are working in China and India or those who intend to move into these markets.

This book is timely; the importance of this field of study cannot be overemphasised. Tourism is now the world's number one industry. As an indication of its size the World Tourism Organisation (WTO) estimates that tourism accounts for 6% of all exports worldwide or 30% of all invisible exports. International arrivals by the year 2020 are expected to be in the region of a staggering 1.6 billion. China and India are both benefiting from and playing their parts in this tourism revolution. Both are experiencing tremendous growth in their economies and at the same time are being opened up to tourism exports and imports. By 2020, it is estimated that China will be the world's number one tourist destination. India, once the "sleeping giant" of tourism is now starting to awaken.

As China and India take their places on the world stage of tourism, changes in their offering to cope with this increased demand are necessary. Not the least of this are the hospitality facilities that exist within the countries. Significant investment both nationally and internationally has poured in to improving hotel stock, food and beverage facilities and transport infrastructures. The tourism and hospitality industries in these countries are becoming increasingly important for existing and developing operators and offer employment opportunities for managers and other employees.

Further the world's attention is now turning to China and India due to their global and economic significance. Despite this attention, the book fills a void in that relatively little has been written about tourism and hospitality in China and almost nothing concerns India.

In summary, the aims of the book are threefold. First, it attempts to provide an authoritative, comprehensive and up-to-date source of knowledge about the fast growing hospitality and tourism industry in China and India and about issues confronting hospitality and tourism management within these countries. Second, it will contribute to a greater understanding of what constitutes, what takes place and what could occur within the industry in these countries. Finally, it will identify the main environmental factors that have, are and will continue to shape development of these industries.

The authors are all founder members of the Centre for International Hospitality Management Research (CIHMR), which is located in the Faculty of Organisation and Management at Sheffield Hallam University. It is one of only a handful of research centres in the UK that is working in the hospitality area and it is exclusively dedicated to the furtherance of hospitality management and the hospitality industry both nationally and worldwide.

The mission is to continue to develop as a leading and reputed international research and business development centre. It is at the forefront of hospitality management research and has undertaken commissioned research from many organisations including government departments, national institutions and multinational companies. Further details of the centre and its work can be found on:
http://www.shu. ac.uk/research/cihmr/

Part One

Chinese and Indian Contexts

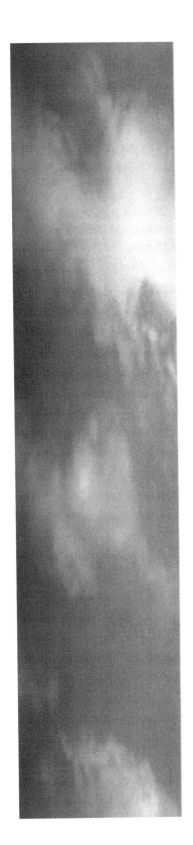

CHAPTER 1

The economies of China and India

> **Chapter objectives**
>
> When you have read this chapter, you will be able to
>
> 1 Analyse the structure of the economies of China and India.
> 2 Delineate key economic indicators of China and India.
> 3 Identify barriers to growth in the Chinese and Indian economies.
> 4 Explain economic issues for China and India.
> 5 Outline economic policy in China and India.

Introduction

The purpose of this chapter is to introduce the reader to the economies of China and India. The chapter is organised in two parts – China and India. All of the issues will be dealt with in the same order in each part.

China

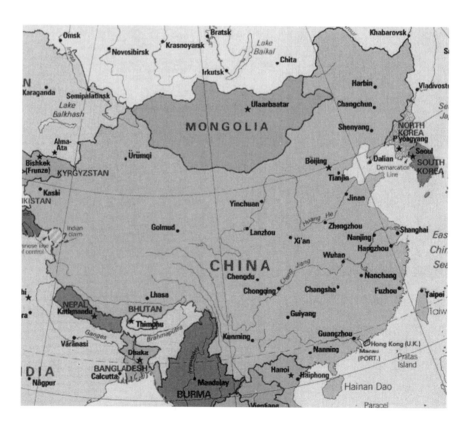

Map 1.1
China

The structure of the Chinese economy

Table 1.1 shows the structure of the Chinese economy. The main agricultural products are rice, wheat, potatoes, corn, tea and cotton. The main manufacturing industries are iron, steel, armaments, petroleum and consumer products, including food processing, toys and electronics. In the service sector, tourism, both direct and indirect, is thought to account for over 12% of Gross Domestic Product (GDP).

The actual labour force was estimated at 760.8 million in 2003 (CIA World Factbook, 2006). Of this workforce, almost half of the labour force is engaged in the primary sector, yet this sector produces only one-eighth of the country's GDP. This points to inefficiencies in agriculture but may also indicate the high proportion of the population that is tied to rural communities. Conversely, the secondary sector produces over one-half of the country's GDP with less than one-quarter of the workforce.

Unsurprisingly, for an emerging economy, the service sector is quite small (33.3%) when compared with economies such as the United Kingdom and Germany. However, this is large when compared with other Asian economies and, due to the ageing population of China, is ripe with opportunities as consumption patterns change.

Two important items that impact upon the performance of the Chinese economy stem from this analysis. First, the differences in productivity within the sectors may account for the large disparity of incomes that is found in China between rural and urban populations. Second, the unemployment rate in urban areas is said to be 9.8%, many of these workers have become unemployed as a consequence of the market reforms. This rate of unemployment, coupled with better wages and living standards in the cities, is causing population migration from rural to urban locations (Garner, 2005). Present statistics estimate that 39.1% of the Chinese population reside in urban locations. This is expected to grow to 49.8% by 2014 and 68.2% by 2024 (Garner, 2005).

Table 1.1 The structure of the Chinese economy – 2003

Sector	Contribution to gross domestic product (%)	Labour force employed (%)
Primary (agricultural and extractive industries)	13.8	49
Secondary (manufacture and construction)	52.9	22
Services (banking, insurance, finance and tourism)	33.3	29
Total	100.0	100

Source: Extrapolated from CIA *World Factbook* (2006).

Garner (2005) believes that this level of migration is likely to be to the large urban conurbations such as Beijing and Shanghai but will move to other areas in the future. There is also a belief that as prosperity in the East of China increases and with it the wages, industry and commerce may relocate from the East to the West.

Key economic indicators • • •

The key indicators in Table 1.2 demonstrate the remarkable growth of the Chinese economy since reforms were introduced. The estimated Chinese GDP growth rate is just under 10%. Some commentators believe that this growth rate has actually been exceeded, and is probably already in excess of, 10% (Cooper, 2006). To reinforce this, the Chinese premier has set a target of 10% growth per annum from 2006 to 2011. Growth at these rates means that if these levels of growth are sustained then the Chinese economy will double in size every seven to eight years.

The expansion of the economy by 9.9% in 2005 made the Chinese economy the fifth largest in the world overtaking that of France. It is estimated that the Chinese economy will overtake Great Britain and Germany by 2008 (Macartney, 2006a). This growth of the economy has been based on investment, consumption and trade. Much of the investment in China has come from overseas. China benefits massively from this and is the major and favoured destination for foreign direct investment.

The official Chinese unemployment rate is 9%, which is high. This high level of unemployment has led to some unrest among the population who believed that they were better off under communism. The CIA (2006) believes that this average employment rate may actually be hiding or obscuring even higher unemployment rates of up to 20% in some rural areas.

The export and import figures indicate that there is a large surplus on the balance of payments. Some observers believe that much of this surplus is thought to be due to exchange rates that are artificially low and to protectionism, thus giving China an advantage in the export markets (see section on China and the World Trade Organisation). This and the rate of growth of the economy have led to calls for a slowdown as the economy could be overheating.

Table 1.2 China key economic indicators – 2005

GDP growth rate	9.9%
Unemployment rate	9%
Exports	$752.2 billion
Imports	$631.8 billion

Source: Extrapolated from CIA *World Factbook* (2006).

However, the economy has been likened to a supertanker that cannot slow down even though there are policies aimed at doing so (Macartney, 2006b).

Economic policy ● ● ●

The main reforms to the Chinese economy were enacted in 1978 when the economy was effectively "opened up" after decades of virtual closure to the outside world. The main architect of the reforms was Diao Xaopeng who intended to move the economy from the communist, centrally planned economy to a more market-oriented system. The main change was to take economic influence away from the state enterprises to non-state organisations.

The main reforms were to

1 Allow a variety of private enterprises in services and light manufacturing.
2 Open up the economy to foreign trade and particularly foreign investment.
3 Move away from central bureaucracy and give more authority to local officials and managers.
4 Move agriculture back from central collectivism to family and village control.

The direct consequence of these and subsequent policies has been to quadruple the size of the Chinese economy in 30 years.

China and the World Trade Organisation ● ● ●

In recent years, the most important step forward in the Chinese economy has been China joining the World Trade Organisation (WTO) on 17 September 2001. After what were described as difficult negotiation conditions for joining were enforced. These conditions were that China was to commit to economic, legal and administrative reforms, to respect international trade regulations and to restructure its administrative system.

Joining the WTO opens the Chinese markets up to international trade and competition. The pessimistic consequence of this could be that Chinese business will lose out to its more efficient competitors. However, the optimistic view is that the lowering of trade barriers coupled with low wages and subsidies will bring in even more foreign investment and that WTO membership will make Chinese privately owned companies more competitive.

Barriers to growth and possible problems in the Chinese economy ● ● ●

The phenomenal growth rate of the Chinese economy makes it appear that the future is extremely rosy. The move to a more market economy coupled with the growth of GDP is not without its problems. The main problems in the Chinese economy are as follows:

1 It is estimated that as a consequence of the move to a market economy, millions of people have lost their jobs with the state enterprises. As many as 100–150 million people exist in low-paid jobs between villages and cities. The population of Shanghai is estimated at 12–13 millions; it is possible that the population may be 4 million higher if the number of itinerant workers is taken into account (CIA, 2006).

2 The problem that China has is sustaining job growth to employ the "laid-off" workers. It is estimated that rural unemployment is 9.7%. These figures also point to a disparity of incomes between urban and rural populations. Incomes in urban areas are estimated to be £550 per annum while incomes in rural areas are less than £200. This has led some to wish for the return of Mao when everyone was equally poor (Macartney, 2006b). China's construction bank has been criticised for making huge profits for its foreign partners.

3 A consequence of the one-child policy is that China has one of the most rapidly ageing populations in the world. This may lead to issues regarding welfare and social benefits (CIA, 2006).

4 Reducing corruption and having corruption-free, mature political systems will be necessary for long-term future success (Smith, 2006).

5 In 1990, China used 3.5% of the world's crude oil; this figure is now 9% and the demand for crude oil is growing at 8.8%. The consequences of this are that this level of use is not sustainable and has enormous environmental impacts (Smith, 2006).

6 There are massive disparities in incomes in China. Incomes per capita in cities such as Shanghai and Guangzhou are much higher than those in the provinces. Righter (2006) says that an aperitif in Beijing may be more than an agricultural worker's monthly wage. This, together with no or very poor pensions and social security, education and health services that are beyond many people's means, may be costing China close to 8% of its GDP and is causing civil unrest at the same time (Righter, 2006).

7 It is believed that the yuan (Chinese currency) has been kept artificially low. As the exchange rate of the yuan rises, this could damage export growth as Chinese exports will naturally become more expensive (Macartney, 2006b).

8 The reduction of import duties will put pressure on Chinese companies and agriculture, as the imports would become cheaper. This would lead to goods and food being imported at the expense of Chinese products (Macartney, 2006b).

9 China's growth is coming with heavy environmental costs. These environmental costs include water shortages, deforestation, soil erosion, desertification and pollution (Edmonds, 2003). It is estimated that 15 of the world's 20 most polluted cities are Chinese (Jacobs, 2006). Many of China's waterways are actually poisonous; the seven major river systems are in the two lowest grades of water quality (Jacobs, 2006; Edmonds, 2003). Edmonds (2003) says that many small rivers in China are anoxic; they are incapable of sustaining aquatic life. This already high level of pollution is exacerbated by household and industrial waste.

India

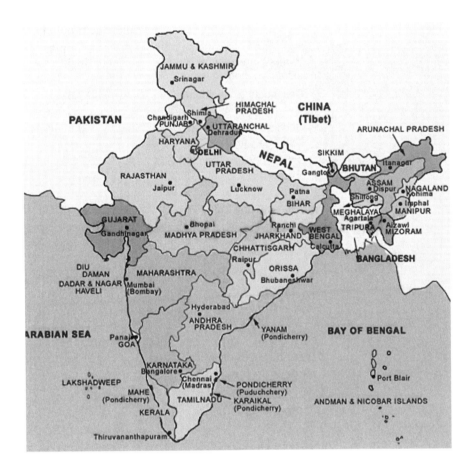

Map 1.2
India

The structure of the Indian economy

India's economy is diverse ranging from handicrafts to high-tech IT industries in the service sector. Table 1.3 gives the structure of the Indian economy. The main agricultural products are rice, wheat, oilseed, jute, tea and cotton. The main manufacturing industries are textiles, chemicals, steel, food processing, cement and software.

The actual labour force is estimated at 496.4 million in 2003 (CIA, 2006). As with China, a huge amount of the workforce (three-fifths) is engaged in the primary sector, yet this produces less than one-fifth of the country's GDP. Similar to China, this may indicate inefficiencies in agriculture but may also indicate the number of the population that are tied to rural communities. Indeed, India has often been referred to as two countries – urban India and rural India.

Table 1.3   The structure of the Indian economy – 2003

Sector	Contribution to gross domestic product (%)	Labour force employed (%)
Primary (agricultural and extractive industries)	18.6	60
Secondary (manufacture and construction)	27.6	17
Services (banking, insurance, finance and tourism)	53.8	23
Total	100.0	100

Source: Extrapolated from CIA *World Factbook* (2006).

As shown by Table 1.3, services are the source of economic growth accounting for over half of GDP while employing less than a quarter of the workforce. Much of this growth in the service sector has derived from highly skilled and educated personnel using their English language skills (CIA, 2006). For an emerging economy, the service sector is unusually large, but this is a reflection of service industry employment that has migrated to India largely from the West over the past decade.

Key economic indicators • • •

Table 1.4 shows the key economic indicators for India. India has been called the "world's fastest growing democracy" (Smith, 2006). Its GDP growth rate has increased from 2.4% to 7.8% over the past 15 years. Reasons for this recent increase have been first, the better performance of agriculture, which has been bolstered by the monsoons (Euromonitor, 2006). Second, global companies have relocated to India to take advantage of lower wages and the English language skills of Indian employees. Third,

Table 1.4   India key economic indicators – 2005

GDP growth rate	7.6%
Unemployment rate	8.9%
Exports	$76.23 billion
Imports	$113.1 billion

Source: Extrapolated from CIA *World Factbook* (2006).

changes in economic policy have allowed, with limited success, foreign investment.

It will be noted that the growth is high at 7.8% but is not as high as China's. One of the reasons posited for this is that India has not had the same level of foreign direct investment as China. As a comparison, foreign direct investment in China in 2003 was $53 billion, and in India it was $4.2 billion, a figure that is less than one-tenth of that of China (Farrell et al., 2005). Due to its younger population, the economy of India will begin to grow faster than that of China by the middle of the twenty-first century (Elliott, 2006).

Notwithstanding all of this, the possible transformation of the Indian economy has come 10 years after that of China. Attention is now being focused upon India's economy and labour market. One reason for this is the migration of a high number of jobs that have been taken from the West in the knowledge-based industries (Farrell et al., 2005).

From Table 1.4, it is noticeable that other key indicators in the Indian economy are not as promising as the growth of its GDP. Similar to that of China, the Indian unemployment rate is high at just under 9%. This could be a possible source of unrest in the future. It may also be another indication of the rural Indian and the urban Indian nations.

The import and export figures show that there is a deficit on the balance of payments; that is, India is spending more on imports than it earns from exports to the tune of over $36 million. Deficits at this level are unsustainable, and the expansion of the economy may be the cure for this. If not, measures will need to be put in place to help prevent these deficits.

Economic policy ● ● ●

India has seen a period of gradual economic liberalisation that began in the 1980s. Economic policy has been liberalised in two main ways; these have been a relaxation of the rules regarding private enterprises and the privatisation of state-owned enterprises (Prasad, 2004). Both of these reforms were aimed at attracting foreign direct investment. Although these reforms have been implemented, it should be noted that these reforms are not total.

Rules regarding private enterprises have been relaxed to allow foreign investment and some foreign ownership of Indian companies. The capital markets have been opened up to foreign investors. It is believed that these reforms have not gone far enough in helping India's competitiveness and must go further if the required amount of foreign investment is to be achieved.

Although India is a democracy, it has a legacy of state-owned enterprises that were generally regarded as inefficient and has lacked investment. Some of these enterprises have been opened up to privatisation with some success, for example, Delhi and Mumbai airports have been privatised and have attracted subsequent investment. This deregulation was conceived in the 1990s to allow for foreign direct investment.

Barriers to growth and possible problems in the Indian economy • • •

Although the Indian economy appears to be developing well and its growth rate is promising, several possible barriers to its future growth have been identified. These are given as follows:

1 The phenomenal growth rate of the Indian economy has come at costs that are both economic and environmental. As India's economy grows so does its demand for crude oil. India now requires 4.5% of total crude oil, and this is rising. The question here is where is this oil going to come from?

2 The growth in the economy and the increase in the wealth of its population will lead to an increased demand for cars. At present, the demand for cars is eight cars to each 1,000 of population, and by 2050, this demand is expected to rise to 382 cars to each 1,000. This increase in vehicles may lead to a devastating increase in greenhouse gas with a subsequent impact on an already polluted environment (Elliott, 2006).

3 If the GDP of 7.8% is to be achieved and sustained, it is argued that there must be reform in the financial sector. The financial system in India is regarded as inefficient as it allocates the majority of its capital to parts of the economy that are unproductive. It is believed that if these funds are redirected, then $8 billion may be allocated to other more productive sectors and then the growth rate will be increased by an additional 2.5% (Economist, 2006a).

4 The transport infrastructure of the Indian economy is believed to be seriously weak. All of it is in need of attention (Economist, 2006b). The road network in India is 65,000 km long and only 9% of this has two lanes. Some effort has been made in what is termed the "golden quadrilateral" of Chennai, Mumbai, Delhi and Kolkata. Notwithstanding this, many Indian villages remain without all-weather roads (Economist, 2006b). Journeys in Indian cities are slow and congested. Major roads are reduced to a crawl by slow-moving lorries. In large, Indian cities' lorries are restricted in daytime hours.

5 There has been a huge increase in domestic air travel, but airports have not improved to meet the increased demand. As a result, airports are operating beyond design limits, and there have been stories of aeroplanes queuing in the skies to land (Economist, 2006b). A similar story emerges with the railways where there has been little investment and a fall in freight due to the high costs.

6 Spending on the infrastructure has reached a 33-year low at 3.5% of GDP. China, which has similar problems, is actually spending 10.6% of its GDP on its infrastructure. Morgan Stanley estimates that investment must reach $100 billion per annum if the growth targets are to be met (Economist, 2006b).

7 The state of the infrastructure in cities has made business difficult to conduct. These difficulties include frequent power cuts, congested roads, crowded hotels and overfull airports. The generating capabilities of the Indian grid are inadequate. At its peak, demand for electricity is

11% more than supply! This figure is compounded when it is realised that 56% of Indian homes do not have electricity (*Economist*, 2006b).

8 India receives a relatively small proportion of foreign direct investment, especially when compared to China. The lack of this investment could hold back its growth plans. An example of how this may slow the economy is that the infrastructure of Indian economy is said to require $150 billion investment alone.

9 As with China, corruption is believed to be widespread. Reducing corruption and having corruption-free, mature political systems will be necessary for long-term future success (Smith, 2006).

10 Much of India's growth could be attained through domestic consumption. However, its economy is primarily agricultural with two-thirds living in rural areas and over half employed in agriculture. There is talk of an Indian middle class that may number from 150 to 300 million. This middle class may need to emerge to fuel consumer spending (*Economist*, 2006c).

Summary

India and China are both experiencing phenomenal rates of economic growth. It is expected that China will be the world's largest economy by the middle of this century and that India will eventually overtake China. India and China suffer from the same problems with regard to large rural populations, pollution, unemployment and income disparities.

Both countries have undertaken economic reform. China was a command economy that has been effectively "opened up" after being closed to the rest of the world and has benefited from these reforms. India describes itself as the world's largest democracy; it has been slow to open up its economy but is now beginning to attract investment.

Both countries have set ambitious targets for economic growth, but both have problems within their infrastructures and systems that must be resolved if they are to meet these targets. The "opening up' of China has led to it being highly successful in attracting foreign direct investment. It has used this to power its economic growth. India has been markedly less successful in this regard; it has made some attempts to open up its economy but may need to loosen further its rules on foreign ownership in order to attract the foreign investment that it requires (Euromonitor, 2006). It does have advantages over China with regard to the education level of its population and the standard of English.

If both countries are to sustain their current rates of growth, it is imperative that they tackle the enormous economic and environmental problems that beset both of them.

References

CIA (2006). *The World Factbook*. http://www.odci.gov/cia/publications/factbook/index.html.

Cooper, K. (2006). Sparkling Growth Fires Up Chinese Shares, *Sunday Times*, 23 April.

Economist (2006a). Safe and Sorry: To Achieve Faster Growth, India Needs Financial Sector Reform, *The Economist*, 6 June .

Economist (2006b). Building Blocks: India's Creaking Infrastructure Still Needs a lot of Investment, *The Economist*, 6 June .

Economist (2006c). From Top to Bottom: There is a Huge Consumer Market Out There Somewhere, *The Economist*, 6 June.

Edmonds, R.L. (2003). China's environmental problems. In Garner, R.E. (ed.), *Understanding Contemporary China*. London, Lynne Rienner Publishers Incorporated, pp. 255–280.

Elliott, L. (2006). World Gears Up for Tension as Emerging Nations Threaten to Put G7 Countries in the Back Seat, *Guardian*, 6 March .

Farrell, D., Kharma, T., Sinha, J. and Wietzel, J.R. (2005). China and India: The Race to Growth, *The McKinsey Quarterly*, 29 September.

Garner, J. (2005). *The Rise of the Chinese Consumer*. Chichester, John Wiley.

Jacobs, B. (2006). Shanghai's on the Run, *Metro*, 4 April.

Macartney, J. (2006a). China's Economy in Fifth Spot and Closing, *Times*, 26 January.

Macartney, J. (2006b). China's Secret Row Bursts into the Open, *Times*, 6 June.

Prasad, R.M. (2004). On economic liberalisation in India. In Prasad, S.B. and Ghaun, P.N. (eds), *Global Firms and Emerging Markets in an Age of Uncertainty*. Westport, CT, Praeger .

Righter, R. (2006). Chinese "Contradictions" Urge Caution, *Times*, February 6.

Smith, D. (2006). Go East, Young Man, to Economy's New Frontier, *Sunday Times*, 29 January.

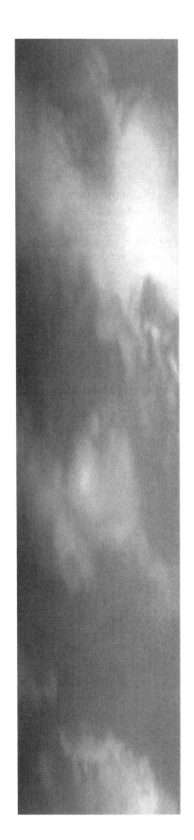

CHAPTER 2

The socio-demographics and governments of China and India

Chapter objectives

When you have read this chapter, you will be able to

1 Analyse the socio-demographic structures of China and India.
2 Discuss the present and predicted population structures of China and India.
3 Demonstrate the ethnic diversity of China and India.
4 Present an insight into the languages and religions of China and India.
5 Explain the political structures of China and India.

Introduction

This chapter is organised to give the reader an insight into the social makeups, population structures and political structures of China and India. The issues of social makeup, population structures and politics that affect China are considered first, followed by India.

China

Population

China is the world's most populous country. One in every five people in the world today lives in China. The estimated population of China in 2005 was in excess of 1.3 billion (CIA, 2006). It is estimated that this population will peak in 2014 and may fall after that (Garner, 2005).

The Chinese call their country Zhong Guo or the middle kingdom. This is significant as it illustrates the Chinese view that it is central (Toops, 2003). China is the Far East only from a Western perspective!

Table 2.1 shows the makeup of the Chinese population by age and gender. It clearly illustrates the youthful nature of the Chinese, where over 20% are under the age of 15, while only 7.6% are over the age of 65. The table also illustrates that men outnumber women by an overall ratio of

Table 2.1 Age and gender of the Chinese population – 2005

Age (years)	Male	Female	Percentage
0–14	148,134,928	131,045,416	21.4
15–64	477,182,072	450,664,933	71.0
65 and above	47,400,282	51,886,182	7.6
Totals	672,717,282	633,596,531	100.0

Source: Own table from figures in CIA *World Factbook* (2006).

1.06:1. The average age of the Chinese population is 32.3 years (CIA, 2006), and the population is increasing by 12–13 million per year or 0.58%. This annual population growth is more than the entire population of European countries, such as Belgium or Greece.

The large and growing population of China is not without its problems. The major problem with such a large population is feeding it. This problem has been compounded with the move to a more market economy. Further, the one-child policy that operates means that China has a population that is rapidly ageing. This rapid ageing could lead to future problems with regard to further economic expansion and welfare problems of an increasingly elderly population.

The rapidly ageing population will have an impact upon consumption. Service industries will benefit as the ageing population are expected to have an increased demand for leisure, tourism and restaurant products and services (Garner, 2005). There will be a decrease in demand for goods and services that cater to the young.

China's one-child policy

The one-child policy was introduced in 1979 in order to limit the then communist China's population. The policy applies to China's Han Chinese population living in urban areas. It does not apply to the ethnic minorities. The consequences of the policy are fourfold. First, it has been estimated that the policy has reduced population growth by 300,000. Second, there is disparity in the male to female ratio; currently, this is estimated to be 114:100. Third, the fertility rate is below replacement level (http://geography.about.com/od/populationgeography/a/onechild). Finally, there has been an increase in the growth of the non-Han population as this is exempt from the one-child policy (Rong, 2003).

There are some signs of a relaxation in the application of the one-child policy. From 2004, Shanghai has allowed divorced couples to have a second child regardless of whether or not they have a child by their first marriage. At this point in time, it is uncertain whether or not other authorities will join in (Garner, 2005).

Ethnic groups

The name China comes from the Qin (pronounced Chin) dynasty that unified China (Toops, 2003). China has an ethnically diverse population. Fifty-six different nationalities live in China (Zhang, Pine, Lam, 2005). The major ethnic groups include Han Chinese, Zhuang, Uygur, Hui, Yi, Tibetan, Miao, Manchu, Mongol, Buyi and Korean (CIA, 2006). Table 2.2 adequately indicates the diversity of the Chinese population. Although more than 9 in 10 are Han (native) Chinese, the variety of other ethnic groups adds greatly to the cultural mix of China. Han Chinese are scattered everywhere, other ethnic groups tend to be located in particular areas, as demonstrated in Table 2.2.

Table 2.2 Ethnic groups in China – 2005

Ethnic groups	Major location
Han Chinese	Everywhere
Zhuang	Guangxi
Hui	Ningxia
Tibetan	Tibet
Manchu	Jilin, Liaoning and Beijing
Mongol	Mongolia

Sources: CIA (2006) and Zhang et al. (2005).

The Han Chinese take their name from the Han dynasty. They are the dominant group in China, although they actually come from different lineages. Toops (2003) says that they are united by their acceptance of Confucius and Confucianism.

Under the Chinese constitution, all ethnic groups are treated equally; they have identical economic and social status.

Languages

The official language of China is Mandarin. This is widely spoken and is the language of the Han Chinese. Cantonese is spoken by the majorities in the Special Administrative Regions (SARs) of Hong Kong and Macau. Of the 55 ethnic minority groups only two, Manchu and Hui, speak Mandarin; the remaining 53 groups each have their own language. Some of these languages have no written form (Rong, 2003).

Religion

Officially, China is an atheist country with no dominant religion. In practice, the main religions are Buddhism, Islam, Taoism and Christianity. Some religions may be particular to specific ethnic groups and regions, for example, the Naxi's Dongba religion, Buddhism in Tibet and Mongolia and Islam among the Hui, Uygur and Kazak peoples.

Hoiman and King (2003) state that unlike many other countries, Chinese society and its culture is not dominated by religion. Those Han Chinese who practice a religion tend to practice Buddhism, Christianity or Taoism. China has 4 million Catholics and 10 million Protestants with over 12,000 churches (CNTA, 2006). This diversity of religion impacts upon tourism and tourism sites and destinations.

The 55 minority ethnic groups are more influenced by religion than the Han Chinese. Of the 55 groups, 4 are Tibetan Buddhists, another 4 are Hinayana Buddhists and 10 are Muslims. The remainder may practice other more primitive religions such as Shamanism (Rong, 2003).

Government

The official name for China is the People's Republic of China (PRC). The People's Republic was established on 1 October 1949. It is (despite recent reforms) a communist state that is divided into 23 provinces, five autonomous regions and four municipalities. Taiwan is regarded as the twenty-third state. Additionally, there are two SARs – Hong Kong and Macau (CIA, 2006).

The government is effectively a one-party state controlled by the Chinese Communist party. There are eight registered small parties, but the Chinese Communist party controls each of them. There is no political opposition; the Chinese Democratic Party and the Falungong (a spiritual movement) are both considered subversive.

China's parliament is the National People's Congress (NPC). It comprises almost 3,000 delegates, the majority of whom are picked by local level officials. All of the provinces, municipalities and autonomous regions are represented, including Taiwan. The Congress meets in March each year to approve budgets and to endorse nominations. It almost always does what the communist party wants and is considered by many to be a rubber stamp. It has occasionally opposed the communist party, usually as a stance against corruption (Watts, 2006).

India

Population

India is the world's second most populous country. The estimated population of India in 2005 was in excess of 1 billion (CIA, 2006). India is sometimes called Bharat (its old name). Its capital city is New Delhi, and its most populous city is Mumbai (Bombay).

Table 2.3 shows the make up of the Indian population by age and gender. The Indian population is more youthful than the Chinese population, where almost one in three of the population are under the age of 15, while only 4.9% are over the age of 65 compared with 7.6% of the Chinese population. This disparity may be accounted for, in part, by marked differences in longevity and China's one-child policy. Life expectancy in China is 72 years compared with 64 years in India. There is no one-child policy in

Table 2.3 Age and gender of the Indian population – 2005

Age (years)	Male	Female	Percentage
0–14	173,634,432	163,932,475	31.2
15–64	356,932,082	333,283,590	63.9
65 and above	26,542,025	25,030,784	4.9
Total	557,108,539	522,246,849	100.0

Source: Extrapolated from the CIA *World Factbook* (2006).

Table 2.4 India's projected population growth rate – 2010–2040

Year	Total population
2010	1,163,500,000
2020	1,287,700,000
2030	1,403,700,000
2040	1,500,600,000

Source: World Bank (2006).

India and as such India has a large and youthful population. It is estimated that by the middle of this century the population of India will be greater than that of China.

Table 2.3 also illustrates that men outnumber women by an overall ratio of 1.06:1. This figure is almost identical to that of China. However, the average age of the Indian population is 24.7 years (CIA, 2006), and the population is increasing at 1.4% per annum, which is almost three times the rate of China.

Table 2.4 shows the projected growth rate of the Indian population from 2010 to 2040.

Table 2.4 shows that India's population is expected to grow by over a quarter in a period of 30 years. As with China, this large and growing population has its problems. The two major problems with such a large population is feeding it and providing the necessary health care. However, importantly, this increased population is expected to become wealthier; this may lead to increased demands for consumer goods and with this, increased oil consumption. This growth may be a source of future long-term problems as it may be something that cannot be sustained environmentally.

There is some talk of a growing Indian middle class. Actually who or what constitutes the middle class is very difficult to define. Deshpande (2003, p. 136) says that middle class is more of a "symbolic rather than a factual description". Indians themselves appear to base the classification upon taxation; those who pay middle levels of taxation are, according to this definition, middle class.

According to Euromonitor (2006), one of the greatest threats to the Indian population is AIDS. At present, the prevalence rate for the disease is 1%; that may seem small but accounts to over 5 million infected people. One per cent is also the level which is regarded as the first warning sign of a significant problem.

Ethnic groups

The ethnic composition of India is divided into Aryan in the North and Dravidian in the South. Table 2.5 shows that Aryan is the largest group followed by Dravidian and Mongoloid.

Table 2.5 Ethnic groups in India – 2005

Group	Percentage of population
Indo-Aryan	72
Dravidian	25
Mongoloid and others	3

Source: Extrapolated from CIA *World Factbook* (2006) estimates.

The divide of the two major racial groupings is based upon colour and language; the Indo-Aryans are lighter skinned and the languages are Indo-European. Conversely, Dravidians are darker skinned with apparently different languages. It is thought by some that the original people of India were the Dravidians and that Indo-Aryans were the invaders. However, there is little scientific proof for this.

What this ethnic mix does give is a country rich in different languages, religions, monuments and customs that gives fantastic variety for the tourist.

Languages

The languages of India reflect the diversity of the country. Hindi is the most widely spoken. It is the national and first language of 30% of the people, mainly spoken in the North. The Indian constitution recognises 15 regional languages; in addition to Hindi, there are 14 official languages that include Bengali, Tamil, Gujarati and Urdu. Many of these languages are regional and indicate the diversity and number of the Indian states. Ten of the major states are organised on linguistic lines.

English, although not an official language, is an associate language and is the language of commerce and politics (CIA, 2006). The intention was to phase out the use of English; however, the prevalence of English as the language of the business has slowed, if not stopped, this process. It is the standard of spoken English in India that has led to many jobs in banking, IT and communications being outsourced to India.

Government

India is described by Euromonitor (2006) as a federation that consists of 25 states and 7 union territories. India describes itself as the world's largest parliamentary democracy. Much of its legislature is, not unsurprisingly, similar to that of the United Kingdom. The head of the Indian parliament is the president, who (theoretically) has full executive powers (CIA, 2006). The president is elected for five years. The president appoints the head of government (prime minister) and the Cabinet on the basis of election results to the lower house. In actuality, the real executive powers are held by the prime minister (the leader of the largest party in parliament) and the council of ministers.

The Indian parliament is divided into two houses. The upper house (Raiya Sabha) has 250 members apportioned mainly by state. The lower house (Lok Sabha) comprises more than 545 members apportioned among the states (CIA, 2006).

The present ruling party is the Congress party and its allies that took over power from the Bharatiya Janata party (BJP) with 219 seats (Euromonitor, 2006).

Summary

This chapter was intended to give an insight into the population, government and social make up of China and India.

China and India are the world's two most populous countries. Almost 40% of the world's population is either Chinese or Indian. Between them, they have close to 2.5 billion people. It is thought probable that India will be bigger than China by the middle of this century. This growth and development makes both countries rich in economic potential. Nevertheless, the growth of such large populations is not without its problems, both countries have high levels of poverty and relatively poor systems of welfare. The countries are similar in that they have divides in wealth between cities and rural communities. Indeed, India is said to be two countries – village India and urban India (CIA, 2006). China is remarkably similar and has many of the same problems.

With regard to politics and religion, they are very different. India is a parliamentary democracy while China, despite its market reforms, remains the world's largest communist countries and is a one-party state. India is rich in many and varied religions (although this is a cause of some tensions), and China is officially atheist.

In summary, both countries offer a wealth of opportunity, while coping with the problems of their demographic structures and globalisation.

References

CIA (2006). *The World Factbook.* http://www.odci.gov/cia/publications/factbook/index.html.

Deshpande, S. (2003). *Contemporary India: A Sociological Perspective.* New Delhi, Penguin.

Euromonitor (2006). *India.* http://www.gmid.euromonitor.com/CountryProfile.aspx, 5 April.

Garner, J. (2005). *The Rise of the Chinese Consumer.* Chichester, John Wiley.

Hoiman, C. and King, A.V.C. (2003). Religion. In Garner, R.E. (ed.), *Understanding Contemporary China.* London, Lynne Rienner Publishers Incorporated, pp. 339–376.

Rong, M. (2003). Population growth, Urbanisation. In Garner, R.E. (ed.), *Understanding Contemporary China*. London, Lynne Rienner Publishers Incorporated, pp. 227–254.

Toops, S.W. (2003). China: A geographic preface. In Garner, R.E. (ed.), *Understanding Contemporary China*. London, Lynne Rienner Publishers Incorporated, pp. 11–28.

Watts, J. (2006). Leaders Tackle China's Great Divide, *Guardian*, 6 March.

Zhang, H.Q., Pine, R. and T. Lam, Tourism and Hotel Development in China: From Political to Economic Success, Bridghampton, NY: Howarth.

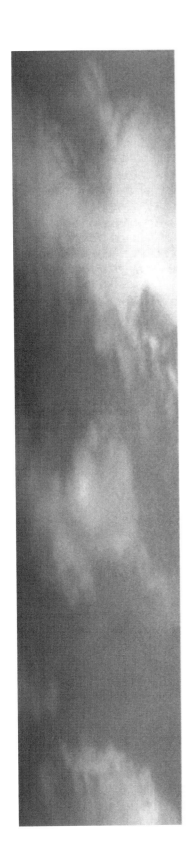

CHAPTER 3

The culture of China and India

> **Chapter objectives**
>
> When you have read this chapter, you will be able to
>
> 1 Explain national culture.
> 2 Evaluate theories of national culture.
> 3 Highlight influences on the cultures of China and India.
> 4 Provide an appreciation of the cultures of China and India.

Introduction

This chapter is organised to give the reader a solid introduction to the theory of national cultures, the influences upon the cultures of China and India and descriptions of Chinese and Indian cultures. The chapter begins by examining models of national culture giving the reader the basis of an introduction to theories of national culture. As the theories are generic, India and China will be dealt with together.

After the introduction to national culture is completed, the remainder of the chapter is divided into cultural issues affecting China and India.

The theory of national culture – an introduction

The purpose of this section is to examine national culture. Specifically, it will seek to establish whether there is evidence that different national cultures differ from one another.

The major works that will be examined in this chapter will be single and multiple dimension models of national culture. All of these models stem from the managerial models of culture. The reason for this choice is that these models, unlike those from other disciplines, deal specifically with the issue of national culture. Importantly, they attempt to identify dimensions that make national cultures different from each other.

Moran and Riesenberger (1998) believe that in the world of business and management, culture in its general sense has become accepted as an important and constitutive element. This importance was given further impetus in a survey in which understanding culture and the national cultures of others accounted for three of the twelve key competencies for the twenty-first century manager (Thunderbird's World Business Advisory).

Arriving at a commonly accepted definition of culture is fraught with difficulties. Williams (1983) warns that "culture" is one of the two or three most complicated words in the English language. As early as 1952, Kroeber and Kluckhohn collected and analysed 164 definitions and well over 100 statements about culture.

Instead of discussing diverse and contrasting definitions of culture, it is more productive to turn immediately to national culture and the work of Pizam (1993). He notes the abundance of definitions of national culture and their apparent lack of consensus. He points out that the definitions have commonality in that national culture is a social mechanism that guides and shapes people's thoughts, values and beliefs, and finally controls their behaviour. This fits quite neatly with Hofstede (1980; 1991 and 2001) who is possibly the most quoted authority on national culture. He suggests that national culture is a collective mental programming of the people of a nationality. He further suggests that people share a collective national character that shapes their values, attitudes, competencies, behaviour and perceptions of priority. In short, people of a nation have a cultural mental programming. This will be used as the working definition of culture within this chapter.

Models of national culture

To answer the question – "Do national cultures differ?"– it is appropriate to consider the models of national culture and to relate them to Chinese, Indian and Western cultures.

Two types of models of national culture can be found in the management literature. These are single dimensional models, where countries are classified culturally on the basis of one variable, and multi-dimensional models, where nationalities are classified on the basis of more than one variable.

Single dimension models of national culture

Three single dimension models of national culture have been identified. The first model focuses upon the dimension of context. Context refers to how individuals in any society find information and knowledge (Hall, 1976; Hall and Hall, 1990). People from high context cultures are thought to obtain information from personal networks, that is, they discuss the matter with friends, acquaintances and relatives. In doing this, they ask questions and listen to gossip. People from low context cultures will listen to the views of others but make decisions on the basis of research. The research will involve general reading, reports, databases, the Internet and other information sources. From Hall's research, Chinese people were the second highest context culture, while British people were the fifth lowest context culture.

The second single dimension model distinguishes between monochronic and polychronic cultures (Lewis, 1992). People from monochronic cultures act in a focused manner; they concentrate on one thing at a time and in a set time span. On the other hand, people from polychronic cultures are flexible; they are able to do many things at the same time. They are opportunistic and do not work to set times. It is argued that in a management setting, a mixture of monochronic and polychronic cultures will lead to culture clashes and disagreement (Morden, 1995). In this research, British people were the fifth-ranked monochronic culture, while the Chinese people were the twelfth-ranked monochronic. This difference between the British and Chinese may mean that Western management practices would not be easily transferred to a Chinese culture.

The final single dimension model distinguishes between low- and high-trust societies (Fukuyama, 1995). High-trust societies organise the workplace on a more flexible group-oriented basis, responsibility is delegated to lower levels of the organisation. Countries classified as high-trust include the United States, Japan and, to a lesser extent, the United Kingdom. In contrast, low-trust societies are bound by bureaucratic rules, they tend to fence in and isolate workers. They are familistic; they have strong family bonds but have little trust in others. Countries classified as low-trust include the Latin Catholic countries, China and Russia.

The main criticism of single dimension models is that they focus on one dimension. National culture is complicated. It is too simplistic to assume that nationalities may be classified using only one dimension (Fan, 2000). While the researchers themselves may acknowledge this shortcoming, comparison along single dimension leads to contradictions between the findings of the models. As an example, on the basis of the high- and low-trust model, the United States and Japan are almost identical. In the other models, they are cultural opposites.

Similarly, in one context, the British and Chinese people are ranked reasonably closely together, which may indicate that culturally they are alike. Yet in another context, they may be far enough apart in other areas to indicate cultural problems, suggesting difficulties in course transfer.

Given this, we can now turn to more complex models.

Multiple dimension models

There are two most frequently cited multiple dimension models of national culture. These models are normally referred to by the names of their researchers. These models are Trompenaars (1993); Trompenaars and Hampden-Turner (1997) and Hofstede (1980; 1991 and 2001). These models will be dealt with out of chronological order, and greater attention will be paid to Hofstede's work. The rationale for this is that although both models are concerned with management, Hofstede's model has, in my opinion, wider applications, is more widely quoted and appears to have a wider acceptance.

Trompenaars and Hampden-Turner

This model identifies seven dimensions of national culture that are used for understanding diversity in business (Trompenaars, 1993; Hofstede, 1996; Trompenaars & Hampden-Turner, 1997; Morden, 1999). The first five of these dimensions concern relationships with others and are known as value orientations. Trompenaars describes these dimensions as abstract. The translations of these dimensions are given in parentheses. The value orientations are universalism versus particularism (rules versus relationships); individualism versus collectivism (individual versus the group); neutral versus the emotional (range of emotions expressed); specific versus diffuse (the range of involvement) and achievement versus ascription (how status is accorded). The remaining two dimensions are "orientation in time" and "attitude to the environment".

Responses by different nationalities to questions related to the seven dimensions showed significant differences between national cultures. From these responses, "advice" on dealing with cultural diversity is given.

Although this model has been attacked as flawed in terms of sample size, commercialism and the construct of the dimensions (Hofstede, 1996), it does, as with the single dimension models, indicate significant differences between national cultures and Western and Chinese cultures.

Hofstede

Hofstede's classification of national cultures is probably the more famous. It is regarded as a classic book and a "super classic" in relation to its impressive citation record. It has averaged 94 citations per annum over the last two decades (Baskerville, 2003; Schneider and Barsoux, 2003). After 30 years, it was updated as a second edition in 2001. Little was changed from the earlier work (Hofstede, 2001). Much of the new edition is concerned with adding in later research and defending against earlier criticisms (Boonghee and Donthu, 2002).

In his original study, Hofstede administered over 116,000 questionnaires in 20 different languages to IBM employees in 40 countries. This he called a "Morale Survey". Each questionnaire contained 150 questions based on the individual's values and beliefs about motivation, hierarchy and leadership. Upon analysis of the responses of the individuals from different countries, Hofstede identified four variables (later extended to five) with which he was able to classify all of the countries within the study into eight distinct national categories.

The four variables identified by Hofstede are the following:

1 Power Distance – the extent to which society will accept differences between the lowest and the highest. High levels of power distance, that is, where large differences are acceptable were found to exist in the Arab countries and in Malaysia, and low levels were found in the West.
2 Individualism – the extent to which society is concerned about the individual as opposed to the group. The extent to which individuals "stand on their own two feet". In this area, the United States. was the most individualistic whilst some South American countries were the most collectivists.
3 Masculinity/Femininity – the extent to which society defines roles in terms of gender, for example, men are lorry drivers, engineers, etc., and women stay at home and bring up the children. In this area, Japan was found to be the most masculine while Sweden and Norway were the most feminine.
4 Uncertainty Avoidance – the extent to which people feel threatened by uncertain situations, that is, the extent to which they need to establish formal rules, accept absolute truths, etc. Greece was found to have high uncertainty avoidance, while the UK and Eire scored relatively low in this area. In general terms, it would appear that societies that have a tradition of one job for life have high uncertainty avoidance.

When these four dimensions were analysed, Hofstede was able to classify countries into one of eight national cultural types depending on the degree of the four dimensions. While not wishing to go into all of the nationality types, two are important to this discussion. The first is "Less Developed Asian". This classification includes Hong Kong, Taiwan, India and Pakistan. These countries are similar as they have low uncertainty avoidance and individualism, medium masculinity and high power distance. The second is "Anglo"; this includes the United Kingdom along with Canada, Ireland, Australia, New Zealand and the United States. These countries were found to have low-to-medium uncertainty avoidance, high individualism and masculinity and low power distance.

The significant point to note with regard to culture differences is that the United Kingdom and India differ in each of the dimensions. It is also interesting to note that China does not exist in this model (see Confucian dynamism later). These cultural differences may be significant as they may impact upon business and commercial dealings, tourist preferences and cultural expectations.

One of the early criticisms of Hofstede's original work was that the questionnaires and the cultural dimensions that resulted from it were derived from the Western cultural tradition. As a result of this, it may be that Hofstede's work was culturally biased and that some important results were missed. A group of academics specialising in Chinese culture put together what they called the Chinese Value Survey. This work concluded that there was a direct correlation with three of Hofstede's dimensions but that another oriental dimension – Confucian Work Dynamism – had been missed, indicating cultural bias in Hofstede's early work (The Chinese Culture Connection, 1987). This dimension included concepts that although stemming from Confucius would be understood by Westerners but would not be given any real importance by them, for example, thrift, perseverance and persistence. This dimension, which is also called long-term orientation, was believed to be the reason for the rise of the Asian "tiger" economies in the 1980s (Schneider and Barsoux, 2003).

Hofstede worked with the main author of the Chinese Value Survey, Michael Bond, to add this fifth dimension – Confucian Dynamism – to his model (Hofstede and Bond, 1988). This dimension applies mainly to China, Korea, Hong Kong, Singapore and Japan. In practical terms, it is long-term versus short-term orientation to life (Hofstede, 1991; Rodrigues, 1998; Schneider and Barsoux, 2003). This fifth dimension was added in Hofstede's work (Hofstede, 2001).

Summary

The models presented in this section are based upon single and multi-dimensions. All of them have been subjected to criticism that has been, in some cases, vitriolic. Indeed, there are at least nine criticisms of Hofstede's work, which vary from its sample to the findings. Nonetheless, what these models do is to indicate that national cultures may differ and give some dimensions upon which they may differ.

This chapter will now turn its attention to specifics regarding the national cultures of China and India.

China

Chinese culture

"Chinese culture" is used as a term to encompass all cultural values held by Chinese people regardless of where they live, that is, people from Hong Kong, Taiwan, Singapore and Mainland China; all share the same culture (Fan, 2000). On the face of it, this statement would appear to be a major generalisation – although it is acknowledged that there are great social, political and economic differences between the Chinese nations. Fan believes that there are core values that are unique and consistent that has been shaped by 4,000 years of history. It is these core values that determine Chinese national culture. This view, although it may appear extreme, is consistent throughout the literature, with little or no attempt made to differentiate the different Chinese nationalities or regions of China. Barron and Arcodia (2002) also subscribe to this view when they describe the enduring significance of Confucianism to East Asian countries.

Traditional Chinese culture stems from a mix of Confucianism, Taoism, Buddhism and many regional cultures. However, Confucianism is undisputedly the most influential and is at the heart of the core values mentioned above (Fan, 2000). As pointed out earlier, the unifying force of the Han Chinese is believed to be Confucianism. Confucianism is a behavioural and moral doctrine that is based on the teachings of Confucius. Confucianism spells out rules for each level of the human interaction. It is argued that these rules of behaviour are instilled into Chinese children even though there may be no direct reference to a Confucian text (Crookes and Thomas, 1998).

The important dimensions in the rules of behaviour referred to above are social harmony and structural harmony. Social harmony is achieved through the *Jen* and the *Li. Jen* implies human heartedness, that is, acting towards others as one would wish to be acted towards. The *Li* concerns behaviour in any situation; it shapes and maintains relationships, and it gives order in hierarchies (Westwood, 1992).

There are two aspects that control social harmony. These are "face" and "shame" that have been likened to opposite sides of the same coin. Face (*mien-tsu*) means that one should act in ways that do not lose face for oneself, one's family or one's superiors. In this situation, one would be expected to agree with a superior's decision and not to make one's own views known. Shame would be felt if the rules of social norms were broken, for example, if a superior's opinion was disagreed with.

Zinzius (2004) says that face has two meanings. These are social standing and personal dignity. It is the respect that they receive from others that is important to the Chinese. Face can be seen as a regulator of social and moral conduct. The impact of face is that open criticism and insults are contrary to social norms. Criticising another results in loss of face as does not meeting expectations and/or promises (Zinzius, 2004). The opposite of losing face is giving face. This may be achieved by paying compliments and praising someone.

In ancient China, scholars spoke of the *ta wo* or "greater self"; this is distinguished from the *hsiao wo* or "smaller self". The smaller self relates to a person's own ambitions and desires. The greater self relates to the wider society or humankind as a whole. The expectation would be that the smaller self is sacrificed for the greater self (Hsu, 1985). It is the belief in the precedence of the greater self together with a belief in hierarchy configuration – the state in which everyone is born into a certain position and is expected to be conscious of that position and behave accordingly. As a result of this, Chinese people do not simply react to overt codes of society. Instead, their behaviour is governed by self-control according to internalised social norms.

Structural harmony is achieved through the management of key relationships. There are five key human relationships in which an individual is defined; these are the love between father and son, the duty between ruler and subject, the distinction between husband and wife, the precedence of the old over the young and the faith between friends. Within relationships, the individual is always the least important. The smaller self must always be sacrificed for the greater self. These relationships are the *Wu Lan* – the duties of hierarchical social relationships. The result of the *Wu Lan* is that superiors can expect respect and obedience from subordinates but in turn must care for and protect them. The roles of each person are clear; each person must stay in role, and the *Li* governs role behaviour. In the Confucian tradition, individuals are identified only in social relationships. The aim of life is to put the world in order; the aim of education is to train the character, to learn to be conscientious and to be altruistic (Cheng and Wong, 1996). Education is perceived as central in forming the person (Barron and Arcodia, 2002).

Relationships are important in the business world. *Guanxi*, which has its basic meaning of relations, is about network and forming connections based upon requirement and reciprocity (Zinzius, 2004). Business is conducted through networks and contacts.

Harmony and avoiding conflict are the ideal in Chinese life and business. Within business, this may cause confusion to Westerners that may be more direct. A direct *ni* (no) would be bad form and would not normally be given. An example of this is that an e-mail is unanswered not because the recipient has not read it but because the recipient does not wish to say no. Conversely, a yes may not mean yes, it could mean no!

This Confucian view of life is that humankind is controlled by social relationships. People are not equal; society is "hierarchical and patriarchal" (Zinzius, p. 121). Chinese culture may be regarded as collectivist, family is important and at its core.

Research into the psychology of Chinese people finds them to be conflict-avoiding, others-centred and searching for harmony. Their personality tends towards introversion, conformity and submissiveness (Bond, 1986). As a result of this, Chinese people tend to be conservative and cautious.

Cheng and Wong (1996) state that there are three aspects of Chinese culture that make it distinctly different from other national cultures and impact upon Chinese communities. These aspects are the individual–community dimension, the effort–ability dichotomy and the holistic–idealistic tendency.

The effect of the individual–community dimension is that the individual submits to the will of the community. The consequences of this are that first there is conformity and uniformity. The whole of society conforms to what is advantageous for the majority.

The second consequence concerns the prime importance of human relations, specifically, the importance of the community as opposed to the individual. The pressure to succeed and to achieve is there for everyone regardless of their parents' educational attainment. Achievement is not for the self but for the family face.

In Chinese culture, there is a tendency to play down genetic abilities and to give a higher regard to effort. This gives rise to the effort–ability dichotomy. Simply put, this means that according to traditional Confucian philosophy everyone can succeed. There is no limit to one's ability; instead, emphasis is placed upon effort (Wong, 2001). This belief in effort too is rooted in a culture that is closely related to social structure. Chinese society is hierarchical, but there is movement within that structure. In ancient China, government officials were selected through public examination and much play was made of people attaining these positions from relatively low classes.

The holistic–idealistic tendency has also been called Chinese systems thinking. This system of thinking tends to be holistic, for example, schools do not stop at knowledge, and they look to the whole idealistic person.

In summary, Chinese culture is highly complex. It is based upon Confucianism and has evolved over centuries. Sixty years of Communism have not changed it. Chinese culture has collectivism, the family, effort, hierarchy, face and relationships at its heart. There are major differences between Western and Chinese cultures that need to be recognised. These are summarised in Table 3.1.

Table 3.1   Comparison of cultural values – China and Western

Value	China	West
Family and society	Family	Individualism
Communication	Subtle and indirect	Direct and open
Status	Gained by position and family	Gained through achievement
Face	Giving, taking and having face are important	No special status
Religion/Philosophy	Confucianism/Harmony	Christianity and democracy
Achievement	Effort	Personal qualities
Conduct of business	*Guangzhi*	Negotiation

Source: Extrapolated from Zinzius (2004).

India

Culture

Unlike China, India does not have a history steeped in Confucianism. Its culture is steeped in its history, its peoples and its religions. This mixture has led to a cultural heritage that is rich in art forms, historic monuments, religious buildings, music, dance and literature.

India is one of the world's oldest civilisations and has diversity within both its religions and its peoples. India is enriched by the number of its diverse and varied religions. Religion plays an important and major part in the life of the country. The main religion is Hinduism that is adhered to by over 80% of the population. This is followed by Islam (13.4%), Christianity (2.3%) and Sikhism (1.9%) and several other religions, such as Jainism, with smaller numbers of adherents (CIA World Factbook, 2006).

Its people may be divided into Aryan in the North and Dravidian in the South. The divide of the two major racial groupings is based upon colour and language, the Indo-Aryans are lighter skinned and the languages are Indo-European. Conversely, Dravidians are darker skinned with apparently different languages. It is thought by some that the original people of India were the Dravidians and that Indo-Aryans were the invaders. However, there is little scientific proof for this.

What this ethnic and religious mix does give is to produce a country that is rich in different languages, monuments and customs. All of these give fantastic variety for the scholar and the tourist.

The caste system

It is impossible to write about culture in India without making a reference to the caste system. There are two viewpoints with regard to the caste system in India. One is that it is an anachronism that has no place in modern. The other is that it exists and preferences are given according to caste.

There are five different levels of the caste system within India. These are the Brahman who are the priests and teachers; the Kshatriya who are the soldiers and rulers; the Vaishya the merchants and traders; the Shudra who are the labourers and Harijan or Achata, these are the outcasts or the impure who are more commonly known in the West as the untouchables (O'Neill, 2005). Within these five levels are the castes into which all people are born, marry and finally should die (Callahan and Pavich, 2006). Within the caste system, everyone should have his place and should accept this.

This perspective, however, is seen as having no place in modern India. It is illegal to discriminate against the Harijans who were called the children of God by Gandhi. Positive discrimination is encouraged, places in universities, for example, are reserved for them. Nevertheless, there remain tales that the Harijans are discriminated against and that the Brahmins are favoured in employment and education (O'Neill, 2005).

Summary

This chapter was intended to be an introduction to the theoretical and practical nature of the national cultures of India and China.

Culturally, both countries have long and fascinating histories that make them rich in language, literature, art, music and architecture. The diversity of India and China's population give rich cultural mixes. The cultures of China and India are different, both in theory and in make up. China's culture is steeped in and founded upon Confucianism and its history. India's culture shows in its diversity of offering, religion, architecture, music and customs.

In summary, both countries offer a wealth of opportunity for the tourist, while coping with the problems of their demographics and globalisation.

References

Barron, P. and Arcodia, C. (2002). Linking Learning Style Preferences and Ethnicity: International Students Studying Hospitality and Tourism Management in Australia, *Journal of Hospitality, Leisure, Sport, Tourism Education*, **1**(2), 15–27.

Baskerville, R.F. (2003). Hofstede Never Studied Culture, *Accounting, Organisations and Society*, **28**(1), 1–14.

Bond, M. (1986). *The Psychology of Chinese People*. Harrow, Longman.

Callahan, T. and Pavich, R. (2006). *Indian Caste System*. www.csuchico.edu, 3 April.

Cheng, K. and Wong, K. (1996). School Effectiveness in East Asia: Concepts, Origins and Implications, *Journal of Educational Administration*, **34**(5), 32–48.

Crookes, D. and Thomas, I. (1998). Problem Solving and Culture – Exploring Some Stereotypes, *Journal of Management Development*, **17**(8), 583–591.

Fan, Y. (2000). A Classification of Chinese Culture, *Cross-Cultural Management*, **7**(2), pp. 3–10.

Fukuyama, F. (1995). *Trust, The Social Virtues and The Creation of Prosperity*. London, Hamish Hamilton.

Hall, E.T. (1976). *Beyond Culture*. New York, Anchor Press.

Hall, E.T. and Hall, M.R. (1990). *Understanding Cultural Differences*. Yarmouth, Maine, Intercultural Press.

Hofstede, G. (1980). *Culture's Consequences: International Differences in Work Related Values*: Newbury Park, California, Sage.

Hofstede, G. (1991). *Cultures and Organisations: Intercultural Co-operation and its Importance for Survival*. London, Harper Collins Business.

Hofstede, G. (1996). Riding the Waves of Commerce: A Test of Trompenaars "Model" of National Culture Differences, *International Journal of Intercultural Relations*, **20**(2), 189–198.

Hofstede, G. (2001). *Culture's Consequences*. 2nd Edition, Thousand Oaks, Sage.

Hofstede, G. and Bond, M.H. (1988). The Confucius Connection: From Cultural Roots to Economic Growth, *Organisational Dynamics*, Spring, 5–21.

Hsu, F.L.K., (1985). "The self in cross-cultural perspectives". In Marsella, A.J., Deves, G. and F.L.K., Hsu. *Culture and Self: Asian and Western Perspectives, Tavistock*, New York, 24–55.

Lewis, R.D. (1992). *Finland: Cultural Lone Wolf – Consequences in International Business*. Helsinki, Richard Lewis Communications.

Morden, A.R., (1995). "International Culture and Management". *Management Decision-Making*, Volume 33, No. 2, 16–21.

Morden, A.R. (1999). Models of National Culture, *Cross-Cultural Management*, **6**(1), 19–44.

Moran, R.T. and Riesenberger, J.R. (1998). *The Global Challenge: Building the New Worldwide Enterprise*. Maidenhead, McGraw-Hill.

O'Neill, T. (2005). Discrimination Against India's Lowest Hindu Caste is Technically Illegal. But Try Telling That to the 160 Million Untouchables, Who Face Violent Reprisals if They Forget Their Place, *National Geographic Magazine*, 21 June.

Pizam, A. (1993). "Managing cross-cultural hospitality enterprises". In Jones, P. and Pizam, A. (Eds.), *The International Hospitality Industry, London*: Pitman.

Rodrigues, C.A. (1998). Cultural Classification of Societies and How They Affect Cross-Cultural Management, *Cross-Cultural Management*, **5**(3), 29–39.

Schneider, S.C. and Barsoux, J.L. (2003). *Managing Across Cultures*. 2nd Edition, Harlow, Pearson Educational.

The Chinese Culture Connection (1987). Chinese Values and the Search for Culture-free Dimensions of Culture, *Journal of Cross-Cultural Psychology*, **18**(2), 143–164.

Trompenaars, F. (1993). *Riding the Waves of Culture: Understanding Cultural Diversity in Business*, London, Nicholas Brearley Publishing.

Trompenaars, F. and C. Hampden-Turner, (1997), *Riding the Waves of Culture: Understanding Cultural Diversity in Business (2nd edition)*, London: Nicholas Brearley Publishing.

Westwood, R.I. (1992). *Organisational Behaviour*. Longman, S. E. Asian Perspectives.

Williams, R. (1983). Keywords: A vocabulary of culture and society. In Tomlinson, J. (1991). *Cultural Imperialism*. The John Hopkins University Press.

Zinzius, B. (2004). *Doing Business in the New China: A Handbook and Guide*. Westport, CT, Praeger.

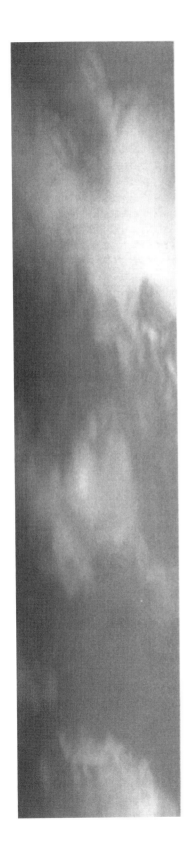

CHAPTER 4

Tourism trends in China and India

> **Chapter objectives**
>
> When you have read this chapter, you will be able to
>
> 1 Explain the nature of tourism in China and India.
> 2 Discuss the economic importance of tourism in China and India.
> 3 Outline future prospects for tourism in China and India.
> 4 Analyse the barriers to tourism in China and India.
> 5 Provide overviews of tourism policy in China and India.

Introduction

This chapter is organised into two parts. The first part deals with tourism trends in China. It begins by considering the tourist resources that China has to offer. It continues by examining the impact of tourism in terms of the number of visitors, both domestic and international, and the impact that this has on China's economy.

It concludes by considering China's tourism policies and the challenges or barriers that the Chinese tourist industry must face in early part of the twenty-first century.

The second part is a mirror image of the first part, but it concentrates upon India.

China

China's tourism resources

China is the world's fourth largest country in area. It covers over 9.3 million square kilometres. Bordered by 14 other countries, it is extremely diverse in climate, culture and terrain. An example of its diversity is its climate that ranges from tropical in the south to sub-arctic in the north. In terms of ethnicity, 56 different nationalities are identified (Shen, 2003).

As a whole, China is rich in tourism resources and covers the whole of the tourism experience. China has major cosmopolitan cities such as Beijing and Shanghai; a wealth of old historic structures such as the Great Wall and the Forbidden City; a diverse geography that includes mountains, deserts, lakes and forests and UNESCO sites. It has a diversity of ethnic groups and is now placing itself firmly in the areas of eco-tourism and sport tourism (Lew, Yu, Ap and Guangrui, 2003). Importantly, China has a long history and is comparable to India, Egypt and ancient European civilisations making it rich in cultural and historic attractions (Zhang, Pine and Lam, 2005). It has a civilisation that is more than 5,000 years old (Shen, 2003). The Olympics, which is the foremost sporting event in the world, will be in Beijing and other lesser known cities such as Qingdao in 2008. The Olympics will be a vast showcase for China's tourism potential.

Tourism is still in its early stages but there are already 119 national parks and 500 provincial parks. Over 4,600 scenic places and places of historic interest have been identified (Shen, 2003). There are theme parks and

Table 4.1 Top tourist attractions by sector on the basis of sales percentage in China – 2004

Rank	Attraction	Sales (%)
1	Theme/amusement parks	30.9
2	National parks/areas of natural beauty	9.4
3	Historic buildings/sites	18.8
4	Theatres	5.0
5	Museums	5.0
6	Art galleries	1.3
7	Zoos/Aquariums	1.1
8	Others	8.5
	Total	100.0

Source: Extrapolated from Euromonitor (2005a).

facilities for sport/leisure, arts, performances and cultural entertainment. Theme parks in particular are booming with the Splendid China, Window of the World and the Chinese Folk Culture Village in Shenzhen, Southern China (Wu, Zhu and Xu, 2000). The popularity of theme/amusement parks is demonstrated in Table 4.1, which indicates that theme/amusement parks account for almost one-third of all tourist attraction spend. The popularity of theme parks continues with new parks planned on the mainland and in Hong Kong and Macau. In 2005, Disney opened in Hong Kong, and there are plans for another Disney in Shanghai by 2010. In Macau, over 90% of the population is employed in tourism, and there are plans to recreate San Francisco's Pier 39 as a tourist attraction.

As is indicated by Table 4.1, aside from theme/amusement parks China's major tourism products are its cultural and historic attractions (Wang and Qu, 2004). It is these attractions that are most popular with international tourists.

Tourism development and policy in China

Zhong, Pine and Zhong (2000) and Gu (2003) identified four stages of tourism development in the People's Republic of China (PRC) from 1949. These include the following:

1 Tourism as a political activity (1949–1966)

In this, stage tourism was not to be encouraged. International tourism was very small and was almost entirely limited to officials of the communist party. Domestic tourism was frowned upon and was regarded as contrary to the doctrine of communism.

2 Standstill (1966–1978)

This period saw the Cultural Revolution and the chaos that was brought with it to China. In this period, the upset and turmoil of the Cultural Revolution effectively closed China to tourism. As expected, the number of visitors in this period, both international and domestic, was almost negligible.

3 Economic reconstruction or "Open Door policy" (1978–1985)

The reforms of Deng Xiaopeng reversed the effects on tourism of the Cultural Revolution and opened up China to tourism. A country that had seen almost no tourists for 12 years was almost overnight open for business. The reasons for this were that after great and lengthy debate, the economic impact and benefits of tourism were recognised. Tourism was regarded as especially important for its potential as a foreign currency earner and as an important economic activity providing employment and income.

4 Tourism as an economic contributor (1986 onwards)

Building on the economic changes of the third-stage tourism and its significance as an economic activity were further recognised by the Chinese government. Tourism was made part of the national plan and enjoyed priority status. Of the 31 provinces and regions, 24 recognised tourism as one of its pillar industries.

As the significance of tourism has increased so has tourism policy been formulated to enable and encourage further tourism development. Tourism policy in China has been described as top-down in that almost all of it stems from the government (Zhang, Chang and Jenkins, 2002). A recent example of this is that the China National Tourism Association has developed the "10th five-year Plan and Long term Goal Outlines up to 2015 and 2020 for Tourism development in China". Over 20 years, the intention is to move China from a "big tourism country" to a "powerful tourism country" (CNTA, 2001). In formulating this plan, specific and ambitious goals have been set – these are that by 2020,

- Inbound tourist arrivals will be between 210 and 300 million. Of these, between 31 and 45 million will be foreign tourist arrivals. The figure for foreign tourist arrivals is to be a minimum of three times greater than the figure for the year 2000.
- International earnings are to be from $58 billion to $82 billion, which must be a minimum of 3.6 times higher than the earnings of 2000.
- Earnings from domestic tourism are to reach 2100 billion yuan, a figure that is six times greater than 2000.

The major tourism policies have concerned standards such as hotel star rating systems and investment in tourism. The major policies are shown in Table 4.2. Tourism has received a further boost in 2001 when China joined the WTO. The impact of this is that this further opened up China to trade and the outside world, thus giving more opportunities for

Table 4.2 Tourism policy in China

Date	Policy	Purpose
1979	Foreign investment	Encourage foreign investment in hotels and travel agencies.
1984	five together	Tourism administrations, government agencies, local government, collectives and individuals to invest in tourism.
1988	Regulations on star ratings and standards of tourist hotels.	Regulatory and quality control.
1996	Regulation administration of tour guides.	Regulatory and quality control.
1996	Regulation administration of travel agencies.	Regulatory and quality control.

Source: Adapted from Zhang et al. (2000).

international tourism development that stems for international business (Lew et al., 2003).

Aside from direct tourism policies, other policies not directly aimed at tourism such as paid holidays have encouraged and helped domestic tourism (see section on domestic tourism). Domestic tourism has been further helped by the increase in prosperity among China's population that has been brought about by China's economic miracle. This combination of economic and social policy has combined to give the Chinese population the prerequisites of time and income that are needed for travel.

Table 4.2 summarises tourism policy in China from 1979 to the present day.

Tourism in China

Tourism is important to China both economically and culturally. As China moves towards becoming the world's largest economy, it is also becoming the world's most popular tourist destination.

Table 4.3 shows the predicted top ten world tourism destinations by 2020. It is predicted that by 2020, China will be the world's top tourism destination overtaking the old favourites such as France, Spain and the USA. One of the main reasons for this is the phenomenal rate of growth of tourism within China. The rate of growth is expected to average a stunning 8% per annum between 1995 and 2020. It should be noted from Table 4.3 that these figures do not include Hong Kong and Macau. Hong Kong itself is predicted to be the fifth most popular tourism destination by the same time. China and Hong Kong together will have one-eighth of the world's market share of tourism by 2020.

The following section explores the impact of tourism on China. It begins by examining international tourism and its impact upon the balance of payments.

International tourism

International tourism concerns tourism across borders. As illustrated by Table 4.4, China has experienced huge but erratic increases in tourism from 1999 to 2004. The downturn in international tourism in 2003 was largely a consequence of the SARS (Severe Acute Respiratory Syndrome) outbreak, when pleasure tourists decided to stay at home or visit other, safer destinations.

Table 4.3   Top ten world tourist destinations by 2020

Rank	Destination	Arrivals (1000s)	Market share (%)	Annual growth 1995–2020 (%)
1	China	137,100	8.6	8.0
2	USA	102,400	6.4	3.5
3	France	93,300	5.8	1.8
4	Spain	71,000	4.4	2.4
5	Hong Kong	59,300	3.7	7.3
6	Italy	52,900	3.3	2.2
7	UK	52,800	3.3	3.0
8	Mexico	48,900	3.1	3.6
9	Russian Federation	47,100	2.9	6.7
10	Czech Republic	44,400	2.7	2.7
	Total	708,800	44.2	41.2

Source: WTO (1997).

Table 4.4   Number of arrivals to China, 1999–2004

Year	Number (1000s)	Growth (%)
1999	27,262.0	
2000	31,872.7	16.9
2001	33,166.7	4.1
2002	36,854.0	11.1
2003	32,700.0	−11.3
2004	34,355.9	5.1

Source: Euromonitor (2005a).

Number of international arrivals • • •

Table 4.5 illustrates the number of arrivals by purpose of visit. The largest increase from 1999 to 2004 has been in business visits. This increase of over one-third shows the importance of China as a business centre and is an indicator of the economic opportunity that is available in China. It is also an indicator of the strength of the Chinese economy that is now greater than that of the United Kingdom and is set to overtake Germany by 2007.

The rate of growth of business travel (33.5% between 1999 and 2004) also illustrates the phenomenal growth rate of the Chinese economy that is doubling in size approximately every eight years.

Table 4.6 gives an interesting perspective on tourism arrivals by country of origin. Almost 60% of tourism arrivals to China are from Hong Kong, Macau and Taiwan. This indicates the ease of travel from these places

Table 4.5 Arrivals to China by purpose of visit, 1999–2004

Purpose	1999	2000	2001	2002	2003	2004	Increase 1999–2004 (%)
Business	7,175.9	7,891.6	8,470.1	10,205.8	10,267.8	10,787.9	33.5
Leisure	18,450.5	21,907.0	22,389.4	22,635.7	20,404.8	21,437.9	14.0
Visiting friends and relatives	1,635.6	2,074.1	2,307.2	3,012.5	2,027.4	2,130.1	23.2
Total	27,262.0	31,872.7	33,166.7	36,854.0	32,700.0	34,355.9	20.6

Source: Euromonitor (2005a).

Table 4.6 Arrivals to China by country of origin – 2004

Rank	Country	Arrivals	Total (%)
1	Hong Kong	15,230.0	44.3
2	Macau	4,234.9	12.3
3	Japan	3,103.4	9.0
4	South Korea	2,583.6	7.5
5	Russia	1,692.1	4.9
6	Taiwan	940.1	2.7
7	USA	931.9	2.7
8	Malaysia	540.1	1.6
9	Philippines	509.1	1.5
10	Mongolia	437.1	1.3

Source: Euromonitor (2005a).

to China; it complements the number of tourists who travel to China to visit friends and relatives. It is also an indicator of the ease of moving between Hong Kong and China. Shenzhen, a city of over 5 million, is on the border with Hong Kong and can be reached in 30 minutes from Kowloon. Guangzhou, a city of over 10 million, is 3 hours from Hong Kong by boat along the Pearl River or 45 minutes by aeroplane. It should also be noted that the arrivals from Hong Kong are almost double Hong Kong's population.

The lack of visitors in the top ten ranking from the West indicates that there are huge markets that are available to China's tourism industry.

The economic importance of international tourism to China

As a major player in international tourism, China is reaping enormous economic benefits. Table 4.7 shows the receipts from incoming tourism. The table shows two figures: the current growth rate and the constant growth rate. Of the two, the more important is probably the constant growth rate as this compares spending although prices have remained the same. The figures illustrate the erratic and demand elastic nature of tourism where the SARS epidemic caused a constant growth rate reduction of 17.6% in 2003.

In 2004, tourism accounted for over 1% of GDP in China. This figure may appear small but when added to domestic tourism spend, it is a major contributor to the economic health and wealth of the nation.

Outgoing tourism

It should be noted that China is not only a major tourism destination but it is also a major provider of international tourists. By 2020, China may be the world's top tourist destination, but it will also be the fourth largest tourist producing country. Table 4.8 goes some way to illustrating this

Table 4.7 China's incoming tourism receipts and growth, 1999–2004

Year international tourism	Receipt		Growth (%)	
	Current (RMB million)	Constant (RMB million)	Current	Constant
1999	116,683.3	116,683.3	–	–
2000	124,318.0	124,001.4	6.5	6.3
2001	132,647.3	131,699.2	6.7	6.23
2002	168,583.0	168,669.0	27.1	28.1
2003	140,495.0	138,959.1	−16.7	−17.6
2004	172,808.9	165,139.9	23.0	18.8

Source: Euromonitor (2005a).

phenomenon. Outgoing tourism has increased year on year from 1999 to 2004. At constant growth, outgoing tourism has increased by 176%. The number of Chinese tourists abroad is already greater than the number of Japanese tourists. It is estimated that by 2020, there will be 100 million Chinese visitors abroad (Macartney, 2006).

This increase in outgoing tourism is a consequence of increased prosperity, the European Union has made travel easier for Chinese citizens, and the ease and relatively low price of travel from China. The Chinese traveller is willing to spend but will save on hotels and food in order to spend on other goods (Macartney, 2006).

Balance of payments

Tourism is a service and as such is an invisible on the balance of payments accounts. Table 4.9 shows tourism exports (receipts) and tourism imports (expenditure). The difference between the two is the travel balance.

Table 4.8 China's outgoing tourism expenditure and growth, 1999–2004

Year	Expenditure		Growth (%)	
	Current (RMB million)	Constant (RMB million)	Current	Constant
1999	76,884.0	76,884.0	–	–
2000	88,601.9	88,376.2	15.2	14.9
2001	102,512.5	101,779.8	15.7	15.2
2002	127,423.5	127,488.5	24.3	25.3
2003	150,736.6	149,088.8	18.3	16.9
2004	222,519.2	212,644.1	47.6	42.6

Source: Euromonitor (2005a).

Table 4.9 China's travel balance, 1999–2004

Year	Receipt (RMB million)	Expenditure (RMB million)	Balance (RMB million)
1999	116,683.3	76,884.0	+39,799.3
2000	124,318.0	88,601.9	+35,716.1
2001	132,647.3	102,512.5	+30,134.8
2002	168,583.0	127,423.5	+41,159.5
2003	140,495.0	150,736.6	−10,241.6
2004	172,808.9	222,519.2	−49,710.3

Source: Euromonitor (2005a).

In the first four of the six years in the study, China had a surplus on its travel balance; that is, it attracted more tourism spend than it spent itself. However, the last two years indicate substantial deficits and that China is importing more tourism than is exporting.

Tourism contribution to the Chinese economy is that it is a major earner of foreign currency that can be used to import other goods and services.

Domestic tourism

Domestic tourism has increased by over 40% from 1999 to 2004 (Table 4.10). Domestic tourism saw a surge in 2002 and a downturn in 2003 that was connected with the SARS outbreak that had been the cause of people staying at home. The first year in the period under study, 1999, coincided with the introduction of the "golden holiday weeks". This alone may have caused much of the increase in domestic tourism in that year (Euromonitor, 2005a).

Spending on domestic tourism stands at over 550 billion RMB in 2004. From 2002, spending has moved away for hotels and transport and has moved towards shopping and entertainment (Euromonitor, 2005a).

Wu, Zhu and Xu (2000) and Wang and Qu (2004) give three reasons for the increase in domestic tourism. They are as follows:

1 The increased growth in income per capita, which has risen greatly over the past 10 years. It should be noted, however, that there are vast regional disparities, and major differences between urban and rural locations.
2 An increase in leisure time brought about by a five-day working week and new national holidays. Public holidays have been increased, and the working week has been shortened fairly dramatically from 1994. In 1994, the working week was decreased from six to five and half days. This was followed in 1995 by a further cut to five along with two weeks of paid vacation. In 1998, three public holidays – Labour Day, National Day and the Spring Festival – were extended to three days each with weekends, and all of these holidays are effectively extended to one week

Table 4.10 Total number of domestic trips in China, 1999–2004

Year	Number of trips ('000s)	Growth (%)
1999	719,000.0	–
2000	744,000.0	3.5
2001	784,000.0	5.4
2002	878,000.0	12.0
2003	857,771.9	−2.3
2004	932,847.2	8.8

Source: Euromonitor (2005a).

each. It is estimated that urban Chinese people each receive 114 leisure days. This is key to stimulating the growth of domestic tourism (Zhang, Pine and Lam, 2005).

3 Structural readjustments of the China's economy.

Domestic tourism has been given further impetus by an increase in car ownership plus reasonable and relatively cheap airport facilities that are widely used by the domestic population. Domestic flights are frequent and airports in China have been constantly upgraded and renewed over the past five to ten years, although there remains room for improvement.

The economic impact of domestic tourism

Gong and Kruse (2003) have evaluated the economic impact of domestic tourism in China. They point to four major economic impacts and benefits of the huge growth in domestic tourism in China. The first is that there is an "interregional transfer of Chinese purchasing power". This means that there is a transfer of incomes from the places in which the domestic tourists reside to the places that they visit. Gong and Kruse (2000) point to the lesser known seaside resort of Beidaine where 70% of all retail sales are generated by domestic tourism. This movement of incomes could go some way in improving regional income imbalances.

The second is that domestic tourism and its expenditure plus its multiplier effects are better for the growth of local economies than international tourism. The reasons that Gong and Kruse (2000) cite for this is that domestic tourism is by its nature less capital intensive, has more local involvement and serves a larger number of people.

Third, domestic tourism provided business opportunities for small businesses. This gives a spur and a boost to local entrepreneurship that would not be gained by international tourism and the multinational enterprises that are attracted by it. Next, the economy may be managed through domestic tourism, for example, consumer spending may be increased by promoting domestic tourism.

Last, domestic tourism may have social benefits. It should not be forgotten that China has vast disparities in income particularly between rural and urban populations. Tourism promotion in rural areas could go some way to alleviating poverty in rural areas.

Although these benefits are given for China, it should be noted that they are fairly general and could also apply to India, which has similar disparities between urban and rural areas.

Problems with domestic tourism

Notwithstanding the benefits of domestic tourism, Zhang, Pine and Lam (2005) point out that there are three problems with domestic tourism in China. The first is that there is a lack of variety in the tourism offering. Chinese domestic tourism tends to concentrate upon sightseeing and natural and cultural attractions. It does not take advantage of the other attractions that China has to offer.

Second, there are problems that concern the knowledge and quality of tourism professionals, this is deemed to be lacking in the Chinese travel and tourism industry. This problem may lessen with the advent of competition in the travel market but may be at the expense of China's domestic businesses.

Last, the average per capita income within China, and especially away from the large cities, is extremely low. This is a major barrier to domestic tourism as high disposable income is a prerequisite to tourism of any kind and is required to sustain it.

Employment in China's tourist industry

The World Travel and Tourism Council, WTCC (2006), estimates that in 2006, an excess of 77 million people are employed directly and indirectly by travel and tourism in China. This is over one-tenth of all employment. This figure is expected to rise to almost 90 million by 2016.

These figures include the multiplier effect; that is, for each employee directly employed in travel and tourism, there are other people employed indirectly servicing travel and tourism. For example, a wine waiter in a hotel could be directly employed by tourism, and the wine supplier would be indirectly employed by tourism. Both parties would experience the benefits or otherwise of tourism.

The employment that tourism brings benefits the individual employee as he/she receives a wage or salary. It also benefits the government as it receives tax on the salary and tax revenues on the spending that the salary is used for.

Challenges to China's tourism industry

China's tourism industry may be booming; however, it faces many challenges in the near future if its growth is to continue and the economic benefits are reaped (Gong and Kruse, 2003; Mak, 2003). These challenges may be described as external competition, environmental costs, infrastructure, seasonality and possible overcapacity.

China will face increased competition from enterprises that are outside of its borders. China has been effectively opened up to competition by its entry into the WTO in 2000. The effect of this is that China's travel market is now open to external competition in the tourism market place. This may be multinational operators in hotels, attractions and transport. The question that this raises is – Can China's tourism enterprises survive this competition when there is no longer any protectionism? (Gong and Kruse, 2003).

Tourism may have adverse environmental impacts upon China. Tourism and travel come at cost, not the least of which is the environment. China already has a very high proportion of the world's most polluted cities. How will tourism's environmental impacts be dealt with? Increased air travel will add to global warming. Historic sites could be endangered. Tourism resources may be insufficient to deal with the increased number of visitors.

Although great strides have been made, problems with its tourism infrastructure remain. Mak (2003) claims that transport remains one of the biggest barriers to tourism and its development in China. The reason given for this is that transport varies in standard across the provinces, and schedules are poor. Across all transport sectors, there are inefficiencies and relatively low economies of scale. Airlines are lacking in punctuality, and there are poor safety records. Roads are poor with few major motorways, cities are congested and there are many accidents leading inevitably to fears about the safety of tourists.

Tourism in China could suffer from seasonality, that is, that demand depends upon the time of year. Domestic tourism in China has its peaks, and these peaks coincide with the three long, major public holidays. Cities with major tourism attractions that attract international tourists, such as Beijing, may be extremely cold and unwelcoming in winter. This can lead to peaks and troughs in tourism that can in turn lead to employment being subject to season and give rise to seasonal unemployment, which would have attendant negative impacts upon incomes.

There is a possibility that there may be overcapacity in the travel and tourism industry. Gong and Kruse (2003, p. 99) suggest that tourism in China has become a "development fad" based upon the notion that tourism is "good everywhere". If tourism becomes too big and grows too quickly, there may be oversupply in the industry that may lead to greater rivalry and competition, which, in turn, may lead to inefficiencies in operations as operations are not at their capacity.

From the international arrivals figures, much of international demand for China as a tourism destination is from compatriots from Hong Kong, Taiwan, Macau and overseas Chinese. Many of these tourists are merely "popping over" the border or are visiting friends and family. Their expenditure may be low when compared to other more "traditional" tourists. The challenge to China is to widen its international tourist base. Further, the foreign tourists tend to concentrate on only a few destinations. These are Beijing, Shanghai, Guangzhou, Xi'an, Guilin, Shenzhen and Hangzhou, and it will be noted that two of these, Shenzhen and Guangzhou, are very close to the Hong Kong border. The remainder indicates a concentration of tourism expenditure in relatively few locations.

China is not the only tourism destination in Southeast Asia. Other destinations such as Vietnam and Cambodia are becoming popular; a consequence of this may be that China faces competition from these emerging destinations.

Opportunities for China's tourist industry

China has many positive growth factors that help its tourism industry. These growth factors include economic growth that is increasing its potential for business tourism, higher disposable incomes and enhanced leave entitlements. Additionally, improved promotion of China's tourism resources and the "opening up" of China through the WTO's agreement may give China's tourism industry the professionalism that it needs.

Due to its vast resources, opportunities exist for other attractions that China may offer. These would include "niche tourism" products such as adventure tourism and eco-tourism.

Summary

China is an emerging nation and is set to become the world's "number one" tourism destination. China has recognised the economic benefits that tourism may bring and has implemented policies in order to receive these benefits.

China has vast, largely untapped tourism resources. It has a long history and a wealth of cultural and historic artefacts. There is a tremendous demand for incoming business and business tourism due to the strength of the economy. Domestic tourism demand has increased; this has been brought about by increases in disposable income and extra leisure and vacation time.

Nevertheless, China does still face problems; despite recent improvements, the infrastructure for tourism is poor. While improvements to airports have been made, road networks remain poor and slow. There are few motorways, and travel into major cities is extremely difficult as they are heavily congested. Tourism is concentrated in relatively few locations leaving some tourist attractions relatively ignored. Demand for incoming international tourism is largely from Hong Kong and other Chinese territories. Marketing to the rest of the world needs to be improved.

In conclusion, China has recognised the importance of tourism to its economy. It is doing relatively well from tourism exports and employment. If this is to continue, it will be necessary to both fund and manage tourism development properly in order to ensure that the benefits are sustained.

India

Introduction

This section on tourism in India effectively mirrors that on China. It considers the tourist resources that India has to offer. As with previous section, it continues by examining the impact of tourism in terms of the number of visitors, both domestic and international, and the impact that this has on India's economy.

It concludes by considering India's tourism policies from 1945 and the challenges or barriers that the Indian tourist industry faces in early part of this century.

India's tourism resources

India has a diversity of offering. It is the world's second most populous country. It has a wealth of tourism resources and should offer something for every type of tourist. Abram, Edwards, Ford, Sen and Wooldrige (1999) state that India is geographically diverse; it has a diversity of landscape ranging from mountains to deserts.

India is one of the world's oldest civilisations and has diversity within both its religions and its peoples. India has a variety of tourist attractions that include wildlife parks, beaches such as Goa, ancient monuments of which the most famous is probably the Taj Mahal, sites of pilgrimage, music and festivals, palaces and forts and hill stations such as Ooty. Yet despite this wealth of offering, India is regarded as a sleeping giant of tourism. It does not, at present, receive the number of tourists that are commensurate with its size and offerings. As Abram et al. (1999) say, it should be a Mecca for tourism, instead it is a sleeping giant. It may, however, be a sleeping giant that is to be awoken.

Table 4.11 shows India's top tourism attractions by type and sales in 2004.

Table 4.11 clearly indicates that historic buildings and sites are by far the most popular tourist attractions in India. They account for well over half of all tourist expenditure on attractions. These attractions include the Taj Mahal (see Table 4.12). The Indian government gave a boost to visits to historic monuments by overseas tourists when it dropped the policy of increased prices to such attractions to foreign visitors. Attractions gaining in popularity are amusement parks (Euromonitor, 2005b).

Table 4.12 shows tourist attractions by visitors. The top five attractions each have visitors in excess of 1 million each year. The Taj Mahal, closely followed by other historic monuments that represent India's historic and cultural tradition, probably unsurprisingly, heads the table.

Table 4.11 Top tourist attractions by sector on the basis of sales percentage in India – 2004

Rank	Attraction	Total sales (%)
1	Historic Buildings and sites	57.4
2	Theme and amusement parks	15.5
3	National parks/areas of natural beauty	9.8
4	Theatres	6.5
5	Zoos and aquariums	4.0
6	Others (includes large temples, sporting events, cultural festivals and fairs)	3.9
7	Museums	1.9
8	Art galleries	0.5
9	Circuses	0.5
	Total	100.0

Source: Extrapolated from Euromonitor (2005b).

Table 4.12 *Major tourist attractions by visitors ('000s) – 2004*

Rank	Attraction	Number of visitors
1	Taj Mahal, Agra	2,494.2
2	Red Fort, New Delhi	2,112.0
3	Qutb Minar, New Delhi	2,105.7
4	Sun Temple, Konark	1,351.4
5	Agra Fort, Agra	1,278.5
6	Ajanta Caves, Eliora Caves, Aurangabad	967.2
7	Golconda Fort, Hyderabad	822.5
8	Bibi Ka Maqbara	807.6
9	Group of Monuments, Mallapuram	800.1
10	Gol-Gumbas	783.2

Source: Euromonitor (2005b).

Tourism development, planning and policy in India

Gupta, Lal and Bhattacharyya (2002) state that tourism planning started in India in 1945, when it was recommended that a separate tourist organisation with regional offices should be established. By 1948, this had become an ad hoc committee, which included representatives from the hospitality, tourism and transport industries.

In the intervening years to present day, the expansion of tourism has led to it being taken more seriously by the government, and increased provision has been made for it in the government's five-year plans. Recently, tourism has been given prominence and status as it has been recognised by the formation of Ministry of Tourism and Culture (Gupta, Lal and Bhattacharyya, 2002). The role of the ministry involves the planning, publicity and programming of conferences, the travel trade, hospitality and accommodation. Additionally, it provides market research (including providing statistical information) and administration. These administrative functions are important as they include activities aimed at ridding tourism of some of its bureaucratic excesses such as simplification of frontier formalities and regulating the various activities that make up travel, for example hotels (Gupta, Lal and Bhattacharyya, 2002). The role of government with regard to tourism has been one of providing direction.

Tourism planning

Gupta, Lal and Bhattacharyya (2002) state that the Indian government has made several plans for tourism. These include the following:

National action plan for tourism (1992) • • •

This was aimed at achieving a growth in tourist arrivals and with it foreign exchange and employment. This was to be achieved by taking away some of the barriers to India's tourism potential. Essentially, this involved improving the infrastructure of tourism and developing certain areas for tourism growth and development. In addition, there were to be improvements to the tourism offering through the creation of heritage hotels and resorts and the introduction of river cruises and trains for tourists. Last, special airline and hotel packages to encourage tourism were to be developed.

National strategy for the development of tourism (1996) • • •

The national strategy was developed after discussion with the planning commission and state governments. The proposals from these discussions included the following:

1 Transport – airports and roads were to be modernised. The rail network was to be improved.
2 Improvements to the tourism infrastructure were to be made alongside environmental planning.
3 The development of new tourism products – cultural and eco-tourism.
4 A focused marketing strategy that includes both publicity and promotion.

Ninth plan (1997–2002) • • •

The planning commission approved funding for the development of the tourism infrastructure. This included product development, manpower development and research. By 2002, there had been a 9% increase in tourism in India, but the performance of India as a major tourism player was poor as it only received 1% of the global market (Gupta, Lal and Bhattacharyya, 2002). The Delhi declaration of 2001 attributed this poor performance to promotion and marketing.

National tourism policy (2002–2007)/the tenth five-year plan • • •

This policy was devised as a framework for tourism that is led by government, is propelled by the private sector and is directly aimed at the welfare of the Indian community. Euromonitor (2005b) summarises the policy by saying that the part of the government is to provide the infrastructure for tourism along with the legislative framework; the private sector, in turn, provides a quality tourism product and the community supplements all of this by providing its support.

The intention of the policy is to establish India as a global tourism brand, and add to and improve the products that the industry offers, for example through adventure and eco-tourism (Gupta, Lal and Bhattacharyya, 2002;

• •

Euromonitor, 2005b). Seven key words to promote tourism were introduced. These are welcome, information, facilitation, safety, co-operation, infrastructure and cleanliness. It also, as with the previous policies, intends to improve the tourism infrastructure. However, this time funds, both private and public, and incentives to invest in tourism are available.

Additionally and importantly, the tenth five-year plan allocated 2,900 crores to tourism. The tenth five-year plan intends to make the following happen (Euromonitor, 2005b).

1 To place tourism firmly as a major driver of economic growth in India.
2 It recognises the multiplier effects of tourism in terms of job creation and economic growth. In doing this, it intends to bind the multiplier effects for their positive economic benefits.
3 To provide a spur for domestic tourism and to enlarge international tourism.
4 To place weight on India's tourism potential, effectively by awakening the sleeping giant and placing India as a global brand.
5 To create and develop new tourist circuits based upon India's culture and heritage.

The tenth five-year plan adds weight to this by providing a series of incentives aimed at encouraging investment in tourism and improving the infrastructure. With regards to the infrastructure, funding is available for the airports at Bangalore and Hyderabad. Money is also available for modernising the airports at New Delhi and Mumbai (Euromonitor, 2005b).

Incentives to tourism have been provided in two forms through lower taxes and incentives to investment. First, lower taxes resulted in the expenditure tax on hotels has been abolished. The obvious and immediate impact of this is to make hotels and therefore the tourism product more affordable. A further cut in taxation, although with a lesser impact, is that the customs duty on imported liquor has been reduced; this will have some impact in the luxury hotels market.

Second, there are significant incentives to invest in the hotel industry. The hotel industry has been given infrastructure status, the effect of this is that the hotel industry attracts a lower rate of interest and borrowing for hotel investment is cheaper. Additionally, financial institutions, for example, major banks receive tax breaks on income from hotel project loans. The impact of this is to make more funds available for building and improving hotels in the three-star categories and above (Euromonitor, 2005b).

The new tourism policy and the tenth five-year plan appear for the first time to be placing a genuine emphasis on tourism and making positive efforts to improve the infrastructure for tourism.

International tourism

Number of international arrivals • • •

Tables 4.13 and 4.14 show that in the years 2003 and 2004, there was a boom in both international arrivals and departures compared with other

Table 4.13 Number of arrivals to India, 1999–2004

Year	Number ('000s)	Growth (%)
1999	2,481.9	–
2000	2,641.2	6.4
2001	2,537.4	-3.9
2002	2,384.4	-6.0
2003	2,750.3	15.3
2004	3,355.4	22.0

Source: Euromonitor (2005b).

Table 4.14 Arrivals to India by purpose of visit, 1999–2004

Purpose	1999	2000	2001	2002	2003	2004	Increase 1999– 2004 (%)
Business	505.9	792.4	608.1	755.8	882.6	1,083.8	105.3
Leisure	1,044.4	1,162.1	1,004.7	1,037.0	1,210.2	1,435.2	37.4
Visiting friends and relatives	612.9	422.6	674.3	377.9	446.3	626.2	2.1
Others (includes pilgrimages, social and religious studies)	318.7	264.1	250.3	213.7	211.2	210.2	-34.0
Total	2,481.0	2,641.2	2,537.4	2,384.4	2,750.3	3,355.4	35.2

Source: Extrapolated from Euromonitor (2005b).

years in which tourism performance was patchy. International tourism increased by over 15% in 2003 and 22% in 2004, while tourism receipts rose by 16% and 32% respectively. Tourism is now regarded as a major driver of the Indian economy for the earnings and the employment that it brings. These figures came at a time when India received international accolades as a major tourism destination.

The reasons for the turnaround in the fortune of the Indian tourist industry are mainly due to improvements to infrastructure and marketing and the alleviation of health fears. With regard to marketing, India has placed much time and effort into evolving the country as a major tourism destination and a global brand. Twenty-nine billion rupees have been allocated to improving the marketing effort of India's tourism. The government has given its support to publicity campaigns.

Improvements have been made to the tourism infrastructure; this has been mostly manifested in improvements to a number of major airports. While these improvements are acknowledged, further improvements need to be made to the road and other transport networks.

Table 4.13 shows that arrivals to India have increased by 35.25% from 1999 to 2004, there have been increases in three of the categories of purpose of travel. The most impressive is in the business category in which travel has more than doubled in six years. These figures reflect the increasing importance of the Indian market on the world stage. The level of English in India is such that it is a favoured destination for the "globalisation" plans of many multinational enterprises, particularly in the world of banking and finance.

The 37% increase in the number of leisure visitors may be a reflection of the marketing of India as a destination.

Incoming tourism

Tables 4.15 and 4.16 demonstrate the growth rates of India's incoming and outgoing tourism receipts. With the exception of 2001 and 2002, tourism receipts are starting to indicate quite vigorous growth. This may be another sign of the sleeping giant awakening. The constant growth rate for 2004 shows a growth in receipts in excess of a quarter in one year.

The upsurge in tourism to India is due to a combination of two factors. First, India has made attempts to improve its marketing of itself as a major tourism destination. Second, the growth of India's economy and its position within globalisation has made it a destination for foreign business travel.

Table 4.15   India's incoming tourism receipts and growth, 1999–2004

Year	Receipt		Growth (%)	
	Current (Rs million)	Constant (Rs million)	Current	Constant
1999	129,510.0	129,510.0	–	–
2000	142,380.0	136,891.4	9.9	5.7
2001	143,440.0	133,009.4	0.7	−2.8
2002	141,950.0	126,0894.7	−1.0	−5.2
2003	164,290.0	140,583.2	15.7	11.5
2004	216,862.8	177,919.2	32.0	26.6

Source: Extrapolated from Euromonitor (2005b).

Table 4.16 India's outgoing tourism expenditure and growth, 1999–2004

Year	Expenditure		Growth (%)	
	Current (Rs million)	Constant (Rs million)	Current	Constant
1999	92,680.0	92,680.0	–	–
2000	131,360.0	126,296.2	41.7	36.3
2001	108,690.0	100,786.4	−17.3	−20.2
2002	167,610.0	148,882.6	54.2	47.7
2003	161,100.0	137,853.5	−3.9	−7.4
2004	202,986.0	166,534.4	26.0	20.8

Source: Extrapolated from Euromonitor (2005b).

Outgoing tourism

The pattern of outgoing tourism has been erratic; outgoing tourism has experienced falls followed by recovery. Over the period from 1999 to 2004 there has been a massive increase in outgoing tourism.

The reasons for this growth are all connected to the economy. First, there have been general increases in disposable income that is a prerequisite of tourism. Second, the globalisation of the Indian economy has led to the need for Indian business people to travel abroad for work (Euromonitor, 2005b).

Balance of payments

Table 4.17 gives India's travel balance. With the exception of 2002, India has had a surplus on its travel balance in each of the years. India is a

Table 4.17 India's travel balance, 1999–2004

Year	Receipt (Rs million)	Expenditure (Rs million)	Balance (Rs million)
1999	129,510.0	92,680.0	36,830.0
2000	142,380.0	131,360.0	11,020.0
2001	143,440.0	108,690.0	34,750.0
2002	141,950.0	167,610.0	−25,660.0
2003	164,290.0	161,100.0	3,190.0
2004	216,862.8	202,986.0	13,876.8

Source: Euromonitor (2005b).

net exporter of tourism and as such tourism is an invisible export that is a major earner of foreign currency. Tourism contribution is such that it accounts for over 5% of all exports. Its contribution as an invisible export is much greater than this.

Given the poor performance of the Indian tourism until recently, the figures indicate the potential of tourism as an earner of foreign currency for the Indian economy.

Domestic tourism

Table 4.18 shows the increase in domestic tourism in India from 1999 to 2004. Over that period, domestic tourism has increased by over 80% (Euromonitor, 2005b). Domestic tourism has seen year on year increases each year from 1999 to 2004. Despite the huge increase, the number of trips remains low when the population is taken into consideration. Notwithstanding, this spending on domestic tourism in 2004 stood at over 538 billion rupees. It should be noted that statistics for Indian domestic tourism trips create a difficulty in that business trips are included within them and are not shown separately (Euromonitor, 2005b).

Euromonitor (2005b) and Mintel (2003) give five main reasons for the increase in domestic tourism. These may be summarised as improved facilities, price competition, better disposable incomes, government policy and improved marketing. First, there has been an improvement in tourist facilities, which could further improve with the budget hotels that have arrived in the Indian accommodation market. Second, competition on price between public and private carriers has resulted in prices being cut, and the first budget carrier – Air Deccan – has arrived in the air transport market.

Third, disposable income has increased, particularly in industry and services. Gross Domestic Product and disposable incomes have grown faster than the population. A sign of the increased disposable incomes is that between 1999 and 2004 spending on leisure services increased by more than 50% at constant prices (Euromonitor, 2005b).

Table 4.18   Total number of domestic trips in India, 1999–2004

Year	Number of trips ('000s)	Growth (%)
1999	190,671.0	–
2000	220,106.9	15.4
2001	234,781.4	6.7
2002	271,328.2	15.6
2003	315,116.2	16.1
2004	346,484.6	10.0

Source: Euromonitor (2005b).

Next, government policy towards tourism has given a boost to tourism. The tenth five-year plan reduced taxation on hotels making accommodation prices cheaper; fiscal policy has been used to increase household spending by reducing personal taxation.

Last, government tourism policy has been aimed at promoting tourism and its infrastructure. To this end, 29 billion rupees were allocated. While it is too early to establish cause or effect, it may be that tourism promotion that has been advocated since 1945 is beginning to work.

The economic impact of domestic tourism in India

Earlier in this chapter, the economic impact of domestic tourism in China was evaluated. Four major economic impacts and benefits of the huge growth in domestic tourism in China were given. These were an inter-regional transfer of purchasing power that may redress regional income imbalances, the multiplier effects of domestic tourism and the management of the economy through domestic tourism. As India has similar regional imbalances and disparities in incomes between urban and rural populations, it is likely that India may experience similar impacts to those claimed for China.

Additionally, India may receive social benefits in that tourism may go some way to alleviating poverty within the country.

Employment in India's tourism industry

The WTCC (2006) estimates that in 2006 an excess of 24 million people are employed directly and indirectly by travel and tourism in India. This figure is approximately 3% of all employment. In percentage terms, it is very low when compared to major international tourism destinations but placed India in second place in the world tourism employment league.

These figures include the multiplier effects that were explained in the section on China. As with China, the employment that tourism brings benefits the individual employee as he/she receives a wage or salary. It also benefits the government as it receives tax on the salary and tax revenues on the spending that the salary is used for.

Challenges to India's tourism industry

Mintel (2003) says that barriers to the growth of tourism in India were identified at the WTCC's India Initiative. The retreat at Agra identified that there are five major barriers that India's tourism industry must overcome if it is to improve its ranking in the world's tourism league tables, and, importantly enjoy the benefits that tourism may bring.

The first barrier, a consequence of civil aviation policy, is that fares are high and schedules can be erratic. The second barrier is that visa processing may be slow and lengthy, leading almost inevitably to significant delays that can be a deterrent to tourist demand.

Third, although much is being done to address it, destination marketing is poor when compared to other major tourist destinations. India does not have an Olympic Games or an Expo to showcase its attractions. Next, the infrastructure for tourism, particularly the rail networks, leave room for a great deal of improvement. The final barrier identified was that India was seen to be slow in responding to and managing both crises that impact upon tourism and opportunities that may arise for tourism.

Opportunities for tourism in India

The opportunities for travel and tourism in India will arise from business and leisure demand. Leisure demand will depend upon India's ability to overcome the barriers that were identified and the ability to open up the tourism products and attractions that it has.

The WTCC's India Initiative identified new products that India could exploit to improve its position in world tourism. These new products and the markets that go with them will need careful marketing if they are to be a success. The potential new markets include cultural tourism (India has 22 world heritage sites), adventure tourism in the Himalayas, eco-tourism in the Himalayas and the Andaman and Nicobar islands and holistic healing and rejuvenation (Mintel, 2003).

Summary

China and India are two emerging nations that appear to be faring very differently in world tourism. China is set to become the world's "number one" tourism destination while the WTCC has described India, with all of its resources, as the "sleeping giant" of tourism. Nevertheless, there are indications that India may be awakening from its slumber as it, along with China, recognises the economic benefits that tourism may bring.

Tourism in both countries has similarities. Both China and India have vast, largely untapped tourism resources. They have long histories and a wealth of cultural and historic artefacts. Both countries have a tremendous demand for incoming business due to the strength of their economies. Both countries have increased demand for domestic tourism brought about by increases in disposable income and extra leisure and vacation time.

The problems that they face are also similar. Both, despite recent improvements, have poor infrastructures for tourism. While both have made improvements to airports, road networks remain poor and slow. Major cities are heavily congested. Similarly, both China and India tend to have tourism concentrated in relatively few locations leaving some tourist attractions relatively ignored.

In conclusion, China and India have recognised the importance of tourism to their economies. Both are doing relatively well from tourism exports and employment. If they are to continue, it will be necessary for both countries to fund and manage tourism development properly in order to ensure that the benefits are sustained.

References

Abram, D., Edwards, N., Ford, M., Sen, D. and Wooldrige, B. (1999). *India: The Rough Guide*. London, Rough Guides Ltd.

CNTA (2001), The Tenth five-year plan and the long-term goals up to 2015 and 2020 for tourism development in China, Bejing: China Tourism Publishing House. Cited in Lew, A.A., Yu, L, Ap. J. and Z. Guangrui (2003). Introduction. In Lew, A.A., Yu, L., Ap., J. and Z. Guangrui (eds) *Tourism in China*, Bridghampton, NY: Howarth.

Euromonitor (2005a). *China: Global Market Factfile*. http//www.gmid.euromonitor.com/CountryProfile.aspx

Euromonitor (2005b). *India: Global Market Factfile*. http//www.gmid.euromonitor.com/CountryProfile.aspx

Gong, X. and Kruse, C. (2003). Economic impact of tourism. In Lew, A.A., Yu, L., Ap, J. and Guangrui, Z. (eds), *Tourism in China*, Bridghampton, NY, Howarth, pp. 83–101.

Gu, Z. (2003). The Chinese Lodging Industry: Problems and Solutions, *International Journal of Contemporary Hospitality Management*, **15**(7), 386–392.

Gupta, S.P., Lal, K. and Bhattacharyya, M. (2002). *Cultural Tourism in India*. New Delhi, DK Printworld.

Lew, A.A., Yu, L., Ap., J. and Z. Guangrui (2003). Introduction. In Lew, A.A., Yu, L., AP, J. and Z. Guangrui eds., *Tourism in China*, Bridghampton, NY: Howarth.

Macartney, J. (2006). Wave of Chinese Tourist Shoppers Floods the High Streets of Europe, *The Times*, 15 July.

Mak, B. (2003). China's tourist transportations: Air, land and water. In Lew, A.A., Yu, L., Ap, J. and Guangrui, Z. (eds), *Tourism in China*. Bridghampton, NY, Howarth, pp. 165–193.

Mintel (2003). *Travel and Tourism – India*, Mintel Publications, July.

Shen, X. (2003). Short and long-haul international tourists to China. In Lew, A. A., Yu, L., Ap, J., and Guangrui, Z. (eds), *Tourism in China*. Bridghampton, NY, Howarth.

Wang, S. and Qu, H. (2004). A Comparison Study of Chinese Domestic Tourism: China vs the USA, *International Journal of Contemporary Hospitality Management*, **16**(2), 103–115.

World Trade Organisation (WTO) (1997). Tourism: 2020 vision, Madrid: WTO.

World Travel and Tourism Council (2006). *China: Travel and Tourism Climbing to New Heights*. World Travel and Tourism Economic Research.

Wu, B., Zhu, H. and Xu, X. (2000). Trends in China's Domestic Tourism Development at the Turn of the Century, *International Journal of Contemporary Hospitality Management*, **12**(5), 296–299.

Zhang, Q.H., Chang, K. and Jenkins, C.L. (2000). Tourism Policy Implementation in Mainland China: An Enterprise Perspective, *International Journal of Contemporary Hospitality Management*, **14**(1), 28–42.

Zhang, H.Q., Pine, R. and Lam, T. (2005). *Tourism and Hotel Development in China: From Political to Economic Success*. Bridghampton, NY, Howarth.

Zhong, G., Pine, R. and Zhong, H.Q. (2000). China's International Tourist Development: Present and Future, *International Journal of Contemporary Hospitality Management*, **12**(5), 282–290.

Part Two

Hospitality and Tourism Management in China

(Including Hong Kong and Macau)

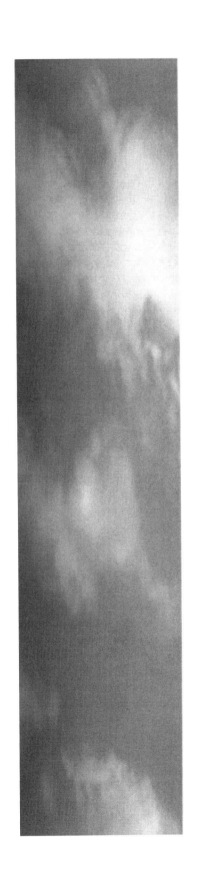

CHAPTER 5

Hotels and resorts – China

> **Chapter objectives**
>
> When you have read this chapter, you will be able to
>
> 1 Explain the nature and the structural characteristics of the hotel and resort sector in China.
> 2 Provide a historical overview of hotel and resort development in China and some of the influencing factors on this development.
> 3 Identify and critically review some of the major development and management issues and operational trends.
> 4 Evaluate the future outlook for the sector.

Introduction

In 1978, when China first opened its doors to international visitors, there were very few hotels in the country. With massive international tourism since that time, especially since the beginning of the new millennium, the hotel industry in China has burgeoned. But it has been a long and steep journey of discovery. There have been barriers to both indigenous hotel company growth and the establishment of international hotel chains. The chains have been considered to be probably of particular significance to the future development of the industry (Pine and Qi, 2004). Yet there are indications that they have been affected by a range of barriers. These have included the economic and political systems that have been in place, and whilst overseas hotel investors were encouraged, up until China's entry into the WTO in 2001, they were under government control. Now China is forecast by the WTO to become the world's top tourist destination by 2020, with an estimated 130 million international travellers, and with government control effectively removed, investors are flooding into such an extent that hotel building is booming (Elegant, 2006).

This chapter begins by providing a historical overview of the development of hotels in China and examines some of the factors that have influenced, and are currently influencing, this development. The chapter will proceed to explain the nature and the structural characteristics of the hotel sector and then analyse some of the major development and management issues. Finally, the future outlook for the sector will be discussed.

Historical overview

Accommodation serving travellers has existed in China since ancient times, but it was not until the 1920s with the improvement of transportation systems that the tourism industry really began to emerge. This was coupled with the first period of hotel growth. However, political wars put an end to this fledgling industry in the 1930s and from then through the foundation of the PRC in 1949 and until 1978, domestic tourism hardly existed and there were virtually no incoming international tourists. The 10 years of the Cultural Revolution from 1966 to 1976 made tourism development a non-issue in China (Chen and Ball, 2005). Visitor arrivals in 1978, for example, were 1.8 million (including tourists from Hong Kong and Macao), which exceeded the total accumulated arrivals from 1949 to 1977. In 1979, the number of arrivals increased by 133% to 4.2 million (CNTA, 2000).

In 1978, the Communist Party of China made a policy change to move away from political struggles to economic reform. This change, along with China's decision to open its doors to the outside world, provided a massive fillip to its tourism industry. The development of the hotel industry commenced at this time, and from this point on, there was no looking back for the tourism and hotel industry.

Before 1978, hotels of international standard were very limited and of poor quality. According to Sun (1992), there were only 76,192 bedspaces in 203 hotels in China in 1978 and only 137 of these, which were all state-owned, could really accommodate international visitors. This rose slightly to 150 in 1979 but was still totally inadequate to meet the basic and modern accommodation needs of this huge surge of tourists (Han, 1994; Wei et al., 1999). The lack of hotel beds was a major problem and so the Chinese government set about increasing the size of the hotel industry (Zhao, 1989). China's five-year plan from 1981 to 1985 focused on hotel development. After 1984, local government departments, collectives and even individuals were allowed to invest in and operate tourism development projects, and foreign investment was introduced into the hospitality industry and was very successful (Tisdell and Wen, 1991). As a result, the total number of hotels increased to 710 by 1985 (CNTA, 2002). Since 1984, China has achieved great progress. There have been large increases in the number of hotels and bedspaces and fundamental changes to facilities and services have occurred, often reflected in the price, as a result of the combined efforts of the national and local governments and of the private and public sectors. This was further stimulated in 1992 as China widened its economic reform and "Open Door" policy (Zhang, Pine and Lam, 2005). However, while foreign involvement in the hotel industry in China was encouraged and aided until 2001, businesses were still under government control. However, after 15 years of trying, China entered into the WTO in 2001. One eventual consequence of this should be the end of such controls.

In 2006, there was a hotel construction frenzy in China, particularly in the larger cities. This has been fuelled by a variety of factors. China is expected to become the second most popular tourism destination within a decade, according to the World Tourism Organisation, and by 2020, it is forecast to become the world's most-visited country, attracting some 130 million visitors a year. This will be aided by the 2008 Beijing Olympics, which will raise the profile of the country on the world's stage – this will bode well for the future prospects of the country's hotel industry. China's burgeoning domestic-tourism market is also important. By 2010, the number of domestic tourists is forecast to soar from 1.2 billion to about 1.8 billion. Further contributing to this domestic-tourism/hotel boom is the dramatic rise in car sales and the rapid construction of a national road network, making travel more practical and appealing. China has about 22,000 miles of roads, a number that is expected to be more than double by 2020. Other developments that are contributing to increased domestic travel and demand for hotels have been the increase in the number of low-cost airlines expanding throughout the country. While in Hong Kong, the arrival of Disney in September 2005 is contributing to hotel performance there.

Many of China's older hotels have failed to survive recent changes, and so the vast majority of hotels today are of recent construction. This is the case of many luxury hotels, which Harper (2001) says are "often tedious and dull on the exterior [but] encase splendid interiors". Such hotels are largely to be found in Hong Kong, Macau, Beijing, Guangzhou and Shanghai but in more recent years have begun to appear elsewhere, as business travel has increased beyond these places.

Size, significance and structural features of the sector

Hotel provision in China ranges from the cheap non-star rated and privately owned hotels to five-star international hotels operated by chains. The Chinese call low-priced hotels binguan (meaning guest house), whereas more expensive hotels are called jiudian (meaning wineshop) or fandian (strangely meaning restaurant) (Harper, 2001).

In China, in 2000, there were 10,481 hotels and 948,182 bedrooms. These fell respectively to 7,358 hotels and 816,260 bedrooms in 2001 when the non-star rated hotels were removed from the statistics (CNTA, 2002). This suggests that there were around 1,500–2,000 non-star rated hotels at that time. By the end of 2002, the number of tourist and star-rated hotels had risen to 8880 (Tables 5.1 and 5.5). Over 18% of these had over

Table 5.1 Comparative statistics of Chinese tourist hotels by ownership type – 2002

Type of ownership	Number of hotels	Number of rooms ('000s)	Average occupancy	Revenue £m*
State-owned	5061	487.1	57.9	2649.4
Collective shareholding	893	71.0	58.2	403.0
Co-operative	172	15.6	60.1	120.0
Alliance	90	9.5	61.0	66.9
Limited liability	732	75.0	63.3	592.4
Limited liability shares	327	41.1	65.6	395.5
Private	559	36.0	59.9	203.5
Others	361	26.4	56.2	148.7
Hong Kong, Macau, Taiwan investors	407	74.8	66.0	1186.3
Foreign investors	279	60.7	64.8	888.5
Total	8880	897.2	60.1	7034.1

* Calculated data. Currency conversion is CNY = £1.
Source: China National Tourism Administration Report web site released on 15/7/03.
Web sites: www.cnta.org.cn, www.ctha.org.cn

300 rooms and nearly a third were concentrated in Beijing, Shanghai, Guangdong and Zhejiang provinces. Wang (2003) states that in 2002, the total revenue from these tourist hotels was over £7 billion and that they supported 1.2 million local jobs and contributed tax revenues of about £374 million.

The structure of China's hotel industry can be analysed in different ways. Table 5.1 divides tourist hotels into 10 ownership categories. State-owned hotels, with their complicated ownership, dominated in 2002 with 57% of the total hotels and just over 54% of all bedrooms. However, these were only responsible for 38% of the total revenue and their average occupancy was less than 58%. Their revenue per available room (revPAR) was approximately £5,439 or £15 per day. In contrast, Hong Kong, Macau, Taiwan and foreign investors were responsible for nearly 8% of the total hotels and 15% of all bedrooms in China, and yet they were achieving almost 30% of total revenue with a revPAR of close to £15,000 per room or around £41 per day and had average occupancies of around 65%.

The weaker performance of the state-owned hotels can be explained by them being unlike commercial businesses, having a lesser/no concern for profits and having a greater interest in social responsibility (Wang, 2003). They follow traditional administrative systems, have central planning still in place and still have too much bureaucracy and have been described as conservative with ideas, lacking in vitality and sensitivity to the changing market and environment (Muxlow, 2006).

In contrast, Wang (2003) claims that the joint-venture hotels owned by Hong Kong, Macau, Taiwan and foreign investors and mostly managed by multinational hotel companies have comparative advantages in financial and management expertise and in business concepts and techniques. These and their favourable taxation position have boosted their performance. Competition between these companies has intensified and the surge of foreign interest in launching and managing new mainland hotels is astounding "It's stratospheric," says Patrick Ford, president of Lodging Econometrics, a U.S.-based industry-research group. "China is the most attractive place in the world right now for hotels. That's why investment capital is racing there and why the major international brands are racing there too". Indeed, 188 new hotels are under construction in China, says Ford, and 145 of them are four- or five-star offerings with more than 200 rooms. Even if some of these projects aren't completed, this building spree could bring as many as 30,000 new rooms to China at a cost of more than $8 billion (Elegant, 2006).

The presence of the multinational chains especially boosted occupancy levels in Beijing and other key cities. For Beijing, Hong Kong and the Asia Pacific Region, occupancy rates were over 70% in 2005 based on survey data collected by Deloitte (Table 5.2).

Many multinational hotel chains have entered the Chinese market and developed their operations rapidly through their branded outlets. Table 5.3 shows selected international hotel chains operating in China in 2006. InterContinental Hotels Group (IHG), with Holiday Inn as its main brand, is the world's largest hotel group by number of rooms,

Table 5.2 Occupancy, average room rate and revenue per available room in Beijing, Hong Kong and Asia Pacific Region generally for August 2005 versus 2004

	Occupancy		Average room rate		RevPAR	
	2005 (%)	Change (%)	2005 US$	Change (%)	2005US$ (£UK*)	Change (%)
Asia Pacific region	71.2	0.5	106	10.8	76 (43)	11.3
Beijing	75.7	7.1	96	14.4	73 (41)	22.6
Hong Kong	79.4	−1.4	146	21.9	116 (65)	20.2

* Calculated on exchange rate of UK£1 = US$1.78 which was approximate rate in July 2005.
Source: HotelBenchmark™ Survey by Deloitte (2005).
Web site: http://www.hotelbenchmark.com/pressroom/pressreleases/12102005AsiaPacific-EN.aspx

Table 5.3 Selected international hotel chains operating in China in August 2006

Hotel chains	Brands	Headquarters/origin	Number of hotels
InterContinental Hotel Group	Crowne Plaza, Inter-Continental, Holiday Inn	United Kingdom	72 (incl. 4 in Hong Kong and 1 in Macau)
Starwood Hotels and Resorts	St. Regis, Sheraton, Westin, Le Méridien Four Points by Sheraton	United States	42 (incl. 1 in Hong Kong)
Accor Hotels	Sofitel, Novotel, Mercure, Ibis	France	36 (incl. 4 in Hong Kong)
Marriott International	Courtyard, Marriott, Renaissance, Marriott Executive Apartments	United States	25 (incl. 4 in Hong Kong)
Shangri-La Hotels and Resorts	Shangri-La, Traders, China World, Kerry Centre	Hong Kong, China	21
Hyatt Hotels and Resorts		United States	8 (incl. 1 in Hong Kong)
Hilton		United States	4

Source: Individual hotel chain Web sites at 4 August, 2006.

and it is the largest international hotel group in Greater China. It has been in China since 1984, and its growth in China has been aided by partnerships with local hotel developers and owners. An example of this is the signing with Chengdu International Exhibition & Convention Group to manage six hotels and 4,500 rooms in Chengdu and Jiuzhaigou in China's Sichuan province. This deal was signed in February 2006, and it strongly positions the group to reach its target of having 125 hotels open in China by 2008. Of the six hotels that are part of the deal, three hotels will be located in Chengdu city as part of the New Century City integrated complex, incorporating a convention centre, shopping and entertainment facilities, offices and residences. The other three properties are located in the UNESCO-listed Jiuzhaigou Scenic Area and include the InterContinental resort in Jiuzhaigou, which is on the Golden Pillow Awards' list of top 10 resorts in China (www.ihgplc.com/index.asp?PageID=6&Year=2006&NewsID=1575-16k-). One of IHG's initiatives in China is its relationship with the Driving Foundation. The Foundation promotes travelling around the country to the Chinese, and this will not only mean new roads but also new hotels both for IHG and other operators (Goodman, 2005).

Almost all international hotel groups operate under management contract and the support of, and connection with, local partners has been, and remains, a key element for the success of international companies. This has reduced the risk for international companies. The foreign chains contribute their names, management expertise and global booking networks and also ensure that the hotels are designed to exacting standards. The local partners tend to provide local knowledge and the funds for construction, while the foreign firms earn steady management fees for running the hotels. Domestic hotel groups are also beginning to grow through management contracts in provincial cities (China Economic Review, 2005). Partnerships have also occurred between foreign and domestic hotel companies. For instance, Wang (2003) reports on Accor growing in China through its partnerships with Beijing Tourism Group (BTG; the parent company of Beijing Kingdom International Hotel Co., Ltd) and with Zenith Hotel International.

There are also a number of indigenous hotel chains operating in China. These have been discussed elsewhere including in Pine (2002), Wang (2003) and Zhang, Pine and Lam (2005). The biggest of these is Jin Jiang International Hotel Management Co., Ltd. Jin Jiang is the largest hotel management company in China and the company has experience dating back to the 1920s. Jin Jiang's heritage Peace Hotel on Shanghai's bund is arguably the most famous hotel in China. Built in 1929, the Peace Hotel was often described as the "number one mansion in the Far East". The company is currently progressing with advanced booking systems and management processes. Jin Jiang International Hotel Management Company Ltd (Jin Jiang Hotels) has made Travelocity® the hotelier's first global online travel marketing partner by joining its Net Rate Hotel program.

Jin Jiang manages over 100 inns and star-rated hotels around China. These include wholly owned hotel and other hotels and inns under management. These hotels and inns are mainly located in the large and medium-sized cities in China, ranging from luxurious five-star hotels to economical Jin Jiang Inns (see Table 5.4). The Jin Jiang Inn brand is the biggest operator in the economy sector. According to its senior vice president of sales and marketing, "... the biggest challenge is change management-culture change, progressively moving from an SOE

Table 5.4 Jin Jiang hotels and inns in China in August 2006

Hotel category	Number of hotels/inns
Heritage	7
5 star	11
4 star	29
3 star	16
2 star	4
Jin Jiang Inn	34

Source: http://www.jinjianghotels.com/portal/en/ab_ji_ji.asp?did=76 (accessed 4 August 2006).

(state-owned enterprise) to a market-driven and competitive organization" (Sin, 2006). It is also the biggest operator in the economy sector, with 120 properties under the Jin Jiang Inn brand.

Hotels can also be categorised according to their star rating. Hotels are graded from one to five stars in China, by the China National Tourism Administration, according to their facilities, services and standards, and the number of stars is usually reflected in the price with the cheapest having only one star and the most expensive five stars. According to Harper (2001), one-star hotels are usually the reserve of the Chinese to direct wealth into the Chinese economy while most hotels of two stars and above will accept foreigners. In some cases, for example, for some five star hotels, the stars are self-awarded while a few foreign-operated hotels "are declining to apply for hotel ratings and letting their hotels speak for themselves" (China Economic Review, 2005, p. 61). Table 5.5 shows

Table 5.5 Comparative statistics of Chinese tourist hotels by star rating – 2002

Star rating	Number of hotels	Number of rooms ('000s)	Average occupancy	Revenue £m*
5 star	175	64.9	66.3	1397.9
4 star	635	143.5	64.9	1838.3
3 star	2846	346.5	60.8	2452.0
2 star	4414	306.0	56.5	1247.9
1 star	810	36.4	49.7	97.9
Total	8880	897.2	60.1	7034.1

* Calculated data. Currency conversion is CNY = £1.
Source: China National Tourism Administration Report Web site released on 15 July 2003.
Web sites: www.cnta.org.cn, www.ctha.org.cn

performance and physical data for hotels based upon their star rating in 2002. According to the China Hospitality News (2006), there are more than 12,000 star-graded hotels in China, and 279 of them are five-star hotels.

Operational and management problems and issues

There are a variety of problems and issues confronting the future development, operation and management of hotels in China. These include issues associated with hotel operation revenue and profit performance (Gu, 2003), barriers to hotel chain development (Pine and Qi, 2004), human resource shortages (Wang, Jameson and Lashley, 2004) and the achievement and maintenance of satisfactory service and other standards (Muxlow, 2006).

Hotel operation revenue and profit performance

Research undertaken by Gu (2003) on the operating performance of the Chinese hotel industry between 1991 and 2000 showed both revenue and profitability to be deteriorating. Three factors were identified as causing this. These were overcapacity, the low efficiency of domestically owned hotels and declining hotel size. During the 1990s, hotel growth outstripped the increase in incoming tourists, and overcapacity was a problem. Gu (2003) proposed that future growth should be more prudent and that new hotel construction decisions should be based on comprehensive feasibility studies and thorough market analysis. Exploiting the growing domestic tourism market through, for example, marketing campaigns was also proposed as a way of combating the excess supply of hotel rooms. Operating performance of domestically owned hotels, which comprised the largest proportion of overall hotel capacity in China in 2000, was inferior to those hotels under, total or part, foreign ownership. Gu (2003) suggested that deficiencies in managerial skills in domestically owned hotels may be the cause of this and proposed that the use of foreign technical and managerial expertise may reduce the efficiency gap between domestic- and foreign-ownership hotels. Finally, average hotel size declined during the 1990s, and this adversely affected operating performance and reduced economies of scale (Gu, 2003).

Barriers to hotel chain development

In common with elsewhere, much of the future growth of the Chinese hotel industry is likely to come from hotel chain developments. While recognising that there are disadvantages, hotel chains have been considered to have comparative advantages, related to economies of scale, transaction costs and management and technology advantages, over independent hotels (Zhang, Pine and Lam, 2005). However, a number of barriers to the development of both indigenous and multinational hotel chains companies have been identified and analysed by Pine and Qi (2004) and by Zhang, Pine and Lam (2005). They identified the barriers as being associated with the economic and political systems in China (i.e., local protectionism, government intervention, policy restrictions and lack of motivation and drive in the indigenous-owned hotels and their access to capital funding), with the complexity and diversity of hotel ownership in China, with weaknesses in hotel management capability and resources and with the competition between foreign and international chains.

Human resource shortages and problems

With the huge and rapid growth of the hotel industry in China has come the need for a qualified and highly skilled workforce in order to meet the requirements of increasing demanding customers and to provide satisfactory service. However, the concept of service has been an alien one to the Chinese workers, and there has been a difficulty in finding trained and knowledgeable Chinese staff (Wang, Jameson and Lashley, 2004).

Furthermore, problems of high labour turnover, low morale, insufficient support from government on human resource development and poor pay compared with other industries have plagued the Chinese hotel industry (Zhang, Pine and Lam, 2005).

An illustration of the human resource problems can be currently seen in Guangzhou, which faces a serious shortage of trained staff. This shortage will become more apparent with the government's plan to increase the number of star-grade hotels from 203 in 2006 to 300 by 2010. The current labour turnover rate in the industry is 30%, and employees often say low salary and high stress are the two main reasons for the high turnover rate (http://www.chinacsr.com/2006/04/21/guangzhou-hotels-face-human-resource-shortage/). The serious shortage of qualified and skilled labour may have an impact on the rapid expansion of the Chinese hotel industry and the maintenance of service levels and standards. This may threaten China's ability to compete in the global market (Tsang and Qu, 2000). In response to the demand in the labour market, thousands of Chinese hospitality students go abroad to be trained and developed. There has been a strong emphasis on training in languages and communication as well as Western and fusion dining. However, this still seems insufficient to satisfy the needs of the growing industry. Further insights into the human resource problems in China's tourism industry can be found in WTTC (2006, pp. 72–74).

The achievement and maintenance of satisfactory service and other standards

The growth in both international and domestic tourism is necessitating the hotels to have high standards, especially at the four- and five-star levels, and that service quality is provided to build customer satisfaction and loyalty. However, as Muxlow (2006) claims, these aims are not so easy to achieve with the main obstacles being physical facilities and service standards. Progress is being made to the product and physical facilities by adapting to and adopting international hotel concepts and design. Moreover, frequent and better property maintenance and sanitation have been recognised as important in hotels along with the use and installation of reliable reservation systems. Other requirements have been for Chinese hotel managers to gain an increased understanding of guest expectations and a thorough knowledge of service quality management techniques.

The importance of hotel standards has been recognised at national level. To maintain the transparency of the standards in assessing star-grade hotels, China's National Star-Grade Hotel Assessment Commission is conducting a new review of all star-grade hotels that have retained their star grade for more than five years. Those star-grade holders that have deficiencies will be required to correct their problems or they will be downgraded (China Hospitality News, 2006). The aim to attain international standards and quality of services and operations is on top of the agenda, on especially given the Summer Olympics of 2008 when international tourists will abound in China.

Future trends and developments

The continued expansion of the hotel industry in China is inevitable. Improved infrastructure, the massive growth of the Chinese economy, increasing affluence amongst the indigenous population and the anticipated proliferation of low-cost carriers will fuel the growth of domestic travel and with it the growth of the hotel industry. The growth for international tourism and therefore demand for hotels is also likely to continue given China's goal to become one of the world's leading international tourist destinations. The run-up to the 2008 Summer Olympics in China is expected to further accelerate development activity. A hotel-building boom is taking place in China, particularly in the primary markets such as Beijing, Shanghai, Shenzhen and Guangzhou, and opportunities for leading international hotel operators to partner with experienced hotel developers and owners to increase their presence in secondary cities are also increasing. However, according to Elegant (2006), it may be 10 years before business really starts to take off in some of these secondary cities, such as Hefei, Harbin and Chengdu. Expansion into China is a priority of many international hotel companies, but there is a risk that this will lead to oversupply, as has been experienced previously, and that many rooms will go empty in secondary cities and possibly even in the major cities.

International hotel companies will continue to identify new and niche markets for development and will compete with Chinese hotel companies for business. The mid-market and budget hotel segments of the industry, defined as three stars and below, are becoming increasingly attractive to the international companies. However, these segments are fast becoming very competitive as several Chinese hotel companies, notably the Jin Jiang Group, are also targeting the same markets. While these emerging markets offer exceptional growth opportunities, they pose unique challenges in politics and ownership, as well as in recruiting, training and retention of local staff (Muxlow, 2006). Branded hotel chains also offer great potential, and the majority of unbranded hotels that exist in China provide a great opportunity for both Chinese and international hotel companies to consolidate and develop branded operations (Yu, 2003). However, there are problems and issues associated with hotel development in China, and an understanding of these is important for any hotel company seeking success.

Learning tasks

1 For each of the hotel chains listed in Table 7.3, access their web site to identify their latest progress in China.
2 Carry out a PEST analysis of influences that could affect local and international hotel markets in China.

Discussion questions

1 Explain the lack of chain hotels in China. With reference to this chapter and Chapter 12 of Zhang, Pine and Lam (2005), what advice would you give for the development of a hotel chain in China?
2 What are the prospects for the independent hotel sector in China?

Mini case study

Kempinski Hotel Shenzhen

After a building phase of two years, the Kempinski Hotel Shenzhen celebrated its official opening ceremony on Saturday, 30 September 2006. This will be Shenzhen's leading luxury hotel, and it is strategically positioned in Shenzhen's Nanshan District, overlooking Shenzhen Bay in the Pearl River Delta at the southern tip of Guangdong Province in southern China. Shenzen is one of China's first Special Economic Zones and is the only Chinese mainland city with a cross-sea bridge over Shenzen Bay (due for completion late 2006), providing easy access to and from Hong Kong. The hotel is ideally located and within 10–30 minutes of Shenzhen Bao'an International Airport, Shekou Ferry Terminal, Shenzhen's International Convention and Exhibition Centre. A new No. 2 Metro Line, just 10 minutes walk from the hotel, is also in progress. The hotel is set in the heart of the city's new commercial development zone, neighbouring Grade A offices, Shenzhen Opera House, branded shopping malls and a world-class entertainment and leisure complex.

The Shenzen Kempinski is the eighth Kempinski-managed property to open in China. The others are in Beijing (2), Chengdu, Shenyang, Dalian, Urumqi, and one is planned to open on Hainan Island in January 2007. Kempinski is the oldest luxury hotel group in Europe, acquiring its first property in 1897. While the Group was founded in Germany, its portfolio is now spread throughout Europe, Middle East, Africa, South America and Asia. Rich in tradition, it comprises a fine collection of hotels and resorts, from the truly historic to the breathtakingly avant-garde. While maintaining a leading position in the business travel market, endorsed by renowned properties in many of the world's key cities, Kempinski has entered the global resort market in response to growing consumer demand. The Group currently comprises many dedicated resorts, each of which offer an exceptional range of leisure facilities, luxury spa and a breathtaking location.

The Kempinski Hotel in Shenzhen is a joint venture between BTG and Shenzhen Sensenhai Industrial Co., Ltd. It is aimed at the business travel market. With an increasing number of visitors to this fast-growing southern Chinese industrial region and the port of Shenzen, the hotel offers 390 luxury guest rooms and suites, all with super-king comfort beds, chic designer bathrooms, flat-screen televisions and broadband access – facilities that business travellers now expect as standard when they travel virtually anywhere in the world. Four Kempinski executive floors are designed with the business travellers in mind, offering exceptional facilities and the highest level of personalised services. One of the executive floors is dedicated to the female business travellers. All rooms are luxuriously appointed and feature 24-hour personal butler services, complimentary high-speed broadband internet access and in-bathroom television. The executive lounge, located on the 25th floor with panoramic city views, serves a fine selection of complimentary food and beverages throughout the day.

Kempinski Hotel Shenzhen boasts an innovative dining option with Seasons, an all-day dining venue offering European, Asian and local favourites and featuring lavish buffets with live cooking stations for breakfast, lunch and dinner. A popular rendezvous in the hotel is the lounge, which serves a fine selection of light meals and drinks accompanied by live entertainment throughout the day. Regional cuisine is served in one of China's largest restaurants, the 8000 sq. m. and independently operated Ocean Pearl Diner's Club, which is located within the hotel podium. The restaurant has seating capacity for up to 6000 guests, including an unprecedented 222 private rooms. Additional dining and entertainment options will be opening in the coming months. There is also a branded retail mall.

In addition, the hotel includes a business centre with private boardrooms and comprehensive tours and travel services, the wellness centre featuring rejuvenating therapeutic massage treatments, hair and beauty salon, well-equipped gymnasium, indoor pool, spa and outdoor tennis court. For meetings, conferences and events the hotel boasts the opulent, pillar-less Kempinski Ballroom and four additional meeting rooms catering for up to 800 guests.

Web site: http://www.kempinski.com/en/hotel/index.htm.

References

Chen, W. and Ball, S. (2005). *Customer Relationship Marketing in State-Owned Hotel in China: A Case Study of Shanghai International Convention Centre*, in Proceedings of CHME Research Conference, May, Bournemouth University, pp. 63–80.

China Economic Review's (2005). *China Business Guide 2006*. Hong Kong, China Economic Review Publishing.

China Hospitality News (2006). *Chinese Hotels Face New Assessment*, 28 April.

Chinese National Tourism Administration (CNTA) (2000). *The Yearbook of China Tourism Statistics*. Beijing, China Tourism Publishing House.

Chinese National Tourism Administration (CNTA) (2002). *The Yearbook of China Tourism Statistics*. Beijing, China Tourism Publishing House.

Deloitte (2005). *China Fuels Growth in Asian Hotel Performance*. 12 October, http://www.hotelbenchmark.com/pressroom/pressreleases/12102005AsiaPacific-EN.aspx.

Elegant, S. (2006). China's Hotel Boom, *Time Asia Magazine*, 3 July.

Goodman, M. (2005). Hotel Giant Makes Room for Growth, *The Sunday Times Business*, 2 October, p. 12.

Gu, Zheng (2003). The Chinese Lodging Industry: Problems and Solutions, *International Journal of Contemporary Hospitality Management*, **15**(7), 386–392.

Han, K.H. (ed.) (1994). *China: Tourism Industry*. Beijing, Modern China Press.

Harper, D. (2001). *The National Geographic Traveler: China*. Washington, DC, National Geographic Society.

Muxlow, S. (2006). *SpotLight: China's Progress Toward International Competitiveness in Hospitality*. http://www.4hoteliers.com/4hots_fshw.php?mwi=1419, 21 June.

Pine, R. (2002). China's Hotel Industry: Serving a Massive Market, *The Cornell and Restaurant and Administration Quarterly*, **43**(3), 61–70.

Pine, R. and Qi, P. (2004). Barriers to Hotel Chain Development in China, *International Journal of Contemporary Hospitality Management*, **16**(1), 37–44.

Sin, L.H. (2006). Jin Jiang Makes Waves – World's Biggest Asian-Owned Hotel Chain Has Global Ambitions, *TTG Asia*, 17–23 February.

Sun, Shangqing (ed.) (1992). *Choices in the 21st Century: China's Tourism Development Strategies*, Beijing, People's Publishing House (original in Chinese).

Tisdell, C.A. and Wen, J. (1991). Investment in China's Tourism Industry: Its Scale, Nature and Policy Issues, *China Economic Review*, **2**(2), 175–194.

Tsang, N. and Qu, H. (2000). Service Quality in China's Hotel Industry: A Perspective from Tourists and Hotel Managers, *International Journal of Contemporary Hospitality Management*, **12**(5), 316–326.

Wang, Y. (2003). Who Owns the Chinese Hotel Industry? *The Hospitality Review*, October, 17–22.

Wang, Y., Jameson, S. and Lashley, C. (2004). *A Comparative Study of the Application of Human Resource Development in State-Owned Hotels in China*, in Proceedings of CHME Hospitality Research and CHME Learning and Teaching Conference, April, University of Wales Institute, Cardiff, pp. 167–174.

Wei, X. et al. (1999). *The Trend of Tourism Industry in China in New Century*. Guangzhou, Guangdong Tourism Publisher.

World Travel and Tourism Council (WTTC) (2006). *China, China Hong Kong SAR and China Macau SAR: The Impact of Travel & Tourism on Jobs and the Economy*, London, World Travel and Tourism Council.

Zhang, H.Q., Pine, R. and Lam, T. (2005). *Tourism and Hotel Development in China: From Political to Economic Success*. London, THHP.

Zhao, J. (1989). Overprovision in Chinese Hotels, *Tourism Management*, **10**(1), 63–66.

Yu, L. (2003). Critical issues in China's hotel industry. In Lew, A.A., Yu, L., Ap, J. and Guangrui, Z. (eds), *Tourism in China*. London, THHP, Chapter 8, pp. 129–141.

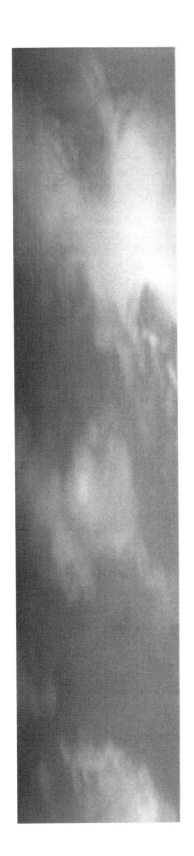

CHAPTER 6

Restaurants, fast food and contract food service – China

Chapter objectives

When you have read this chapter, you will be able to

1 Recognise the nature and the structural characteristics of the restaurants, fast food and contract food-service sectors in China.
2 Identify the origins of eating out and chronicle the historical development of restaurants, fast food and contract food service in China.
3 Highlight some of the influencing factors on this development.
4 Critically review major issues and operational trends.
5 Discuss the future outlook for restaurants, fast food and contract food service in China.

Introduction

Eating good food plays a central role in the lives of Chinese people and, increasingly, restaurant culture is developing not only in the major cities but throughout China. Today food service represents one of the most dynamic industries in China. As Ken Hom says, "food is more than a passion, it is an obsession and good eating is essential to good living . . . and the processes of cultivating, selecting, cooking and consuming it are completely embedded into Chinese culture" (Stevens, 1984). The wealth of literature in the subject, whether it be related to technical matters or literary aspects, is evidence of how knowledgeable the Chinese are about food. Today the most ordinary person in China displays a deep knowledge of food and the pursuit of good food and eating out is axiomatic, particularly during celebrations. Food features significantly in Chinese holidays with its appearance being regarded by many as symbolic. For example, a whole chicken represents family unity and is therefore commonly served during Chinese New Year while noodles are often eaten at birthdays and at New Year as their length symbolises longevity. This chapter begins by briefly reviewing the historical development of eating out in China and the distinctive culinary styles or regional cuisines, which underpin both indigenous food-service provision and the domestic consumption of native food. The chapter then proceeds to consider the growing influence and development of the international, mainly Western, food-service sector in China and some of the issues in the development, operation and management of this sector.

Historical development and regional cuisines

According to Newman (2000), "To understand the food and meals of the Chinese, knowledge of the physical aspects of the country and its history and traditions, as well as the nature of the Chinese people, is needed." This understanding is needed for both an appreciation of domestic consumption of food and for eating out. Dining out of the home has a very long history in China. The proper and thoughtful production and service of food by specialists outside of the home is believed to date back to at least the period from AD 618 to 907. Ackerman (1990), for example, claims that it was then, in the Tang dynasty, that the first serious restaurants began to operate in China.

It was during this time that tea drinking, a fundamental part of Chinese life, was popularised; and today teahouses can be found everywhere in China. The commercialisation of agriculture, increasing agricultural productivity and other industrial and economic developments fuelled urbanisation during the Song dynasty from AD 960 to 1279. These in turn facilitated the rise of the restaurant industry. Rice cultivation had spread from AD 800 and, with the overthrow of Northern China by the Mongols, rice replaced wheat, in the North, as the staple crop. Improvements in the transport infrastructure enabled foodstuff to be moved across China more easily, and the restaurant industry continued to develop during the Ming dynasty (AD 1368–1644). More recently, the Revolution in China and the founding of the PRC in 1949 brought great political, economic and social effects. As Stevens (1984, p. 11) said,

> Within China the great cookery tradition became for quite some time almost moribund. Revolutionaries deemed the art of cooking an elitist and reactionary enterprise, a reminder of Imperial days and therefore best repressed. Only recently (circa 1980's) has an effort been made to revive the tradition, to train young chefs and to allow small private restaurants to start or re-open.

Although changes to Chinese food have occurred over the years, Chinese cooking has developed many of the traditions and fundamental principles have not altered (Hom, 1989). Chinese food culture is much the same today as it has always been with food and eating being a central part of everyday living as well as of celebrations and other events. The preparation and consumption of food are two of the joys of life to the Chinese, and as Dewald (2002) claims, in his detailed account of menus, table etiquette and food ordering in China, food is served with a combination of ceremony and tradition.

China has great diversity in climate, agriculture and available foods and ingredients. The many different peoples (Han Chinese, Mongols, Tibetans, etc.) in China result in there being different traditions, no single language and no one religion. While ginger, scallions and soy sauce are common features of Chinese cooking and cabbage is eaten across the country, variations abound throughout China. Even rice is traditionally grown and consumed in southern China while noodles, wheat and millet are traditional to the North. So these variations make it difficult, if not impossible, to define Chinese food in one unifying way. The food and cooking of China has been divided into five main regions (Grigson, 1988); however, most gourmets and Chinese scholars have broadly divided the style of cuisine within China into four geographical regional categories. These divisions occur because of geographical, climatic and cultural differences and are reflected both in domestic cooking and in the menus of restaurants and other eating outlets (Map 6.1). These differing styles have been termed: the Southern School, the Northern School, the Eastern School and the Western School (Stevens, 1984).

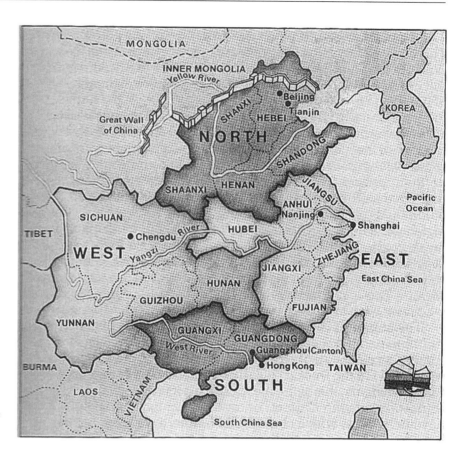

Map 6.1
The four cuisine regions/schools (South, North, East and West) of China.

Southern school

For most people in the Western world, Cantonese food from the Guǎngdōng region in the south of China is the best known. This is because in the nineteenth and twentieth centuries many Chinese families emigrated from southern China and opened take-away and/or eat-in restaurants serving Cantonese cuisine in America and Europe.

Cantonese food is considered by many as the haute cuisine of China, and stir-frying, along with boiling and steaming, is the distinctive cooking method used. Dim sum, little snack foods, which are now to be found worldwide, originated from this region and are served on plates and steamers alongside an array of sauces in many restaurants offering Chinese food both in and outside of China. The Guǎngdōng region is also famous for sweet and sour dishes. The ingredients used in Cantonese cooking are varied, and the freshness, appearance and textures of dishes are all important elements. The exotic tastes of the southerners for such things as dog meat, snake's blood, bird's nests and turtle shells have earned them a reputation around China.

Northern school

In contrast to the Southern School, northern-style food has a reputation for being austere, unsophisticated and bland. A distinguishing feature is the use of corn, wheat and millet in the production of noodles, bread, dumplings and pancakes. Wheat pancakes are commonly served with Peking duck, perhaps one of the most famous of Chinese dishes, and in contrast to most northern foods are more subtle and sophisticated.

The harsh climate means that fresh vegetables are not available throughout the year, and so preservation through drying, smoking and pickling are commonplace. Steaming, baking and sizzle-frying are the most common cooking methods in the northern region, and the influence of the Mongols can be seen in two of the region's most famous culinary exports – Mongolian barbeque and Mongolian hotpot.

Eastern school

While there are a variety of cooking styles and cuisines in the Eastern region, cooking from the region is typified by Shànghǎi cuisine featuring soups and seafood. The extremely fertile land in the area enables the production of a vast variety of ingredients and fresh fruits and vegetables. It is therefore no surprise that the region is noted for vegetarian cuisine. The main cooking techniques are wok stir-frying, sizzle-frying, steaming and red-stewing (slow simmering in dark soy sauce, sugar and spices). Possessing a long coastline and the Yangzi river, fresh fish and shellfish are plentiful, and one restaurant on the shores of West Lake in Hángzhōu the Lóuwàilóu Càiguǎn restaurant dates back to 1848.

Western school

The Western region is landlocked and mostly surrounded by mountains. Pork, poultry, legumes and soya beans tend to be the most commonly used food items supplemented by mushrooms and bamboo shoots. The region is particularly known for its use of red chillies, and its cuisine has a reputation for being down-to-earth, with stir- and sizzle-frying being commonplace methods of cooking. Sìchuān cuisine, with its very strong and spicy flavours, lies at the culinary heart of the region, and one expression, roughly translated from the Chinese, says, "China is the place for food, but Sìchuān is the place for flavor" (Jackson, 2004).

Size, significance and structural features of the sector

The food-service sector can be basically divided into two broad concept types:

- Chinese style food-service operations, and
- The more modern international, and mainly Western style, food-service operations.

Together, these operations form a large sector and one of the most dynamic sectors in the Chinese economy. It was estimated in a study of the Chinese food-service market that in 2003 there were more than 3.5 million restaurants in China employing more than 15 million people, that is, on average four staff per restaurant (Sin, 2005). Some of the main factors driving the continued growth of the sector include the following:

1 Continuing urbanisation of the population.
2 Increasing wealth of the population, generally, and the rapidly expanding consuming middle class, which is estimated at around 100 million people.
3 Rising educational levels of the population encourage increasing sophistication and changes of tastes related to eating out and food consumption generally.
4 Busy lifestyles.
5 The entrepreneurial activities of the owners of small independent food-service operations, including noodle and dim sum shops, and tea-houses.
6 The influx of Western and other international branded fast food and other chains and the growing desire for their offerings.
7 The growing expatriate community.
8 Increasing domestic and international travel, partly encouraged by a better and growing transport infrastructure.
9 The growing demand for healthy and safe food in hygienic surroundings.
10 The increase in domestic and inbound tourism including the interest in the forthcoming Beijing Olympics.

Interviews conducted by Credit Suisse with over 2,200 people in eight major mainland Chinese cities (Beijing, Shanghai, Guangzhou, Shenzen, Shenyang, Chengdu, Xi'an and Wuhan) in 2004 indicated that on average, consumers go to restaurants in general 4.6 times per month and that average personal spending is RMB 49.9 per meal (Garner, 2005). For these eight cities, and based on this data, Garner (2005) estimated the market size per year to be RMB 74 billion (approximately US$9 billion). This is about 10% of total food-service sales in China, which have been estimated at about US$90 billion.

Chinese style food-service operations

The "Chinese restaurant" is an institution worldwide, but providing a detailed analysis of the indigenous restaurant sector in China is problematic when the country is still in a state of flux. Food-service outlets turn over relatively quickly and, like everything else, the food-service sector is changing so fast. Little that is new seems to have any real permanence.

There are a myriad of indigenous food-service outlets in China. Based upon work from Harper et al. (2005), these can be simply categorised as listed below:

- Large-scale restaurants that may or may not offer accommodation (a fàngdiàn).
- Smaller restaurants specialising in one particular type of food (a cānguǎn).
- Informal restaurants with low prices (a cāntīng).
- Cafés and family-styled restaurants offering set meals.
- Self-serve cafeterias (a zìzhù cān).
- Street and market stalls/kiosks selling all manner of cheap traditional fast-food snacks and regional specialities for eating "on the run".
- Hotel restaurants.

Most food-service outlets cater for Chinese clientele with restaurants tending to be noisy, crowded and seemingly chaotic places. For the Chinese, eating and eating out are very much about socialising and making friends, and typically, when eating out, several dishes are ordered and shared by a group, each using chopsticks.

Virtually, all hotels in China have restaurants with four- and five-star hotels in larger cities usually having an international as well as a Chinese restaurant. International tourist-friendly restaurants can increasingly be found near tourist locations and sights often with signs and menus in English. Price and hygiene are two particular issues for foreign tourists, however. Such people can be charged inflated prices and cleanliness may be a concern, particularly in smaller restaurants.

Guo Yoe, in being interviewed by Moss (2006), says about Beijing that there are a number of types of restaurants evident in the city. He says,

> The Chinese say the first is "high class", meaning you pay a lot of money. This is for the new rich, and surroundings are lavish, but the food lacks character. The second kind is the most popular in Beijing, the middle ground between two extremes.

He paints a picture of the second kind as being more traditionally Chinese with skilled chefs, long menus and delicious food. Designer dining restaurants are another kind of restaurant in Beijing, which are growing as such dining becomes more fashionable. Last, he mentions the many little restaurants around the alleys. In contrast to this personal categorisation in Shanghai, an official scheme was announced by the Shanghai Food and Drug Administration in 2005 to categorise its estimated 40,000 food-service outlets into super-large, large, medium or small fast-food and hotpot/barbecue outlets.

> In Taiwan and Hong Kong cuisines from most provinces have been available for a number of years. In Hong Kong there are thousands of places to eat and drink with the most popular Chinese cuisines being Cantonese and Shanghainese. (Time Out, 2004)

Most eating is done outside the home in Hong Kong mainly because the apartments, where most people live, are too small and cramped for group social eating. Added to this, restaurants are significant venues for corporate entertaining and business. This is also the case in mainland China. With the recent rise of tourism in mainland China and with the growing affluence and sophistication of the indigenous population, the availability of non-local Chinese cuisine is spreading, and restaurant culture is awakening particularly in major cities like Beijing, Chengdu, Shanghai and Shenzen. However, a division still often remains between restaurants for the local people and tourists.

International, mainly Western style, food-service operations

A recent phenomenon has been the influx of modern multinational and strongly branded fast-food chains and concepts. These chains, which have come principally from the West, have revolutionised eating out in China and have had an enormous influence upon the nature and size of the fast-food sector. Research by A.C. Nielsen in 2005 found China to be one of the leading five of 28 fast-food markets it surveyed in Asia pacific, Europe and the USA (Sin, 2005).

Traditional Chinese style fast-food operations, for example, dumpling shops, remain attractive to Chinese consumers because of their menu items and inexpensive prices but, increasingly, they have been forced to modernise to compete with the new entrants. Kentucky Fried Chicken (KFC) entered China in 1987 and McDonald's arrived three years later. These were the beginnings of the modern fast-food sector in mainland China. The cities of Shanghai, Beijing and Guangzhou were the starting points for this development, and strategic concentrations of restaurants belonging to a brand are now commonplace in the cities. Gradually KFC, McDonald's and other chains, which originated mainly in the USA, have moved onto attractive sites in new localities and inland. A further trend has been the appearance of new types of cuisine and increased menu choices, and in some locations, especially the large cities, fast-food business has become extremely competitive. The new chains have not just had food as the core menu item but the coffee chain Starbucks has also sprung up throughout the country and has become popular among the fashionable youth in urban areas. The Credit Suisse research gives some idea of the impact of the Western fast-food brands. From their research in the eight major Chinese cities in 2004, Western fast-food restaurants were visited by 50% of respondents with the average frequency being 1.2 occasions per month and average personal spending being RMB 39.1. This, if extrapolated for the population generally, would make the market size RMB 15 billion for the eight cities (Garner, 2005). From this research, the average visiting frequency for McDonald's, KFC and Pizza Hut was 0.6, 0.7 and 0.3 times per month, respectively (Garner, 2005).

This research also suggests that there is opportunity for growth of Western fast food as in the eight major cities, only fast-food sales represent 21% of total restaurant sales, which compares with 25% for Germany, 30% in UK and 50% in the USA (Garner, 2005). Furthermore, the research showed total restaurant frequency is 4.6 times per month and 1.2 times per month for Western fast food, whereas in the USA the frequent fast-food customers can visit up to four times per week.

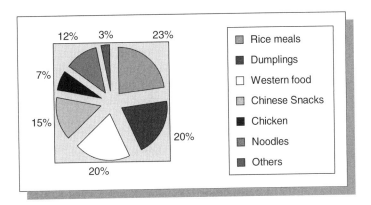

Figure 6.1
The nature of fast foods consumed in Coastal cities
Source: Global Business Alliance, Inc in Bitar (2005).

One of the consequences of the arrival of the Western brands has been the development of modern Chinese style fast-food chains and the entry of chain restaurants from other countries, for example, Japan, Korea and Thailand. What consumers eat at fast-food restaurants in Chinese coastal cities is shown in Figure 6.1 and the leading restaurant chains in China are shown in Table 6.1.

Despite the increasing prominence of the modern chains, traditional Chinese fast-food stands, kiosks and other operations still dominate the fast-food market with an estimated 80% or more of total sales (Bitar, 2005).

Coffee shop/café businesses have been thriving in China and Hong Kong with on-trade coffee consumption generally doubling between 1998 and 2003 (Lee, 2004). This is largely an urban phenomenon with

Table 6.1   The leading restaurant chains in China in – 2005

Brand	Outlets*	Country of origin
KFC	1200+	USA
McDonald's	600+	USA
Malan Noodles	400+	China
Pizza Hut	150+	USA
Starbucks	130+	USA
Xiao Shaoxing	100+	China
California Beef Noodle King	100+	China
Yoshinoya	100+	Japan
Yonghe King	95+	China/Philipines
Café De Coral	60+	Hong Kong

Source: Bitar (2005).

most on-trade coffee consumption being confined to coffee shops/cafés (independent and chained), internet cafés and fast-food restaurants. Starbucks is the leading coffee shop chain. It represents modern lifestyles and affluence in China, but it continues to face increasing competition, particularly from other foreign operators, in this lucrative market.

Food service in mainland China goes beyond commercial street outlets and can be found in hospitals, nursing homes, schools and colleges, factory and office canteens (the provision of food for workers is compulsory in China), prisons and other institutions. In the four cities of Beijing, Shanghai, Guangzhou and Shenzen, the total number of food-service outlets serving only meals in such institutions in 2002 and 2003 was estimated by BIS Shrapnel to exceed 28,000 and in 2004, as much as 40% of hotels, restaurants and institutions (HRI) expenditures in China came from institutional food service. In the past, most institutions were state-owned and ran their own cafeterias, but now services are increasingly being outsourced and international companies are increasingly joining the market. The opportunities for food and service management (otherwise known as contract catering) companies in China are enormous. Yet the food and service management business is still in its infancy in China, and the market penetration by foreign companies are low. Compass along with Sodexho, who entered China before both Compass and Aramark, the other two global companies operating in China, only account for less than 1% of the total institutional food-service market. The food and service management business faces major challenges such as competition from cheap regional and local lunchbox providers, virtually nil access to prisons, military and certain other public sector institutions and very low average meal prices (mainly because of low individual meal budgets) they are able to charge in mainland factories compared to in Hong Kong. Compass entered the market in China in 1997 and is now one of the leading operators in the country and also has almost 70% of the market in Hong Kong. In 2005, Compass had 130 contracts in 25 cities, including in Hong Kong, served in total on average 100,000 meals a day, largely through its Eurest and Shanghai Railgourmet brands (Wachholz, 2005a). Its contracts include that awarded by the Shanghai Railway Administration.

Operational and management issues

Food supplies and distribution

As the disposable income of the rural Chinese people increases, it is probable that they will improve their diet by supplementing chicken to the staples of rice or grain and vegetables. As these people continue to emigrate to the urban areas, where the population is expected to grow by over 10 million every year and more than double to over 800 million by 2020, and as they get wealthier and their tastes and lifestyles change, they are likely to demand different foods and more processed and convenience foods. This includes demand for fast food and other food-service products. One of the consequences of these changes is an increased demand for grain for animal feeding, for meat, for sugar, for coffee and for other foodstuff. If the Chinese mirrored the meat consumption of their U.S. counterparts, their total meat intake would increase from 64 to 181 million tonnes per year or grow to the equivalent of 80% of current global meat consumption (Webb, 2006). Thus, the impacts of changing food consumption patterns and an increased fashion to eat out in food-service outlets upon the food supply chain will be enormous. There will be considerable issues for governments, for food producers and distributors and for food retailers and food-service providers. Not least, food-service providers will need to reflect upon their food purchasing practices and policies to ensure the continuous supply of ingredients at the right price to their operations. Distribution remains a major challenge for foreign companies wishing to expand and to growing indigenous businesses. Some of the hindrances include

- The mountainous terrain covering much of China.
- The variable quality of the roads, which in the cities, particularly, are often congested.
- The fragmented nature of the trucking industry.
- The inadequate storage facilities of Chinese distributors.
- The inadequate refrigerated and frozen food distribution and storage system.
- The reliance upon a variety of suppliers because of the lack of a single supplier covering all ingredients and food items.
- The difficulties of the food-service sector accessing the tax-free wholesale wet markets, which are the major wholesale food supply channel for independent Chinese food-service operators.

Healthy eating

The relationship between food and health is at the core of Chinese culinary art, and food has always been used as a preventative and curative medicine. The use of traditional ingredients and the consumption of the two basic food groups, yin and yang, in a balanced manner have long been believed as important by the Chinese people.

More recently, health awareness has been on the increase in China and Hong Kong, particularly among the growing middle class. Improving living standards and the aftermath of recent outbreaks (see section on Hygiene and food safety) have made consumers all the more concerned over how they can manage their health. However, increased disposable income and changing lifestyles have resulted in the increased popularity of Western fast food, particularly among young Chinese living in urban areas. This has led to a rise of obesity and a decline in the consumption of traditional snack foods (Knowles, 2005). According to Garner (2005), across the world, generally, dietary trends tend to evolve from traditional foods to Western-style food and then on to convenience before progressing to a focus on health. In the urban city areas of China, and especially those in the coastal areas that have been at the forefront of the developments in the food-service sector, the fast-food market is approaching maturity and so it might be expected that the emphasis on health is yet to come. In rural areas, the diet is still more oriented towards the consumption of traditional Chinese foods, and so some of the problems associated with the excessive consumption of Western and convenience foods would seem less of an issue. But this may change, if people in rural areas follow the dietary trends previously mentioned.

Hygiene and food safety

The Chinese have becoming increasingly aware of food safety and the measures to ensure it following the outbreak of SARS in 2003 and the avian (bird) influenza epidemic. The bird flu outbreak in February 2004 had little damage upon the food-service industry, although chicken sales were affected for a short time (Euromonitor, 2006). However, the combined effects of SARS, bird flu and problems with adulterated and unsanitary foods have resulted in food safety and hygiene becoming important considerations for Chinese consumers eating out. Today, they commonly regard hygiene and cleanliness in food-service operations their key priority (Bitar, 2005; Sin, 2005) and the recent problems have, according to Yang (2006), "spurred consumers to patronize larger, cleaner restaurants serving higher-quality, more hygienic, healthier foods".

Managers of food-service businesses have also become increasingly concerned. This is particularly so after the outbreak of SARS when more attention was placed upon improving hygiene in food-service outlets, and during the bird flu outbreak when strict controls were imposed by some restaurants on sourcing products for food safety reasons. The latter has encouraged some of China's food producers to consider new production management systems. In addition, a number of restaurants also launched new dishes to attract customers (Euromonitor, 2006) while others have introduced Hazard Analysis and Critical Control Points (HACCP), which is being promoted in China. Employee training in food handling and hygiene has been stepped up in some operations, especially the chains, and the pressure is on for food-service operators to reconsider, if they have not already done so, equipment specifications and operational procedures. Bitar (2005, p. 44) also reports that the national government is investigating the enforcement of hygiene and safety laws to ensure food safety. The example of Shanghai shows how seriously local government is taking the situation. Here the Food and Drug Administration announced the launch of a scheme to rank restaurants by cleanliness. The number of inspections per year will then be determined according to the ranking awarded to a restaurant (Sin, 2005).

Future trends and developments

According to an old Chinese proverb, "To the ruler, people are heaven; to the people, food is heaven". Certainly food service has been heaven to the Chinese population in recent years as demand has burgeoned, particularly during holidays. This interest has been largely fuelled by improvements in consumers' income levels and by the Chinese government's efforts to improve living standards of the rural population. The consequences have been rapid development of the restaurant industry in China, an upgrade of the industry structure and innovation of products, grouplisation of restaurant businesses and the noticeable influence of Western cuisine culture (Ming, 2005).

In the last two or three years, multinationals, especially those from the West, have been at the forefront in China's food-service environment in terms of sales, benefiting from standardisation, branding, the emphasis on quality control and hygiene and, more generally, on effective management. In the fast-food market, these have included McDonald's, and KFC and Pizza Hut, both part of Yum! Restaurants International, Inc., whereas the leading business in the contract catering market has been Compass. While there have been similarities in approach, different brands have pursued different strategies. For instance, in the fast-food market KFC has focused on selling chicken products, has localised some of its menu items to suit local tastes and has given great importance to a healthy diet. McDonald's, on the other hand, has chosen to concentrate on the provision of Western-style rather than Chinese-style food to consumers when they dine out.

China's food-service industry is still in its infancy, yet over the last decade, momentum has been growing, first in the major urban areas of Beijing, Shanghai, and Guangzhou, and more recently in other cities with high business and tourist traffic. The future is very promising for food-service businesses in China due to sustained and strong economic growth – the improvement in overall living standards across China and the boom in tourism. Euromonitor (2006) claims that the fast pace of life throughout the country will lead to a growth in demand for fast-food products in China. The increased exposure to Western lifestyles will provide higher than average sales growth in food-service outlets with Western features and cuisine, such as in coffee shops and cafés and Western restaurants. This increased exposure will also lead to the further development of such outlets, particularly away from the coastal cities. For Chinese-style restaurant businesses, there are also opportunities. These relate to developing local brands, focusing on the "greening" and sustainability of businesses, innovation in Chinese cuisine and the globalisation of Chinese food-service brands.

However, the difficulties associated with the standardisation of ingredients and preparation, are serious impediments to Chinese restaurant and fast-food development. Many ethnic fast-food chains offer Mongolian hotpot, dim sum, Beijing- or Shanghai-style dumplings, and Cantonese and Sichuan foods in new locations. There are further opportunities here. But for all food-service businesses in China and Hong Kong, threats continue to exist, not least of which is the potential return of SARS or avian flu. However, recent guidelines, aimed at food-service businesses, which attempt to streamline procedures and tighten health and hygiene standards, may help to prevent or reduce any ensuing difficulties.

Learning tasks

1 Look at the web sites for each of the leading restaurant chains listed in Table 6.1 and identify their expansion plans for China and any opportunities and challenges they foresee regarding Chinese developments. Try to determine what presence each of the chains has in Hong Kong and Macau.
2 Go to your local public library or university/college library and search for books on Chinese cuisine or food. Make notes on their content, for example, utensils used in cooking dishes, the techniques used, the ingredients used, any regional differences and similarities in cuisine and the techniques used, and any influences on cuisine. Note the background of the authors and their connection to authentic Chinese cuisine.
3 Record some details about dining/eating out in China.

Discussion questions

1 To what extent do you think Chinese restaurant/takeaway food sold in the UK is similar or different to that consumed in China? If there are differences, why do you think this might be? What are the possibilities of finding Chinese regional styles of food being sold in the UK?
2 Given the vigorous expansion plans of many of the fast-food chains, what is the future for small businesses in China? What recommendations do you have for small fast-food businesses to succeed in the future?
3 Are there opportunities for food and service management (contract catering) companies in China, Hong Kong and Macau? What is the evidence and if you think so, what challenges might they face, and how could these be overcome?

Mini case study

Yum!

Yum! Brands is a US parent company with over 30,000 outlets worldwide. In 2005, Yum! Brands operating in China comprise more than 1250 KFC outlets and 140 Pizza Hut restaurants. In Shanghai, it also has two Taco Bell outlets. Yum! outlets in China totalled far more than McDonald's, which currently has around 600 restaurants, with 1000 planned to be open by the time of the Beijing 2008 Olympics. Yum! operates in about 300 mainland cities, opened in 48 new markets in 2004. The Yum! company is well situated for growth, with it adding about 300 new, and mostly KFC, restaurants every year. The company is highly profitable making about US$200 million operating profit in China in 2004 from revenues of over US$1 billion. Seven years previously it had been US$20 million. The revenues are such that growth can be self-financing with an export profit potential to the parent company.

Yum! Brands entered the Chinese market with a KFC outlet in Beijing in 1987 and now KFC operates in about 280 mainland cities with Shanghai and Beijing having about 100 outlets each. The KFC currently performs particularly well in China with the average outlet volumes in China being greater than the averages for KFC internationally and in the USA. The costs to build outlets are also lower in China and because of lower operating costs, the profit margins higher. According to AC Nielsen, KFC is the leading consumer brand in China in any sector, and its popularity has been gained in part by adapting the menu to include items unique to China. These include breakfast congee, winter soup made of egg, spinach and tomato, oven roasted wings, dragon twister and seasonal vegetables including a salad of shredded carrots or cucumbers or bamboo shoots or lotus roots. The inclusion of such items was aided by the use of a local management team with an appreciation of local eating preferences. The average turnover per Chinese KFC outlet was US$1.2 million in 2004 and 2005 compared to the average for a USA outlet of US$0.9 million.

Yum! Brands Strategic Strengths
Continuity in people and process
Restaurant support centre in Shanghai since 1993
Strong government and media relations
Resource deployment against supply chain
High flexibility to adapt to local needs/preferences

Source: Yum! Brands China.

Yum! Brands in China owns its own food distribution system and employs one of the largest retail estate development teams of any retailer in the world. Eighty percent of its own management are at least college educated and very motivated. The company is advancing quickly in China and developments include trialling home delivery and, opening new brands including a Chinese-style brand with the Chinese name for East Dawning.

Source: Garner (2005) and Wachholz (2005b).

References

Ackerman, D. (1990). *The Natural History of the Senses*. New York, Random House.

Bitar, R.W. (2005). *In the Fast Lane*. Foodservice Europe & Middle East, Trend Edition, pp. 40–44.

Dewald, B. (2002). Chinese Meals in China: The Menu, Table Etiquette and Food Ordering, *The Hospitality Review*, April, **4**(2), 21–26.

Euromonitor (2006). *Consumer Foodservice in China*. London, Euromonitor.

Garner, J. (2005). *The Rise of the Chinese Consumer: Theory and Evidence*. Chichester, England, John Wiley.

Grigson, J. (ed.) (1988). *The World Atlas of Food: A Gourmet's Guide to the Great Regional Dishes of the World*. London, Spring Books.

Harper, D. et al. (2005). *China*. 9th Edition, London, Lonely Planet.

Hom, K. (1989). *Fragrant Harbour Taste*. New York, Simon and Schuster.

Jackson, A. (2004). *Food of the World*. Bath, Parragon Publishing.

Knowles, C. (2005). *China*. 6th Edition, Farnborough, England, AA Publishing.

Lee, H. (2004). *Coffee Brews a Future in China?* Euromonitor Archive. London, Euromonitor, 13 September.

Ming, H. (2005). *China Restaurant Industry Overview*. Presentation given at 42nd annual International Hotel & Restaurant Association Congress, Beijing.

Moss, C. (2006). *Beijing on a Plate*, interview with Guo Yue, Saturday, *Guardian Travel*, 28 January, p. 8.

Newman, J.M. (2000). Chinese Meals. In Meiselman, H.L. (ed.), *Dimensions of the Meal; The Science, Culture, Business, and Art of Eating.* Gaithersburg, MD, Aspen Publishers, pp. 163–175.

Sin, L.H. (2005). *At the Head of the Pack.* Foodservice Europe & Middle East, Trend Edition, pp. 46–50.

Stevens, J. (ed.) (1984). *Ken Hom's Chinese Cookery.* London, British Broadcasting Corporation.

Time Out (2004). *Hong Kong.* 2nd Edition, London, Penguin.

Wachholz, M. (2005a). *Foreign Companies a Major Sales Vehicle.* Foodservice Europe & Middle East, Trend Edition, pp. 68–69.

Wachholz, M. (2005b). *The Colonel's Chinese Career.* Foodservice Europe & Middle East, Trend Edition, pp. 52–56.

Webb, M.S. (2006). I've Worked Up an Appetite to Make a Profit from Food, *The Sunday Times*, Money, 8 January, p. 7.

Yang, M. (2006). *China's Food Service Sector Continues Sustained Growth.* FAS Worldwide: An online review of Foreign Agricultural Service initiatives and services, July. http://www.fas.usda.gov/info/fasworldwide/2006/07-2006/ChinaHRIOverview.pdf.

Tourism
business – China

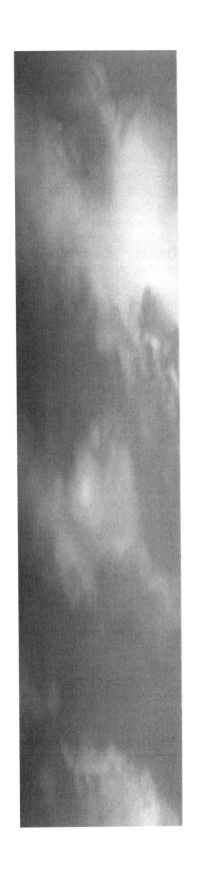

> **Chapter objectives**
>
> When you have read this chapter, you will be able to
>
> 1 Contribute to a greater understanding of what constitutes, what takes place and what could occur within the inbound and domestic tourism business in China.
> 2 Explain the development and economic importance of the tourism business in China and some of the influencing factors on this development.
> 3 Provide a critical insight into issues confronting tourism development and management within China.

Introduction

From being a country with closed doors to inbound tourism before 1978, mainland China has become a major international tourism destination. A combination of Deng Xiaoping's introduction of market reforms, the government's recognition of the economic value of tourism and the opening up of mainland China to the rest of the world have been key drivers behind the continuous and spectacular growth of China's tourism industry. And, what many consider to be, some of the world's greatest tourism experiences, including the Forbidden City in Beijing, the Great Wall, the Terracotta Warriors in Xian and the Three Gorges of the Yangtze River, have become increasingly popular attractions to international business and leisure travellers. Such experiences have been complemented by the opening of new sightseeing destinations in mainland China. Furthermore, the growth in inward visitors to mainland China has been accompanied by a constant increase in domestic tourism.

By 2000, China's international tourist arrivals and receipts were such that it had become the leading country in Asian tourism and, according to the WTO, since 2004, China has overtaken Italy's traditional position as the world's fourth most-visited destination. In 2004, the WTO also reported that with its tourism receipts of US$25.7 billion, China was ranked seventh in the world. From 1995 to 2005, tourism grew in China at a pace of close to 9% a year (Hong Kong experienced a similar growth rate). This was to such an extent that in 2005 tourism was booming in inbound, outbound and domestic markets, and it was a major industry and earner of foreign currency. Even the decline in overseas visitors in early 2003 due to the outbreak of the SARS virus between November 2002 and June 2003 was only short-lived, and the industry quickly recovered. In 2004, the China National Tourism Administration (CNTA) recorded that there were nearly 42 million inbound international visitors to China. This excluded inbound arrivals from the Hong Kong, Macau and SARs, which accounted for another 67 million arrivals. According to the WTTC (2006), China's travel and tourism economy, both directly and indirectly, was expected to account for over US$301 billion, that is, over 13% of total Chinese GDP in 2006. So from virtually nothing in 1978, tourism in China had grown significantly by 2006. This "explosive development was triggered by newly opened international destinations, considerably improved domestic transportation and infrastructure, and by the energetic economic development and stable social environment in China" (Euromonitor, 2006).

The expectation is that the growth in Chinese tourism will continue with the WTO forecasting 130 million annual international tourist arrivals in China and 57 million inbound arrivals in Hong Kong by 2020. This forecast figure for China will make it the world's top tourism destination. Furthermore, the Chinese economy will by then become dependent on tourism.

This chapter concentrates on inbound and domestic tourism and begins by reviewing tourism in China before and after 1978. The latter review will include consideration of tourism policies and their implementation and tourism movements. Transportation and tourist attractions are key elements of the tourism infrastructure and as such will be briefly analysed. Tourism development in China is confronted by a number of challenges and issues. This chapter will discuss some of these. Finally, future prospects for the sector will be discussed.

Tourism in China before 1978

Historical literature indicates tourism and travel dating back thousands of years in China. In ancient times, tourism in China could be considered an individual activity consisting of tour or travel activities organised by individuals for themselves or activities arranged by individual people for others. These activities have been classified and analysed by Zhang, Pine and Lam (2005) into tours by emperors and officials, travel by scholars and scientists and travel for trading purposes, religious reasons and festivals. Tourism for the ordinary people, however, did not really exist and, as such, neither did a tourist industry, with tourism businesses such as travel agents and tourism operators being absent.

In the nineteenth century, China witnessed significant political, social and economic changes. One result was the increased demand to travel both within China and, as it opened up more to the outside world, into the country. The last quarter of the nineteenth century saw the start of modern travel in China, and small travel businesses began to slowly open. These were mainly operated by foreigners for foreigners. The first commercial tours to China began in 1909 through Thomas Cook and Sons. However, it was not until the 1920s and 1930s that the beginnings of what could be called "the tourism industry" started to emerge. International travel companies started to establish themselves in China. These included Thomas Cook's company, who opened offices in Shanghai and Beijing (Hibbort, 1990). Another development was the first Chinese travel agency owned and operated by the Chinese in China. This became known as the China Travel Service and first opened in Shanghai in 1923 (Zhang, 2003, p. 13). However, such developments came to a halt between the late 1930s and the mid-1940s as China plunged into a succession of wars.

Following the Communist victory in 1949 and the establishment of the PRC and through to 1978, when China decided to shift emphasis from political struggle to economic reconstruction and to "open its doors" to the rest of the world, tourism in China was restricted. During this period, the economy was centrally planned and state-owned enterprises dominated any development. Private ownership was almost non-existent. Up to the beginning of 1966, and what has been termed the "Great Cultural Revolution", domestic tourism hardly existed and what little tourism did exist in the country was carefully controlled and undertaken for political reasons rather the economic purposes. Then between 1966 and 1978, travel and tourism came to a virtual standstill as China shut its doors and concerned itself with internal political struggles.

Tourism in China after 1978

A watershed in the historical development of tourism in China took place in the late 1970s. It began in 1978 when the Communist Party of China made a number of historic economic reforms. These were founded on the so-called four modernisations of agriculture, industry, science and technology and national defence.

The country started to move away from a planned economy to a market economy and adopted an Open Door policy, which opened up the country to foreign investment and international visitors. Private ownership was also permitted by the government. Since then, tourism has developed rapidly as the government has emphasised particularly, through a range of policies, the economic importance of tourism (especially since 1986) and the need to earn foreign exchange, provide employment and promote regional development through tourism. Table 7.1 shows some of the major tourism policies and regulations implemented in China between 1978 and 1996.

From 1978 to 1985, when the reforms were in their early stages, tourism policies and practices still often prioritised political gain over economic benefits, but this was to change in 1986 when the government declared tourism to be a comprehensive economic activity and included it for the first time in its national plan for social and economic development (Zhang, 2003, p. 25). Tourism is now considered a key growth area in economic development in provincial, regional and national terms.

In addition to the increased recognition that tourism has been an economically important and successful industry, it has also changed in a number of other major ways since 1978. These, detailed by Zhang, Pine and Lam (2005) and Zhang (2003), include

- less administrative control and micromanagement of tourism by government and more macromanagement through the development of tourism plans for the whole country and through service. The main tourism body, the CNTA was set up in 1981 and focuses on the macro-management of tourism;
- a shifting emphasis from inbound tourism between 1978 and 1985 to both international and domestic tourism. Domestic tourism lagged behind international tourism from when it was first initiated in China in 1978 until the early 1990s when it started to thrive;

Table 7.1 The major tourism policies and regulations implemented in China between 1978 and 1996

Year	Policy and regulation	Target areas	Implementation status
1979	Introduction of foreign investment	Initially in hotels and then to travel agencies	Successfully implemented
1984	Decision to allow tourism administrations, individual government agencies, local governments, collectives with individuals to invest in tourism	Investment in tourism industry	Successfully implemented
1985	Provisional regulation on the administration of travel agencies	Travel agencies	Not well implemented and replaced by 1996 regulation of travel agent administration
1988	Regulations on the star standard and star rating of tourist hotels	Hotels	Successfully implemented
1992	Development of state-level resorts	Tourist attractions	Successfully implemented
1993	Provisional methods on the administration of hotel management companies	Hotels	Successfully implemented
1995	Provisional regulations on the administration of quality service guarantee funds of travel agencies and Quality supervision bureau	Travel agencies – service quality and customer satisfaction	Successfully implemented following initial resistance
1996	Regulation on the administration of tour guides	Travel agencies – qualification and licensing of tour guides	Implemented
1996	Regulation on the administration of travel agencies	Travel agencies	Implemented

Source: Zhang, Chong and Jenkins (2002).

- increasing reliance of short-haul international markets over long-haul markets;
- the development of outward travel and tourism in addition to inward tourism;
- movement away from the state monopolisation of international tourism business, including tourism operators, travel agencies, airlines and hotels, towards a decentralised restructuring with a more open industry and more diverse sources of investment;
- transition from product-oriented tourism provision towards market-oriented provision.

Tourism and the economy

In 1986, China's tourism industry was included in the National Plan for Social and Economic Development. This was the first time this had happened. Since then, the industry has been regarded as an important element of the national economy, and today, the industry is becoming an important driving force in the economy (Mintel, 2006). Tourism is now viewed as a way of attracting foreign exchange from international visitors and stimulating economic growth (Yan and Wall, 2002). Investment in tourism has been increasing to facilitate these. According to the tenth five-year (2001–2005) plan for Tourism Development and Programme for Long-Term Goal up to 2015 and 2020, by 2020, "the tourism industry will become a real pillar industry in the national economy, making a 11% contribution to the country's GDP" (Zhang, Pine and Lam, 2005, p. 91). In fact, the WTTC expected China's travel and tourism economy both directly and indirectly to account for over 13% of total Chinese GDP in 2006. This national picture is also increasingly being recognised regionally with many local governments now regarding tourism as a leading industry in their local economies and important for regional development.

In addition to the contribution to GDP, tourism's contribution to the national economy of China can be seen from its inbound tourism earnings (Table 7.2) and its ability to bring jobs. From 1990 to 2005, China's international tourism earnings increased from US$2.2 billion to US$24.8 billion and the annual percent change over the previous year was, apart from 2001, at or above 10% for every year. The most-visited tourist destinations by inbound tourists are the major cities, and as a result, Beijing generated the highest amount of international tourist receipts followed by Shanghai and Guangzhou.

According to Mintel (2006) in 2005, the industry was expected to generate US$265.1 billion of economic activity, which represents 11.7% of GDP, and then grow to US$875.1 billion by 2015. Between 2006 and 2015, annual tourism demand was predicted to increase by 9.2%. In 2005, the industry was expected to grow by 10.1%, which in absolute terms represented 4.3% of world's market share. Mintel (2006) claims that according to the WTO, "in 2005, of 174 countries measured, China's Travel & Tourism economy ranked seventh in size worldwide, 74th in relative contribution to national economy, but second in long-term (ten-year) growth". Of the international

Table 7.2 International tourism receipts, 1990, 2000–2005

Year	US$ billion	Change over previous year (%)
1990	2.2	19.20
2000	16.2	15.08
2001	17.8	9.67
2002	20.4	14.60
2003	17.4	14.61
2004	25.7	47.87
2005	24.8	17.06

Note: 2005 figure January–October only.
Source: CNTA in Mintel (2006).

tourism expenditure in 2004, 26% went to long-distance transport in China, 23% to retail trade, 13% to accommodation, 8% to food service, 7% to entertainment and 4% to local transport (CNTA, 2005).

Comprehensive and reliable data on tourism employment in China do not exist (Gang and Kruse, 2003). However, the WTTC (2006) claimed that in 2006, travel and tourism was expected to account for 77.6 million jobs or 10.2% of total Chinese employment. This figure included over 17 million employees directly employed in travel and tourism.

Domestic tourism has grown rapidly in China from the early 1990s and can be regarded as being beneficial for regional economic development, improving local economic structures, assisting the development of related industries, providing employment and increasing domestic demand.

Tourist movements

In May 2005, China was the world's fourth most-visited destination, according to the WTO, and it accounted for 5.5% of world market share, equating to three arrivals per 100 of the population (see Table 7.3).

Mintel (2006), drawing upon CNTA data, recorded the following movements:

- Visitor arrivals to both China and Hong Kong grew at a pace of nearly 9% per annum between 1995 and 2004. With an increase in the number of countries gaining Approved Destination Status (ADS), more outbound is likely, with a positive knock-on for inward tourism. The WTTC (2006, p. 60) argues, however, that the situation would be even better if ADS requirements were removed completely "allowing unlimited access to the Chinese market by foreign NTOs and tour operators, and by removing restrictions on travel agency outbound sales".
- The total number of inbound tourists from January to October 2005 was 100.2 million.

Table 7.3 The top eight world tourism destinations

Rank	Country	Arrivals (m)			Change (%) 2004/2003	Market share 2004	Population (m) 2004	Arrivals per 100 of population
		1995	2000	2004				
1	France	60.0	77.2	75.1	0.1	9.9	60	124
2	Spain	34.9	47.9	53.6	3.4	7.1	40	133
3	USA	43.5	51.2	46.1	11.8	6.1	293	16
4	China	20.0	31.2	41.8	26.7	5.5	1299	3
5	Italy	31.1	41.2	37.1	−6.4	4.9	58	64
6	UK	23.5	25.2	27.7	12.1	3.6	60	46
7	Hong Kong	10.2	13.1	21.8	40.4	2.9	7	318
8	Mexico	20.2	20.6	20.6	10.5	2.7	105	20
9	World	545.0	686.0	760.0	10.0	100.0	6376	11

Source: World Tourism Organisation Data as collected by WTO May 2005.

- Most arrivals to China were from Hong Kong, Macau and Taiwan, accounting for 84% of total market share in 2004. Foreigners accounted for the other 16%. However, significantly, in 2005, foreign arrivals increased by 1% to 17% of the total and represented the highest increase in visitor arrivals.
- The majority, 63%, of visitors to China are from Asia, although in 2004 and 2005, visitors from Africa, Oceania and Europe, all showed strong growth.
- China's leading tourism-generating markets are Korea, Japan, Russia, USA and Malaysia. Japan and Korea accounted for a combined market share of 35% in 2005.
- Growth of the domestic market outstripped international arrivals, from 694 million in 1998 to 1102 million travellers in 2004.
- From 2003 to 2004, there was a growth of 84.8% in domestic tourism. The majority of this was business travellers, but to try and increase domestic leisure travel, paid flexible holidays are being introduced to encourage tourism and three-week long holiday per year, the so-called Golden Weeks, have purposely been developed. These focus on the Chinese Spring Festival (29 January–12 February in 2006), Labour Day and the National Day holiday from 1 October.
- Over 46% of foreign visitor arrivals were for leisure purposes and nearly 23% for business in 2005.
- International tourism receipts are lowest in January–March. The average length of stay of foreign visitors is nearly seven days. The majority (over 65%) of international tourist arrivals are males aged 25–44. Most international visitors tend to travel in groups.

Tourist infrastructure

Since the late 1970s, when tourism began to be promoted in China, the tourism infrastructure in China has greatly improved in both amount and standards through the combined efforts of the state and local governments, public and private sectors. Prior to this accommodation, tourist transportation systems and tourist attractions were inadequate and hindered China's tourism development.

Tourist products

In the late 1970s, following the opening up of China to the outside world, there were only a restricted number of regions and cities open to foreign visitors. This was slow to change, but in the 1990s, the situation altered with most cities and regions opening up for foreign visitors. However, the Eastern coastal areas and particularly the coastal cities remain the most popular destinations for tourists, especially foreign tourists, and much has still to be done to attract visitors to other parts of China. An expanding tourism infrastructure has seen city breaks to Shanghai and Beijing becoming more popular.

China offers visitors what many consider to be some of the world's great tourism experiences, and it is traditionally, a once in a lifetime holiday for many international visitors with tours taking in the most famous sights of the Golden Triangle of Beijing, with the Great Wall and the Forbidden City, the 600-year-old Terracotta Army at Xian and fashionable Shanghai. Chinese cultural heritage tourism is currently the main attraction for foreign visitors and has been argued to be a priority in future international tourism product development (Zhang, Pine and Zhang, 2000). However, the need for greater innovation in international tourist products and catering to the requirements of contemporary tourists who are seeking more flexibility and choice will be vital in the future. This will require increased segmentation of the tourist market to realise the maximum benefits both for and from each tourist group.

With the active involvement of local governments, different tourism concepts were launched in 2004 and 2005 to promote tourism in different regions (Euromonitor, 2006). Some limited innovation has taken place. Middle China, represented by Sichuan and Chongqing, has built an integrated package of attractions including promoting tickets covering neighbouring attractions. Whereas Shanxi, Jiangxi, Hunan and other provinces began to respond to the Red Tourism concept introduced by CNTA and have recognised the potential of the Long March of the Communist Party.

In 2003, there were a total of 29 World Natural and Cultural Heritage Sites across the country. Natural attractions include the Three Gorges cruise on the Yangtze River, the limestone cliffs of Guilin in the South and Kunming City of Eternal Spring, as well as the indigenous people in Yunnan province. The world's largest Buddha is at Leshan. More adventurous attractions include, following the Silk Road bordering the countries of Central Asia, the Gobi desert and the steppes of Inner Mongolia and Tibet. The diverse natural environments of China's untapped regions offer tremendous market potential in the future, both for the domestic and international market.

Other tourism potential exists related to cruise tourism, which has been earmarked for development from 12 coastal cities to the meetings, incentives, conferences and exhibition (MICE) market – which has witnessed substantial investment in recent years – and to theme/amusement parks. Further insights into MICE activity in China can be found in WTTC (2006, p. 10, pp. 62–63). Walt Disney Company is planning to open a new theme park in Shanghai. Subject to government approval, construction is anticipated to start in 2008, with opening in 2012.

While most visitors to China come to see the sights, it also has beaches and there are resorts on tropical Hainan Island, which has been referred to as "the Chinese Hawaii". Many Asian visitors also come for cheap shopping in the major cities and for the Chinese regional cuisine.

Other new forms of tourism product have emerged related to, for example, industrial tourism, folk tourism, eco-tourism, tourism festivals and events, and on sporting tourism including white water rafting, skiing, climbing and golf. Many of these have been attractive to the domestic tourism market (Wu, Zhu and Xu, 2000), but they also have generated interest from the overseas market. For instance, golf is a major sporting activity in China and growth has been significant in recent years with more courses, clubs and players. China has the largest golf course in the world. During the last decade, China has become one of the world's most attractive golf destination.

A major forthcoming event to be held in China in 2008 is the Olympic Games. The year 2005 was designated "Olympic Promotion Year", and China is very optimistic about the Games, which are seen as a great opportunity to promote China internationally and thereby increase its share of the leisure market. Approximately US$37 billion is being spent on the Games as China prepares to receive 4.6 million international visitors and 150 million domestic tourists. Further opportunities to promote China come from its hosting of the Asian Games and the World Expo, in Shanghai in 2010, at which China expects to receive 70 million international visitors in the same year.

> Competition amongst travel agencies has been increasing in recent years, especially with the arrival of international travel agencies in China. As a consequence domestic agents have been setting up new services to retain and attract new market shares. These include more flexible holiday packages and new conceptual packages such as customized honeymoon tours (Mintel, 2006).

Transportation

Travel into, and around, China has been extremely problematical due to the inadequate transportation system. This has hindered tourism development in the early years after the opening up of the country and the economic reforms of the late 1970s. But over the last two decades, the situation has changed. Improvements have occurred in the aviation and railway industries and many new roads and motorways have been constructed, improving speeds and convenience.

The growth of the aviation industry is currently soaring in China. In 2005, there were 36,000 flights per week in and out of Chinese airports, over double the amount of 2000. This has been aided by the discount strategy the airlines adopted, which has made air tickets available to more Chinese. Furthermore, according to the WTTC (2006), the Chinese government aims to allow airports in western China to receive international aircraft. This would mean increasing the current 32 airports in the western region to 60 by 2020 – Boeing estimates that China's aviation industry will be operating a fleet of approximately 22,000 passenger aircraft by 2019. This would represent 10% of the world's total. The major airlines are Air China, China Southern and China Eastern, but many new airlines are being set up. These have included private airline companies, for example, OK airways, and the first discount-fare airline in China, Spring Airlines, which made its first flight in July 2005. Another development has been the open skies policy, which will see increasing numbers of low-cost airlines entering China. On the negative side, regulations on minimum fares, which these new airlines have been allowed to advertise, have restricted their competitiveness.

There are over 70,000 km of railways in China of which nearly 40% are electrified. In recent years, the railway authorities have been making great progress in improving timetables, shortening journey times and making travel more convenient and comfortable. This has been particularly beneficial to domestic tourism and special tourist, and chartered trains to key destinations have increased in popularity.

Nevertheless, concerns remain about transportation. Dr. Mak from Hong Kong Polytechnic University has said, "Transportation remains one of the major barriers to tourism development in much of China but especially in rural areas, even though improvements during the last two decades have been significant. Low efficiency, poor economies of scale, poor management, and the poor safety records of air transport, railways, and road services have hindered tourism development in China" (WTTC, 2006).

Accommodation

Great strides have been made to tourist accommodation since 1978. More details of accommodation in China can be found in Chapter 5. One of the big developments, since 2005, has been the construction of the Internet platform, which has increased the availability of accommodation online and facilitated greater communication and Internet selling from both direct sellers and intermediaries. Discount and luxury accommodation markets have been particularly targeted for selling (Euromonitor, 2006).

Tourism issues

There are numerous strategic and other issues confronting tourism in China. The WTTC (2006) has identified and explored a number of these, including structural features that are constraining China's potential tourism development, factors that are preventing business investment, the need for sustained and effective marketing, the insufficiencies of tourism statistics and market research information in China, Hong Kong and Macau, and policies and actions that support the environment and local communities. Other issues that have been identified elsewhere include human resource issues in the development of provincial tourism in China (Qiu and Lam, 2004), the need for ongoing tourism product development tailored to the differing needs of tourists (Zhang, Pine and Lam, 2005), the negative social and environmental impacts arising from the growth of tourism (Zhang, 2003) and issues of sustainability, and an over-reliance on the tourism industry in the face of potential susceptibility to such threats as avian flu and SARS (Mintel, 2006). Some of these issues will now be briefly discussed.

Organisation and administration of tourism in china

While in a very short period the Chinese government has reformed itself and changed the way it operates, much of tourism policy-making is still centralised in the CNTA. This inevitably means decisions and actions are slower than they might otherwise be "and overcoming outdated gov-ernment structures in the fast pace of tourism development remains an ongoing challenge, according to the WTTC" (Mintel, 2006).

The WTTC (2006) argues that tourism structures need to change further with the public and private sectors sharing a new vision of openness, collaboration and co-operation, so that tourism development in China can progress to the next point in the life cycle.

Regional development

Economic growth and development across China has been uneven with the urban areas, particularly those on the eastern coast, developing the fastest. Tourism is increasingly being seen as important to the accelerated development of the western and middle areas of China. However, while the tourism industry in China has grown, its development has also been very uneven regionally. Inward tourism has tended to concentrate in the three coastal cities of Shanghai, Guangzhou and Beijing, and the proportion of total tourism receipts earned in coastal localities has greatly exceeded the proportion of national population in these areas. Thus, as Wen and Tisdell (2001) suggest, tourism growth appears to have increased regional disparity. So for tourism to succeed in encouraging increased economic growth in the western, middle and more rural regions, new initiatives may be required to capitalise on this opportunity to further enhance tourism in China. Reliance on the traditional rural tourist product may be insufficient, and the development of new and innovative products may be required, such as the ecotourism products that Wen and Tisdell (2001) propose.

They also claim that for tourism to become, what they call, "a regional growth pole" in inland China, it will need strong government support and industrial cooperation. The WTTC (2006) points to other requirements:

Particularly with regard to western China, it is critical that tourism infrastructure, strategic plans and objectives be followed by detailed action plans for tourism marketing and promotion, training and education, and sustainable development. The economic business model for western China's tourism must be sustainable. Otherwise, China will be forced to provide onerous investment and ongoing subsidies.

Environmental impacts/pollution

Environmental impacts are often exacerbated as tourism expands, and these impacts in turn are likely to adversely affect the tourism product and demand. These impacts of tourism are varied and include increased air and water pollution, the implications of large volumes of tourists on the wear and tear of facilities and historic and other sites, and increased consumption, waste and resource utilisation.

Increased industrialisation and economic growth already contribute to environmental problems in China. According to the *New Republic Online* dated 23 August 2004, 16 of the world's 20 most polluted cities are in China; five of China's biggest rivers are not suitable for human contact, and two-thirds of China's cities do not meet World Health Organization air-quality standards (WTTC, 2006). Beijing suffers from four principal sources of polluted air. These are cars, building dust from construction and demolition sites, coal burning power plants and factories and dust storms that blow in from the Gobi desert. Hong Kong is not immune, and it has experienced soaring smog levels. The authorities have been so worried about the levels of air pollution adversely impacting upon athletes and visitors attending the forthcoming Olympics that dozens of restriction orders have been drawn up to curb pollution. Moreover, the *China Daily* newspaper has reported that the Communist Party has warned its citizens not to embarrass their country during the Olympics by spitting, littering or shouting into mobile phones (*Daily Mail*, 18 August 2006).

Concerted efforts must be made to prevent the negative impacts that tourism can bring on the environment and to China. Sustainability in Chinese tourism is vital and must be central to all policy-making and development planning. It also must be accepted throughout the country and amongst all stakeholders in the tourism industry. For sustainability to be realised, there needs to be a balance between product development and environmental concerns and a balance of private initiative, economic incentives and regulation for environmental protection.

In 1997, the Hong Kong Tourist Association in conjunction with the Industry Department commissioned the design of an environmentally sustainable development strategy for Hong Kong's travel and tourism industry. Later research revealed that while many in the industry were aware of, or had adopted, environment-friendly practices, awareness of the strategy was low. This suggests that even in what might be considered a more advanced part of China, more needs to be done to raise awareness levels with regard to the strategy (WTTC, 2006).

Future trends and developments

China, like India and other Southeast Asian countries, possesses one of the fastest growing economies in the world, and tourism development in China has paralleled that of the economy more generally. There is no doubt that the development of the hospitality and tourism business in China has been rapid and pronounced and it follows the opening of its markets to the outside world in 1978 and its entry into mainstream economic and political life, including into the WTO in 2001. Since the late 1970s, China's tourism infrastructure and quality standards have been greatly improved, and it has become more accessible to international tourists.

China has significant potential to become the world's greatest tourism economy – in terms of inward and domestic tourism and also, although not considered in this chapter, in outbound tourism. By 2020, China's GDP is projected to increase fourfold and is expected to receive a projected 230 million visitors. This potential has been recognised within China, and the future vision of tourism can be seen in the National Tourism Policy, which is incorporated in the CNTA document "Building a world tourism power and developing a new mainstay industry – The compendium for China tourism development in the early 21st century". Key points from this are shown in the summarized version (see Case Study) produced by the WTTC (2006). The expectation is that the planned developments of tourism in China will put it, according to the WTO, in top position in the world by 2020 as the country will become the world's number one tourist destination.

There are many challenges to realising this potential though, and further developing public–private partnerships and dealing with the ongoing education and skills training shortage are amongst some of the major obstacles to be overcome to ensure that the country progresses to the next level of development and towards becoming the global tourism power.

Potential also exists in Hong Kong and Macau as Hong Kong continues to develop itself as a leading aviation transport hub and broadens and deepens its tourism product base. Whereas in Macau opportunities lie in its changing emphasis from a minor gaming operation to a world-class, mega-entertainment and tourism destination.

Learning tasks

1 Go to the web site of the World Travel and Tourism Council (2006) China, China Hong Kong SAR and China Macau SAR: The impact of travel & tourism on jobs and the economy (http://www.wttc.org/regProg/china.htm), and read the report. Compile your own view of the implications of the report for the Chinese national Government, for local governments, for the sustainability of tourism in China, for hotels and for tourists.
2 Read recent issues of trade journals (such as *Caterer & Hotelkeeper, Hospitality, Tourism or Travel G.B.I.*) and "quality broad sheet" newspapers and identify articles and stories about Chinese tourism developments. Analyse the articles or stories in order to

- Identify the nature and size of any developments.
- Comment on issues and challenges confronting tourism in China.
- Identify the source(s) of the information.
3 With reference to the sources listed (References), make recommendations as to how China can overcome the increasingly evident skills deficit that exists in its tourism industry.

Discussion questions

1 What steps should be made to enable China to meet the serious challenge of competition from other major tourist destinations?
2 Why might the recent extraordinary success of the Chinese tourism industry and the country's newly discovered reliance on the tourism industry become a problem?

Mini case study

China's important natural scenic areas

With its spectacular natural scenic attractions, China has much to attract a range of tourist market segments, and tourist requirements. China has an amazing diversity of natural scenic attractions scattered across the country and many of these are recognised as Nationally Important Scenic and Historic Interest Areas, which are the exact equivalent of the term 'national park' applied to the rest of the world, as specified by the Ministry of Construction in 1994.

The first nature reserve was established in 1956 and now there about 2000 more parks protecting about 14% of China's land area and offering tourists a variety of landscapes and a diversity of wildlife. Many protect endangered animals – for example, golden monkey, giant pandas and South China tigers – or sacred areas.

China has 187 National Parks. Other national-level protected areas include 265 National Nature Reserves, 138 National Geoparks, 28 National Mineparks, 627 National Forest Parks, 2 National Wetland Parks, 10 National Urban Wetland Parks and 192 National Water Parks.

Sources: Harper, D. et al. (2005) *China*, 9th Edition, London: Lonely Planet.
Web site: http://en. wikipedia.org/wiki/List_of_national_parks_of_the_People's_Republic_of_China.

References

China National Tourism Administration (CNTA) (2005). *Yearbook of China Tourism Statistics*, Beijing, China's Tourism Press.

Euromonitor (2006). *Travel and Tourism in China*. London, Euromonitor International.

Hibbort, P. (1990). *Cook's Peking Home*. Time Traveller 15, UK: Thomas Cook Travel Archive and Library, pp. 8–9.

Gang, X. and Kruse, C. (2003). Economic Impact of Tourism in China. In Lew, A.A., Yu, L., Ap, J. and Guangrui, Z. (eds), *Tourism in China*. London, THHP.

Mintel (2006). *Travel and Tourism – China*. London, Mintel International Group.

Qiu, H.Z. and Lam, T. (2004). Human Resources Issues in the Development of Tourism in China: Evidence from Heilongjiang Province, *International Journal of Contemporary Hospitality Management*, **16**(1), 45–51.

Wen, J.J. and Tisdell, C.A. (2001). *Tourism and China's Development: Policies, Regional Economic Growth and Ecotourism*. Singapore, World Scientific.

World Travel and Tourism Council (WTTC) (2006). *China, China Hong Kong SAR and China Macau SAR: The Impact of Travel & Tourism on Jobs and the Economy*. London, World Travel and Tourism Council.

Wu, B., Zhu, H. and Xu, X. (2000). Trends in China's Domestic Tourism Development at the Turn of the Century, *International Journal of Contemporary Hospitality Management*, **12**(5), 296–299.

Yan, M. and Wall, G. (2002). Economic Perspectives on Tourism in China, *Tourism and Hospitality Research*, **3**(3), 257–275.

Zhang, G. (2003). China's Tourism Since 1978: Policies, Experiences, and Lessons Learned. In Lew, A.A., Yu, L., Ap, J. and Guangrui, Z. (eds), *Tourism in China*. London, THHP.

Zhang, G., Pine, R. and Zhang, H.Q. (2000). China's International Tourism Development: Present and Future, *International Journal of Contemporary Hospitality Management*, **12**(5), 282–290.

Zhang, H.Q., Pine, R. and Lam, T. (2005). *Tourism and Hotel Development in China: From Political to Economic Success*. London, THHP.

Zhang, Q.H., Chong, K. and Jenkins, C.L. (2002). Tourism Policy Implementation in Mainland China: An Enterprise Perspective, *International Journal of Contemporary Hospitality Management*, **14**(1), 38–42.

Part Three

Hospitality and Tourism Management in India

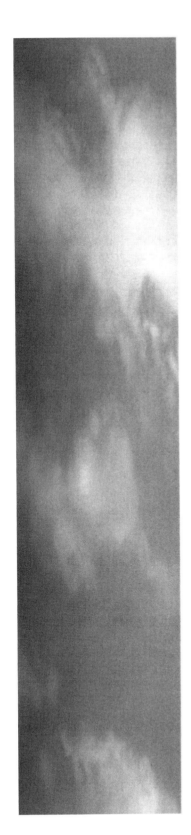

CHAPTER 8

Hotels and resorts – India

Chapter objectives

When you have read this chapter, you will be able to

1 Recognise the nature and the structural characteristics of hotel and resort sectors in India.
2 Chronicle the historical development of the hotel sector in India.
3 Highlight some of the influencing factors on the development of the hotel and resort sector in India.
4 Critically review major issues and operational trends.
5 Discuss the future outlook for the hotel and resort sector in India.

Introduction

The Indian hotel sector is in a period of rapid growth and change. There has been an recent explosion of hotel development in recent times particularly in the major cities of India. This development has been fuelled by the rapid expansion of business activities in these centres as a result of the Indian economy growing and a resulting increase in business travel around India. This chapter will consider this growth and evaluate the types of hotels that have developed and the likely future direction of the Indian hotel industry. It will also consider the strategic and operational issues that are currently important for organisations in the sector. We will start by considering the supply side of the sector and who are currently the major players in the market.

The historical development of the Indian hotel sector

The development of the Indian hotel and resort sector has occurred as a result of tourism trends in the country. The number of tourism arrivals to India has shown a steady growth over the last 50 years. In 1950, for example, there were 15,000 tourist arrivals in India compared to the boom year of 1986 when tourist arrivals exceeded 1 million (Bansal, 2001). The growth of tourism has been considered in some detail in previous sections of the book, and current arrivals to India are now in excess of 3 million with numbers of leisure tourists slightly exceeding numbers of business tourists (Euromonitor, 2005). This growth in inbound tourism, coupled with the increase in domestic tourism due to the economic growth of the country, has meant that there has had to be a steady development in different types of accommodation infrastructure according to the requirements of the different market segments. This has included the development of everything from luxury hotels and resorts to one- and two-star hotels for the domestic tourist.

The strategic development of the infrastructure required to support tourism growth in India has been controlled by the India Tourism Development Corporation (ITDC). The ITDC was established by the Government of India through its Departments of Tourism in 1963. The ITDC has played a major part in the development of the accommodation sector in India.

The historical development of much of India's hotel sector has relied on key entrepreneurs who had a vision of how the accommodation sector could be developed and used to underpin rapid tourism development. More recently, the development has relied on foreign investors and international chains, which are trying to establish their brands in this rapidly developing economy.

The Indian hotel sector

The Indian hotel sector has had a long history of development, which has been characterised by the work of major leading entrepreneurs. Some of these entrepreneurs will be considered in this chapter and in the case studies later in the book. It is estimated that the tourism and hospitality industry in India employs large numbers of people who are often inexperienced and untrained (Jauhari, 2006) and that the Indian hotel industry accounts for 50% of all foreign exchange in India. It is therefore of substantial economic importance (Capitaline, 2005). The Indian hotel industry gains approximately 75% of its income through the major metros and as a result the hotels in the major metros are developing at remarkable rates every year as the economy booms. It was estimated in 2003 that the premium hotel category had 30% market share, the mid-market sector had 25% market share and the budget sector had 25% share. It was also thought that the budget sector contributed minimum revenue despite the market share (Capitaline, 2005).

It is estimated that the tourism and hospitality industry in India employs 25 million people and that this will grow to 100 million people in the next 25 years. It is vital that professional training of the staff in this sector has a major priority and this will be considered later in this chapter. The Federation of Hotel and Restaurant Association of India (FHRAI) was set up in 1955 with an aim of representing and promoting the hospitality industry in India. The organisation carries out research on the Indian hospitality industry and publishes reports on different aspects of the business. All hotels and restaurants in the country are encouraged to join the FHRAI and in 2001 the organisation had 2676 members of which 1794 were hotels, 758 restaurants and 120 associate members (Gupta, Lal and Bhattacharyya, 2002). The FHRAI carries out an annual report on the hotel industry, which includes both approved and unapproved hotels. The Ministry of Tourism of the Indian government grants approval to hotels at the project stage and then places them into star categories. The approval status is voluntary but brings the hotelier a number of advantages such as incentives and other benefits from the government. Table 8.1 shows the growth of the different categories of hotels in India by rooms and hotels between 2000 and 2005.

It can be seen from Table 8.1 that there has been a steady growth in the five-star, deluxe and three-star categories of hotel over the period 2000–2005. The fastest growing sector is the heritage category of hotels over the same period. The interest in heritage tourism and the development of heritage hotels to underpin this trend is something that will be considered in the next chapter. There were substantial gains to the Indian hotel industry in 2004–2005 and this has fuelled the development and expansion plans of

Table 8.1 The growth of different categories of hotels over the period 2000–2005

Category	2000		2005		Average annual rooms growth 2000–2005 (%)
	Hotels	Rooms	Hotels	Rooms	
Five-star deluxe	57	12,556	78	18,625	12
Five-star	73	9,051	77	9,326	3
Four-star	92	7,232	124	8,693	9
Three-star	379	19,785	468	24,401	13
Two-star	244	9,135	212	8,242	1
One-star	46	2,253	44	1,504	−9
Heritage	66	2,372	75	2,567	22
Approved	263	10,560	333	13,426	17
Unapproved	493	18,350	470	18,286	−10
Total	1,713	91,294	1,881	105,070	4

Source: Indian Hotel Industry Survey – FHRAI (2006).

investors and hotel operators – this trend is predicted to continue (FHRAI, 2006). Great interest has been shown in the Indian hospitality industry by international hotel operators and foreign investors and this trend will be considered later on in this chapter. The presence of international hotel chains has been a fairly recent phenomenon in India and they are becoming an increasingly important feature of the Indian hospitality sector. They are predicted to grow further in the next decade.

Major hotel chains

Of the small number of hotel chains in India many are Indian-owned with a long history of development. This situation will probably change over the next decade as international chains continue to gain in importance and increase their share of the market. The liberalisation of the market and the growth in travel has fostered the entry of international chains into the Indian market. This includes Country Hospitality (with its brands Regent, Radisson, Country Inns), Marriott, Hilton, Park Plaza and Four Seasons. There has also been an expansion of international brands that were already established in the country including Sheraton, Holiday Inn, Hyatt, Inter-Continental, Meridien, Quality Inns, Best Western and Kempinski. A sample of the major hotel chains that are operating in India is shown in Table 8.2.

It can be seen from this table that the number of hotel chains in India is relatively small and are usually Indian-owned. It is important to link this table to the previous sections of this chapter where it was seen that there has been a recent growth in the five-star and heritage category of hotels. It is in these categories that the chain hotels are concentrating their efforts. The existing chains are looking for new acquisitions and more international

Table 8.2 Major hotel chains in India – 2007

Ambassador hotels	3 hotels in Aurangabad, Mumbai and Chennai.
Ashok Hotels	The Ashok group relies on traditional Indian values and impeccable service to national and international customers. The company operates under three brands – the Ashok Elite hotels in New Delhi and Mysore, the Ashok Classic hotels in six cities and the Ashok Comfort hotels in six cities.
Best Western	17 hotels under the brand
The Casino Hotels	7 hotels and resorts in Kerala
Choice Hotels	17 franchise operations under the Quality Inn and Comfort Inn brands.
Clarks Hotel	Small chain with hotels in Agra, Jaipur, Khajuraho and Lucknow.
Hindustan International Hotels	The Hotel Hindustan International in Kolkata and the Best Western Hindustan International in Varanasi.
Historic Resorts and Hotels	Based in Udaipur and owns 75 star heritage palace hotels and resorts in Rajasthan.
ITC Welcomgroup Hotels India	ITC-Welcomgroup is a company that incorporates investment from India and input by the Sheraton Hotels Worldwide brand. It Includes 9 hotels under the ITC-Welcomgroup Sheraton Hotels name, 5 hotels under the ITC-Welcomgroup Hotels name, 20 hotels under the WelcomHeritage name and 9 hotels under the Fortune name.
Le Meridien Hotels (joint strategic alliance with Japanese based Nikko hotels)	Owns 7 hotels in major cities of India – Le Meridien Bangalore, Cochin and Delhi and Pune, Le Royal Meridien Chennai and Mumbai and Hotel Nikko New Delhi.
Oberoi Hotels	See case study at end of the chapter for more details on this group.
Park Hotels	See mini case study in the text.
Sarovar Park Plaza Hotels	A hotel group set up by Mr Anil Madhok an ex-employee of the Oberoi Group. Owns hotels in Bangalore, Amritsar, Ahmedabad and Agra.
Taj Group	See separate description under leading hotel groups.
Tulip Hotels	Operates 7 hotels in Goa, Bangalore, Vadodara, Kollam, Munnar and Chennai.

Source: Incredible India (2005).

groups are planning entry into the Indian market. These include Accor Asia with the Ibis brand, Marriott's four-star brands Courtyard, Shangrila groups Traders and Sol Melia of Spain (Incredible India, 2005). One of the most important hotel chains in India is the Taj Group that is owned by the massive Indian conglomerate, the Tata group. This company has hotels in the major metros of India and focuses both on the leisure and business tourist in their hotel developments. A summary of the main chain, the Taj Group, that is operating in different regions of India is shown in the mini-case study.

The growth of the chain hotels in the Indian hotel sector has been accompanied by the explosion of hotel development in the major metros of India. The visitor to Bangalore, for example, will see new hotels being built on every commercial corner of the city. The growth of hotels has been a result of the explosion of the computer and high-tech industries in the city. Many of the hotel chains have hotels in the city, and it is interesting to note that one of our Sheffield Hallam University graduates is involved with the Chancery Group of hotels, which owns a small number of hotels in the city. The Chancery Group has recently opened its new five-star Chancery Pavilion hotel, which has put a particular emphasis on new and exciting food and beverage offerings. Case 4 shows details of the expansion of hotels in Bangalore as a whole.

Resorts

Certain regions of India have developed resort areas based on their beach location and encouraged package holidaymakers to visit and stay in specially designed resorts that often operate on an all-inclusive basis. This type of development has not only brought increased prosperity in largely rural areas, but also much controversy as beautiful areas of India have been developed and industrialised. The most famous resort area of India is Goa but other areas such as Kerala are also developing beach-based resort tourism.

The development of these regions of India as resorts has been accompanied by the explosion of beach-based resort hotels that are often in the hands of foreign investors and offer non-stop products and services to attract the inbound tourist who has often bought a package tour from a tour operator in their own country. This type of tourist is very different from the cultural tourist who is attracted to the more authentic and heritage style of hotels. The development of the Goan resort hotels is explored in detail at the end of the chapter, but the mini case study below shows the type of accommodation that beach resorts offer.

Heritage hotels

India has a very well-developed range of heritage hotels that have a particular attraction to the leisure visitor. The heritage hotels in India have usually been converted from a palace or grand home into a hotel to welcome guests. Some of the heritage hotels in India are run by chains and others by royal descendants. The rich cultural history of India has meant that there are a large number of thikanas (small forts or palaces) and havelis (the mansions of once aristocratic families). The idea of turning thikanas into hotels started in Rajasthan and there is a wide range of heritage hotels in this region as a result of this development. Other states such as Madhya Pradesh, West Bengal, Kerala, Uttaranchal, Karnataka and Himachal

Pradesh have also developed heritage hotels. The heritage hotels offer the guest luxurious and often original surroundings and have concentrated on offering the guests a full range of local food and drink. The hotels have also developed a heritage hotels association based in Jaipur that handles marketing and public relations on behalf of the heritage hotels in the country.

The customer

The changing scene of the Indian hotel industry has meant that the customer of hotels has changed over recent years with a growing number of business guests, particularly in the major metros of India. The FHRAI looked at the market segmentation of guests in a sample of the different categories of hotels in the period 2004–2005. Domestic and foreign business travellers contributed a major part of the business for the five-, four- and three-star hotels in India. The domestic business traveller was also an important customer for the two- and one-star hotels in India. The same report also looked at guest analysis of hotel customers in more depth and the details are shown in Table 8.3.

It can be seen from this table that the four- and five-star hotels had high levels of both domestic and foreign guests. The one-star hotels attracted higher numbers of domestic guests. Heritage hotels relied very heavily on leisure guests and this is linked to tourism trends that will be discussed in the next chapter. There appeared to be high levels of repeat business, in particular, in the one-star hotel category. Repeat business in the other categories was also relatively high and illustrates why some hotel chains are introducing loyalty cards. One example of this is the Taj Card offered by the Taj Group of hotels mentioned earlier.

The next part of the chapter will consider the major factors that are facing the Indian hotel sector at the present time.

Major issues facing the Indian hotel sector

The Indian hotel sector is faced with many challenges with regards to improving the profitability of operations and exploiting the new opportunities that have arisen due to the growth in the economy and the changing nature of tourism in India. It is clear that an effective marketing strategy will have to incorporate ambitious marketing plans and branding strategies. All of these marketing strategies will require effective human resource strategies if they are to be successful. It seems that the weak internal markets that were identified in China (Zhang and Wu, 2004) are mirrored in India (Jauhari, 2006). The weak labour market is characterised by excess labour, lack of minimum wages, long working hours and bureaucratic organisation structures. There is also a mismatch of supply and demand in certain areas of the hospitality industry in India. Graduates are prepared to work for low wages and this leads to a myopic vision of the jobs available in the hospitality sector. There are also worries that the current curriculum on offer in universities in India does not address the global issues that the modern hospitality manager needs to understand (Jauhari,

Table 8.3 Guest analysis of Indian hotels

Composition	Five-star deluxe	Five star	Four star	Three star	Two star	One star	Heritage	Others	2004–2005 all-India average
Number of responses	37.0	41.0	34.0	247.0	83.0	28.0	31.0	245.0	746.0
Domestic guests (%)	48.7	58.6	68.8	76.9	76.1	82.1	51.8	82.5	71.7
Foreign guests (%)	51.3	41.4	31.2	23.1	23.9	17.9	48.2	17.5	28.3
Total	100.0	100.0	100.0	100.0	100.0	100.0	100.0	100.0	100.0
Total business guests (%)	62.8	66.4	70.2	59.8	52.5	59.5	25.1	53.1	58.6
Total leisure guests (%)	37.2	33.6	29.8	40.2	47.5	40.5	74.9	46.9	41.4
Total	100.0	100.0	100.0	100.0	100.0	100.0	100.0	100.0	100.0
Average stay of domestic guest (days)	2.3	1.9	2.4	3.0	2.6	2.7	3.7	2.5	2.6
Average stay of foreign guests (days)	3.3	3.0	2.7	3.2	2.5	3.2	3.2	3.0	3.0
Average stay of business guests (days)	2.1	2.1	2.0	2.6	2.8	3.6	1.9	2.1	2.4
Average stay of leisure guests (days)	2.3	2.2	2.0	2.4	2.3	2.3	2.1	2.5	2.3
Total repeat guests (%)	47.4	48.2	36.6	53.2	52.2	66.6	32.9	49.4	49.9

Source: Indian Hotel Industry Survey – FHRAI (2006).

2006). The importance of the hotel management function in India will now be considered in more depth.

Hotel management in India

The chapter has already considered the way in which the Indian hotel industry has undergone a rapid expansion in recent years. The local hoteliers have been faced with increased competition from foreign hotel companies and there has been a need to create global brands on account of this increased competition and the need to expand on an international basis. There has been a change in the type of consumer who has demanded different products and services and increased technology both in the booking service and in the design of the products and services.

New product development has been critical and it has been necessary to create new products and services for an increasingly discerning customer who has become used to new trends and innovations. One example of a new type of hotel that has emerged in the Indian market in recent years is the boutique hotel which has already grown in popularity in the U.S. and Europe but is yet to establish itself as a trend in other markets (Swarbrooke and Horner, 2006). The case study of the Park hotel group in India (Case 6) shows how this chain has developed by the concentration on designer image and innovative food and beverage offerings.

This type of strategic hotel development illustrates one response by a company in answer to the critical factors that are considered necessary if a hotel is to grow and become effective in the changing Indian market. These critical factors are shown in Table 8.4.

It is clear that all of these critical factors need to be addressed by all hotel groups in India. The growing use of information technology in Indian hotels will continue to be an important factor to enable the hotels to address the aforementioned critical factors (FHRAI, 2006). Hotels can also address a number of the factors together to create interesting and new approaches to their operations. One of the ways in which hotels can combine two of these critical factors together is to create an energy efficiency programme that will offer a badge that can be used for marketing purposes. One type of scheme is the ECOTEL® certification programme that has been developed by HVS International, details of which are shown in Case 7.

Table 8.4 Critical factors necessary for the growth of hotels in India

---

Customer orientation
Outstanding service
Flawless operations management
Well thought out marketing strategy – positioning, markets and media
Cost management – energy, marketing costs, attrition costs

Source: Adapted from Jauhari (2006).

The only way to underpin this type of development is to establish an effective human resource strategy to develop all of the different aspects of hotel management. It is necessary for Indian hotel groups to invest in their staff to create higher productivity, foster creativity and ultimately improve market share. It is recognised that this is a major challenge for the Indian hotel industry and one that will increasingly challenge hotel managers over the next decade (Nagar, 2005). A research study carried out by the FHRAI in 2001 showed that there were a lot of issues to be tackled by the hotel sector in particular amongst junior managers who were often leaving their jobs to take on other opportunities in the sector abroad or moving sideways to other jobs offered in the service sector more generally. This report highlighted the need for improved pay packages and improved working conditions particularly for the junior managers. The hotels that came out well in the research had adopted more advanced staff training systems and improved welfare systems. The report also highlighted the need for more advanced curriculum development in the educational institutions offering hospitality courses in India (FHRAI, 2001).

The success of hotels in India in the future will depend on whether the industry can attract, manage and retain creative managers in an increasingly competitive job market. The international hoteliers such as Marriott emphasise, on this human resource function and will increasingly compete for staff in the Indian market. It has been suggested that hotels in India will have to move out of a frame of mind of "recruitment" to adopt a more holistic picture of the human resource function (Nagar, 2005) Some companies have already started to do this and the case study of the Oberoi Hotel company (Case 3) considers some of the ways that this more holistic approach can be achieved. Others still have far to go in this process and need a well-established educational sector to underpin their own development (Chung-Herrera, Enz and Lankau, 2003).

Learning tasks

1 Conduct a small-scale piece of research on one of the major hotel chains. Identify the key strengths and weaknesses that you think the chain has at the present time and how it will exploit these in the next decade.
2 Critically analyse the key factors that currently affect on the Indian hotel sector.

Discussion questions

1 Discuss the role of innovative food and beverage operations in the development of hotels in India.
2 Discuss the ways in which hotels and resorts can offer the business and leisure tourist a complementary range of products and services.

Mini case study

The Taj Group of hotels India

The Taj Group of hotels is India's largest chain. The group is part of the Tata company, a conglomerate that owns companies in the car industry, engineering, consumer products and services sector. The company opened their first hotel in 1903, which was the Taj Mahal hotel in Mumbai. Taj Hotels Resorts and Palaces is the operating name of the Indian Hotels Companies Ltd, and is listed separately on the stock exchange. The company owns hotels, resorts and palaces and has diversified into other areas such as airline catering.

The company has a strongly branded strategy and aims to combine high levels of personal service with tradition and heritage. The company runs a loyalty scheme – the Taj InnerCircle – to encourage loyalty amongst its customers. The company has divided its properties under three brand headings as follows:

Taj Luxury Hotels
These hotels are positioned in the main cities of India. A number of the properties are in the Leading Hotels of the World group. These include the Taj Mahal Hotel (Mumbai), Taj Palace Hotel (New Delhi), Taj Mahal Hotel (New Delhi), Taj Bengal (Kolkata), Taj West End (Bangalore) and The Taj Coromandel Hotel (Chennai).

Taj Business Hotel
These hotels (often called Taj Residency) are aimed at the domestic and international business traveller and are usually located in towns and cities. These hotels offer excellent business facilities and a range of food and beverage outlets.

Taj Leisure Hotels
These hotels are aimed at the leisure traveller and include resorts, wildlife sanctuaries, palaces, historic monuments and pilgrimage centres.

The Taj Group is planning a major expansion strategy with China and Russia being the first countries that the company will target. It is also thinking about expansion into the U.S.

Source: Mintel (2003).
Web site: www.hotels-in-india.com (2006).

References

Bansal, S.P. (2001). *Tourism Development and its Impact*. Delhi, Jagdish C. Gossain.

Capitaline (2005). in Jauhari, V (2006) Competencies for a Career in the Hospitality Industry: An Indian Perspective, *International Journal of Contemporary Hospitality Management*, **18**(2), 123–124.

Chung-Herrera, B.G., Enz, C.A. and Lankau, M.J. (2003). Grooming Future Hospitality Leaders: A Competencies Model, *The Cornell Hotel and Restaurant Administration Quarterly*, **44**(3), 17.

Euromonitor (2005). *India: Global Market Factfile*. http//www.gmid.euromonitor/CountryProfile.aspx.

FHRAI (2001). *Human Resources Practices in the Indian Hospitality Industry*. New Delhi, India.

FHRAI (2006). *Indian Hotel Survey in Cooperation with HVS*. New Delhi, India.

Gupta, S.P., Lal, K. and Bhattacharyya, M. (2002). *Cultural Tourism in India.* Delhi, D.K. Printworld Ltd.

HVS International (2006). ECOTEL®. For more information, see FHRAI (2005). *Incredible India.* New Delhi.

Jauhari, V. (2006). Competencies for a Career in the Hospitality Industry: An Indian Perspective, *International Journal of Contemporary Hospitality Management,* **18**(2), 123–124.

Le Meridien. http://www.hotels-in-india.com.

Mintel (2003). *International Hotel Industry.*

Nagar, N. (2005). *Indian Hotel Industry – New Paradigms and Shifts.* HVS International, http:www.hvsinternational.com.

Oberoi Hotels and Resorts. www.hotels-in-india.com.

Swarbrooke, J. and Horner, S. (2006). *Leisure Marketing: A Global Perspective.* Oxford: Elsevier Butterworth Heinemann.

The Ashok Group of Hotels. www.hotels-in-india.com.

The Park Hotels (2006). www.hotels-in-india.com.

Darlington, J.H. and John, S. (20 May 2005). Bangalore to get Platter of New Hotels. *The Times of India – Times City.*

Zhang, H.Q. and Wu, E. (2004). Human Resource Issues Facing the Hotel and Travel Industry in China, *International Journal of Contemporary Hospitality Management,* **16**(7), 424.

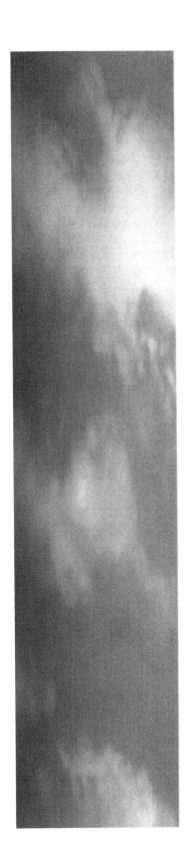

Restaurants, fast food and contract food service – India

Chapter objectives

When you have read this chapter, you will be able to

1 Recognise the nature and the structural characteristics of the restaurants, fast food and contract food-service sectors in India.
2 Identify the origins of eating out and chronicle the historical development of restaurants, fast food and contract food service in India.
3 Highlight some of the influencing factors on this development.
4 Critically review major issues and operational trends.
5 Discuss the future outlook for restaurants, fast food and contract food service in India.

Introduction

Having been to India on numerous occasions and, at every turn, experienced a new and exciting form of Indian cuisine I wonder how it is possible in this short chapter to give you a comprehensive view of the cuisine of India and the food-service business across such large geographic boundaries. It is important as a starting point that you reflect on the opening chapters that gave you a background to the economic and social development of India as a whole. You will remember from this that India is a diverse country with a huge variety of religions and cultures spread over a vast geographic area that experiences a wide range of climates. This, coupled with the long and interesting history of India, has had a major influence on the development of traditional foods and the variety of cuisines that exist in India today. India can be viewed as a melting pot of food and cuisines. The growth of the middle classes in India, particularly in the urban areas such as New Delhi, Bangalore, Mumbai and Chennai, have also fuelled the development of the service industries with restaurants being at the forefront of this development (Shurmer-Smith, 2000). The growth of tourism and the trend to globalisation has also meant that as trading barriers came down new international players could enter the restaurant business and this has been particularly evident in the fast-food business. But more of this later, the history of India and how this has influenced food choice and cuisines will now be considered.

Historical development and regional cuisines

The development of Indian cuisine has a very long and turbulent history and is ever changing even today as Indians try new cuisines and are exposed to new influences and people from other nations. Sen (2004) traced the historical origins of Indian cuisine and a summary of these different influences is shown below:

Prehistory	Early cultivation of plants and spices couple with early domestication of animals.
3000–1500 BC	Crops such as wheat, barley and lentils are developed and meat and fish are staples.
2000–800 BC	Aryan tribes migrate to northern India. Sugar cane is grown and processed in southern India.
1000–500 BC	Hinduism develops and castes develop. This leads to a rejection of eating meat, and particularly cows.
6th century BC	Buddha and Mahavira found Buddhism and Jainism. Jains practice strict vegetarianism.
1st century AD	Christianity arrives in India.
5th century AD	Ayurveda (system of medicine based on food) develops.
1206–1536	Central Asian dynasties introduce Central Asian and Persian cuisines.
Late-15th early-16th century	Portuguese arrive in India, found an empire, and bring new ingredients such as tomatoes, chillies, potatoes etc.
17th century	East India Company is formed.
1830–1850	Tea plantations established by British in Assam and Darjeeling.
1857	British crown takes over government of India and hybrid foods begin to develop.
1947	Tandoori chicken invented in Delhi.
1977	Indian food grows in popularity in UK and the first Balti restaurant opens in Birmingham.
1996	McDonald's and Pizza Hut open in India.
2003	Restaurants continue to open offering new international cuisines as the Indian economy grows and urbanisation develops at a rapid rate.

Source: Adapted from Sen (2004).

It can be seen from this historical review that Indian cuisine has developed over centuries and has drawn inspiration from many customs, traditions and religions. This has resulted in a number of features of the cuisine in general, which are very interesting to note:

Eating out Eating out is a relatively new development in India, which has developed despite traditional values because of the growth of the middle and upper classes that have changing work and leisure patterns and the income to eat out in commercial restaurants. This has fuelled the growth of a vast range of restaurants, particularly in the cities of India, offering a full range of international cuisines. Eating out by tourist, particularly in the tourist areas such as Goa, has also been an important trend.

Links of food to culture   The food eaten by Indians is inextricably linked to the individual's religion, caste, social status and where they live. This includes the avoidance of particular foods by religious groups such as Hindus and fasting, which is a part of most religions practiced in India.

Links of food to health   The ancient system of Ayurveda gave the foundation of the idea that food and health are inextricably linked together. The idea that different foods can also be hot or cold depending on their psychological effect is an idea that is thought to have developed in India and then travelled to other countries such as China.

The caste system in India had a major effect on the development of food culture but the major religious groups have also had a major effect on the cuisine as a whole. It was estimated in the 1991 census that 82% of the population were Hindus, 12.1% were Muslims, 2.34% were Christians, 1.94% were Sikhs, 0.76% were Buddhists and 0.76% were Jains (Shurmer-Smith, 2000). A summary of the different religions and food choices is given below:

Hindus   The Hindu religion could be seen as the unified force of India but it is not one religion with one sacred text or doctrine and it incorporates many different traditions in food according to the caste of the individual and where they live. The one common integrating feature is the fact that food is linked to health and well-being and forms a very important cornerstone of the Hindu faith. It is also considered very important in the Hindu faith to provide food to others as an act of hospitality. In fact, the giving of food to others is considered to be of a higher spiritual significance than eating it oneself.

The Hindu religion encourages a number of important food practices. For traditional Hindus, the caste that you are in determines the type of food you can eat and who you can receive it from. A person from a lower caste can never provide food to a person in a higher caste. This is the reason that people from the Brahmin caste have often become cooks because they can provide food to people from the lower castes. It is also a tradition that Indians from higher castes cannot eat left over or sour food because it is considered unclean. Indians from higher castes also tend to be vegetarians, although there is no hard and fast rule about this, and it is estimated that only 25–30% of all Indians are vegetarian. Cow slaughter is illegal in most parts of India and alcohol is avoided by a large part of the population. Hindus often engage in fasts during certain festivals and at particular times of the year.

There are changes that are apparent, however, in the urban areas. Younger people are beginning to change their eating habits and taking on new approaches to food preparation and eating habits. They are eating out more and experiencing new cuisines and this is bringing about changes, although these changes are very limited in terms of the whole population at the moment.

Muslims   The Muslims represent a small proportion of the population but an influential one. It is also important to recognise that there has been a growth in the number of Muslims in India and that this population is one of the largest Muslim populations in the world. Muslims do not eat pork and intoxicants such as alcohol. They eat meat that has been slaughtered in the traditional way, which is called halal meat. They also observe fasts, particularly during the ninth month of the Islamic lunar calendar called Ramadan when a fast is observed from dawn to dusk.

Christians   Christians represent a small part of the population and observe few food restrictions. Some Catholics do fast during Lent.

Sikhs   Sikhism originated in Punjab in the late fifteenth century. It preaches universal equality and rejects the caste system and idol worship, which are both associated with Hinduism, it also recognises equality of the sex and has a holy book. Sikhs are not vegetarian but they do not encourage meat eating per se. They do believe that there is a strong link between body, mind and food. The Sikh temples do provide food to all visitors regardless of class, caste or religion. This food is always vegetarian so that all people can partake.

Jains   The Jains who represent a small percentage of the population have adopted the strictest views on food choice. They prohibit the consumption of meat, fish and eggs as well as all things that are considered to contain a germ of life. This means that many plants are not eaten and even honey is not eaten since it leads to the death of bees, it is argued.

Jews   The Jewish community, which is small in terms of percentage, is centred in the areas around Cochin, Bombay and Calcutta. The Jews do not eat pork and insist that meat is slaughtered in the traditional way.

Indian cuisine

We have now considered the historical development of the food habits of India as well as the influence of different religions but we now need to think about the special nature of Indian cuisine, the ingredients used and the reasons for a worldwide interest in the production of authentic Indian meals.

Indian food is unique in terms of the ingredients used and the dishes that are created. The arrival of the Europeans to India, already considered earlier on in the chapter, had an enormous effect on the cuisine of India since they brought ingredients with them that had not been previously used in Indian cuisine but have now become an important part of it. The cuisine has travelled well, particularly back to the European countries when Europeans returned from India bringing the spices and other ingredients that they had experienced while they had stayed there. The growth of Indian restaurants in the UK is an example of the diffusion of the Indian cuisine to European palate. It has to be recognised, however, that the cuisine was subtly modified from the traditional to suit the European palate.

Anyone who has visited India recently will recognise that there are similarities between the European version of Indian cuisine and the "real thing" but will also know that the ideas and recipes have been changed to suit a different market. So what makes up the typical Indian dish? What are the mystical ingredients that make up the range and variety of cuisines that can be found in India today?

There is no such thing as a typical Indian meal because the country is large and each region of India relies on the crops and spices that are grown in the particular region. The components of Indian food have been well documented in the UK by well-known cookery experts such as Madhur Jaffrey who produced her famous book on Indian cuisine way back in 1982. She documented the different ingredients that make up Indian dishes and these can be summarised as follows:

Cereals   India has been traditionally divided into two geographic regions in relation to cereal consumption. In the north of the country the staple cereal is wheat, which is used to produce a range of breads. Bread is eaten traditionally with every meal and there is a large range of breads linked to their geographic origin. Chapatis or roti are the most popular form of bread in northern India and bread is often also baked in large tandoor ovens. Naan bread, which is crisp on the outside and soft inside, is also popular in this region. There are a vast range of different Indian breads, which have developed on the basis of the staple cereal in the region.

In the south and east, the staple cereal is rice, which is used to accompany a range of meat and vegetable-based dishes. Indians like rice that has long slender grains and is firm in texture once cooked, which is different from the Chinese like of small-grained sticky rice. The best rice is the basmati rice, which is grown in Uttar Pradesh. This rice is aged for six months to improve its flavour. Rice is also used to make breads and snacks and in special dishes such as biryanis, which are mixtures of rice and other ingredients such as vegetables and meat.

Legumes   Indian cuisine uses a tantalising mixture of legumes such as chick peas, beans, peas and lentils to produce a range of dishes that are recognised as forming an important part of an Indian meal. This includes the range of dals that are made from lentils and differ in colour and texture according to the type of lentils used. One of my favourite dals in India is the black dal, which is made by soaking and cooking dark lentils and adding salt, spices, chillies and ghee (clarified butter). This dal is then eaten with one of the delicious Indian breads.

Dairy products   Dairy products contribute an important source of protein in a vegetarian diet. This includes different forms of yoghurt, ghee and milk. These are added to some dishes but form an important component of other dishes such as paneer, which is a pressed milk solid.

Fruits and vegetables   Fruits and vegetables form an important part of Indian cuisine, particularly in the vegetarian dishes. They are found in main dishes, side dishes, pickles, snacks, breads and desserts. Many of the vegetables such as potatoes, peppers, and tomatoes were introduced to India by the Portuguese and now they have become an important part of the cuisine. There is a huge range of fruits available in India to utilise in main dishes, desserts, pickles and so on. Bananas and mangoes are particular favourites in Indian cuisine. Mangoes and other fruits are often combined with yoghurt to produce the refreshing drink lassi.

Meat and fish   The consumption of meat and fish is low relative to other parts of the world. Chicken is a very important ingredient in North Indian cuisine and fish is very important in coastline areas such as Goa and Kerala, where there is a wealth of special recipes cooking fish separately or combining it with other ingredients in elaborate curries.

Spices   The heart of Indian cuisine is the creative use of spices. This was proposed by Jaffrey in 1982 as follows:

> There is something so very satisfying about Indian cookery, more so when it is fresh and home-cooked. Perhaps it is the unique blending of herbs, spices, seasonings, as well as meat, pulses, yoghurt dishes and relishes that my ancestors determined centuries ago would titillate our palates. At the same time it preserves our health and the proper chemical balance of our bodies.

The range of spices that are used in Indian cuisine is large and complex and we only have a small amount of space here to cover the main spices that are used. Sen (2004) summarised the types of spices used according to the region of India and the type of dish. A brief summary of four of the areas of India, their cuisine and the spices used is as follows:

- North India/Pakistan: Meat dishes, Ginger, garlic, onions, red chillies, coriander seeds and leaves, saffron, black pepper, asafetida, black cumin, cumin, cardamom, cloves, cinnamon, poppy seeds, turmeric powder, chilli powder, paprika, nutmeg, mace
- Punjab: Tandoor cumin, coriander, cinnamon, cloves, chilli powder, ginger, turmeric, garlic, mace, red dye
- Goa: Meat, fish, vegetables, vinegar, black peppercorns, green cardamom, cloves, green and red chillies, cumin, garlic, ginger, turmeric, coconut
- Rajasthan: Vegetable dals, Mango powder, turmeric, cumin, asafetida, curry leaves, ginger, green and red chillies, cardamom and cloves

Note: For a fuller discussion, see Sen (2004).
Source: Adapted from Sen (2004).

You can see from the four regions mentioned above and their cuisines that there is some overlap between the spices used, but the most important thing is the subtle blending of spices to produce distinctly different flavours.

Some of the important components of Indian cuisine have been documented by Wickramasinghe and Rajah (2003). These are as follows:

Tiffin Tiffin was the food of colonial India but the word and the practice of taking Tiffin, which is composed of a series of snacks taken between meals, has become very Indian. Tiffin carriers often bring small dishes of food from homes to offices today, and as such are an important part of the hospitality industry. Indians tend to eat dinner late so Tiffin is used to bridge the gap between lunch and dinner. It consists of snacks such as samosas, bhajis or dosas and often with a variety of chutneys and small side dishes.

Thali Thali is named after a meal platter and is the term to describe a set lunch, which will consist of a number of dishes, breads, chutneys and so on. The thali will also include some form of dessert or sweet as an ending. It is more usual for the dishes to be brought separately at a thali rather than being brought altogether, which is a feature of Chinese cuisine. No Indian dinner is complete without a thali and it is this style of cuisine that many high-class restaurants have adopted.

Tandoor Tandoor ovens had their origins in the Middle East and hence it is a popular form of cooking in Punjab. The tandoor oven is a clay oven that is heated to high temperatures. It was unusual for a home to have an oven rather the local community would have one oven that would be shared within the local community. Meat is first of all tenderised with a marinade of complex spices and then heated at high temperature in the oven. The result is a meat that is tasty and well cooked, accompanied with bread and chutneys. Tandoor cooking in the restaurant trade has become popular, particularly in the UK, since it is often Punjabis who own Indian restaurants.

Sweets The Indian sweet shop is called the mithai and Indians buy the exotic confections from these shops usually for special occasions or as a gift. The Indian sweet-making tradition is unique and uses a range of interesting ingredients to produce an array of tempting morsels. These ingredients include rice, dairy products, sugar fat and flavourings. Typical sweets include barfi, which is like fudge, karanji, which are sweet pastries and the famous rossogolas, which are milk balls in a sweet syrup.

The cuisine of India has a rich and interesting history and has drawn on many influences. The interesting thing to reflect on now is how this cuisine is reflected throughout the hospitality industry in India.

Size, significance and structural features of the sector

We have already seen earlier that the food-service business in India is in a period of rapid growth with new businesses opening daily in every major urban conurbation. This growth has been fuelled by a series of factors. Continuing urbanisation of the population and increased commuting times to work has meant that eating habits have had to change. This has led to the growth in eating establishments outside the home, particularly in the large cities of India. The increasing wealth of the population, generally, and the rapidly expanding consuming middle class, which is estimated at around 300 million people also meant that the desire to eat outside the home has grown.

The rising educational levels of the population have encouraged increasing sophistication and changes of tastes related to eating out and food consumption generally. This is coupled with the growth in busy lifestyles and changing work patterns. Indians are increasingly outsourcing their dining needs to a growing number of restaurants, street sellers, cafes, fast-food shops and convenience stores. It is also interesting to note that young people are motivated by healthy eating messages but are not able to make decisions about health when purchasing food out of the home. This is leading to a growth in obesity among Indians (Nielsen, 2006).

The entrepreneurial activities of the owners of small independent food-service operations including coffee and teahouses, sweet shops and street vendors has meant that there has been an explosion of hospitality outlets including an influx of Western and other international branded fast food and other chains as a result of a growing desire for their offerings. There has also been a growth of international travellers visiting new areas of India as a result of an improving transport infrastructure and this has led to the need for more international food outlets. There has also been a growing demand for healthy and safe food in hygienic surroundings, which is still a challenge for India.

It is clear from the previous section that the cuisine of India is very varied according to the geographic area and the local supply of ingredients. India is a big country with many traditions and religions. Sen (2004) has categorised the restaurants that exist across India into three main categories. The first category is the small hole in the wall or street business that serves the local community. The second category is the upmarket restaurant establishment that is often located in a hotel and targets the Indian middle and upper classes, business travellers and incoming tourists. There has also been a growth in the third category the fast-food restaurant in India in the major cities, with both local and international players competing for this new business. Urban Indians are amongst the top 10 most frequent consumers of fast food across the world and it is estimated that 70% of all urban Indians consume food from a takeaway establishment once a month or more (Nielsen, 2006). We have already mentioned the importance of coffee shops, tea shops and sweet shops as part of the traditional Indian scene.

Many of the food businesses are family-run, particularly in the small category. Many of the larger restaurant businesses are run by large Indian companies or increasingly by new foreign competitors. A number of brief illustrations will explain this point.

Illustration 1 Global Franchise Architects (GFA) India

Global Franchise Architects is a company that was set up by a Lebanese billionaire in 1996. The company currently has three brands that will be established further in India over the next decade, these are as follows:

Pizza Corner This is a pizza restaurant that has 30 outlets in India. The pizza chain started in Chennai and has outlets in New Delhi, Hyderabad and Bangalore. It is expected to expand into Kochi, Manipal, Mangalore and Coimbatore.

Coffee World Coffee World offers a comfortable café décor for young executives and families. The outlets have a Wi-Fi zone and offer a wide range of different coffees. The first outlet was on the prestigious Brigade Road in Bangalore but future expansion is planned in other major cities in India.

The company also owns other brands, which it hopes to introduce in India in the near future. These include New York Deli and The Cream and Fudge Corporation.

The growth of this chain illustrates the importance of targeting the more affluent Indian business person or family. It also heralds the introduction of other world cuisines into a market that has been very traditional to date. Other coffee shops that have opened in Bangalore to satisfy the growing demand from young people include Cafe Coffee Day, Barista and Javagreen. The absence of Starbucks in the country to date has fuelled their growth.

Sources: *The Hindu*, 17 February 2005; Reuters India (2006).

Illustration 2 KFC expansion in India

KFC, the fast-food chain that specialises in chicken has had a presence in India for some time with 11 outlets at the end of 2005. It has recently announced expansion plans, which will be underpinned by the reopening of the recently refurbished New Delhi restaurant. The company is planning to spend US$55,000 on their expansion plans in India with the opening of 14 new restaurants through franchising and self-owned agreement.

The company has recently opened its first restaurant in eastern India, with its KFC outlet in Calcutta, in June 2006. The company has recognised that the culturally active and intellectually evolving city of Calcutta is ready for their new brand of fast-food offering.

Source: *World of Food India News* (2006).

> ## Illustration 3 TGI Friday's
>
> The U.S.-based global restaurant chain TGI Friday's, which is a subsidiary of Carlson Restaurant Worldwide, is currently expanding its business in India. The company recognises that India is a market that is coming of age and this leads to a profitable business for fast-food operators.
>
> The company has bought a 25% share in the Indian master franchisee Bistro Hospitality and plans to open 60 restaurants across India in the next five to seven years. The new restaurants will be in the cities of Chandigarh, Jaipur, Pune, Hyderabad, Chennai and Kolkata with new outlets also being opened in New Delhi and Mumbai.
>
> The company is also thinking of introducing their branded Chinese chain – Pick up Stix – to the Indian market in the near future.
>
> *Source*: *The Economic Times* (2006).

Contract catering and food service

The contract catering and food service has been developing at a slow pace in India as a result of the issues surrounding the complexity of the food chain. There are a small number of companies that have started to develop the food-service business in India and these companies have huge potential for growth in the next decade as the hospitality industry develops further and requires more reliable food suppliers. One of these companies – Hallmark Foods – is a division of Agri Solution and Services (India Pvt. Ltd). The company has a 20-year experience in cold storage, warehousing and distribution and offers a one-stop solution to the food service and retailing industries. The company has contracted farmers to provide food ingredients and has established international norms and practices such as quality control, traceability, HACCP, good agricultural practices and cold chain and food safety mechanisms.

Two other companies that have established a food-service business in India include the French company Sodexho which has established Sodexho Pass Services India, a subsidiary of Sodexho Alliance. This company already caters to over 3,000 corporate clients and over 300,000 employees. The third company that has a major interest in the food-service business is the Radhakrishna Hospitality Services Pvt. Ltd (RKHS), a joint-venture company with the UK-based Compass Group Plc. This company was originally started by Mr Radhakrishna Sheté in 1966 and became the distributor to McDonald's in 1993. It established a joint venture with the Compass group in 1995 and established the first training institute for the staff in the same year. The company has established a chain of food retail stores – Foodland Fresh – in major cities of India and has also formed a joint venture with Accor France to set up the business of ticket restaurant vouchers.

It is predicted that there will continue to be a growth in the food-service business in India as the sector requires more sophisticated solutions to hospitality services.

Food supplies and distribution

India can become the food supplier to the world but it is hampered at the moment by the poor development and fragmented management of the food supply chain network across the country. The problems with the lack of an efficient cold chain system means that about 20% of all food that is grown or produced in India is wasted (Viswanadham, 2006). The key points that are presented in Viswanadham's report.

- India is a rich source of cereals, fruits, vegetables, milk, fish, meat and poultry. There is a surplus of all these ingredients in the food chain and India needs to develop new food processing systems to cope with these surpluses.
- India has vast natural resources but is currently ranked only tenth in terms of food exports in the world.
- Indian people are increasingly looking for processed foods and are increasingly eating in restaurants, which requires a reliable food chain system.
- The food processing industry has lagged behind other industrial sectors such as IT in its development and it is still largely in the hands of small operators.
- There are some multinational players that have entered the food processing industry in India such as Cargill and Congra in agri-inputs, Tropicana in food processing and Metro in food retailing. Multiple restaurant chains include McDonald's, Pizza Hut, Dominos, Coffee day, and Qwicky's.
- The lack of superstores in India means that there is a vacuum in relation to supply chain management. Problems such as country risk, monsoon risk and crop or raw supply failure have also put off new entrants into the supply chain management business.
- The Indian government has put a high priority on the establishment of cold chains and has implemented major financial incentives to encourage investment in the area. Work needs to be done on the cold chain infrastructure, third-party logistics, and the retail sector to improve total food-chain systems.
- There have been examples of limited private sector initiatives in the food supply chain management business. This includes McDonald's India, Amul, which is a cooperative dairy in Gujarat, and E-choupals, which is a procurement company.

Source: Adapted from Viswanadham (2006).

This series of points illustrates that India has a huge potential to develop its food supply chain systems to a much greater extent to enable the country to use its raw ingredients much more effectively and avoid wastage. This needs government intervention and input from private investors to enable effective and efficient systems to be developed. The first signs that the food chain is becoming more sophisticated and secure has recently been shown by the opening of the first nationwide supermarket chain in the city of Hyderabad. The store has air-conditioned aisles, uniformed staff and offers one-stop supermarket shopping for the increasingly discerning consumer. The company is owned by Reliance, India's biggest business house and the company plans to open a network of more than 3,000 stores in 780 cities and small towns by the year 2010. Reliance has managed to cut out the middlemen of the Indian food chain and deal directly with the farmers, cooperative and integrated food chains. The development of the food chain is coming under scrutiny of the Indian left wing parties who say that it will cut out small, family-run food businesses. It is, however, predicted that the rules that restrict foreign investment in retail in India are likely to be relaxed in 2007 opening up the opportunity for increased foreign investment (*Daily Telegraph*, 4 November 2006).

Healthy eating

We have already considered the link between food and health in the Ayurvedic system of treatment early on in this chapter. It is interesting to reflect on the links of health to food and the likely spread of obesity that will occur amongst urban Indians if their diet changes and they eat more fast food and convenience food. Research by A.C. Nielsen has found that Internet users in India who are urban dwellers with higher incomes have become very interested in the nutritional content of foods, particularly when they are buying food for their children. It was found that 41% of Indians check the nutritional labels when they purchase food and they are most interested when they purchase the food for the first time (Nielsen, 2006). This suggests that Indians are very interested in the foods they eat and the effect that it has on their health.

Hygiene and food safety

Hygiene and food safety is a real issue in the food supply chain system in India. It is very critical for India to comply with international standards of food hygiene if it is to export more food and develop a more reliable hospitality sector. This involves the development of more effective hygiene standards. The standards can be improved by the introduction of training systems on supply chain management; and effective methods of food processing and distribution need to be developed. This is also necessary in the restaurant sector. The Indian government is taking a major role in the improvement of food hygiene standards across the country (Viswanadham, 2006).

The development of the McDonald's food chain gives us an interesting example of how this has been achieved by one hospitality business.

Illustration 4 McDonald's India – The food supply chain challenge

The growth of the fast-food chain McDonald's in India has occurred over the last 10 years and has relied on the development of a reliable food chain management system for all the ingredients. An early quote illustrates this point as follows:

"Our growth plan for the next three years is more a function of getting our logistics and cold chain right rather than going to far off places" (Amit Jatia Managing Director McDonald's India Mumbai joint venture). The McDonalds' success in India has been as a result of developing a limited menu, fresh food and affordable prices. The business has grown as a result of joint ventures between McDonald's India and Hardcastle Restaurants Pvt. Ltd Mumbai, and Connaught Plaza restaurant, New Delhi.

The establishment of the restaurants in India meant that the company had to spend 10 years working on the establishment of the food chain for their business before they entered the Indian market. Quality, safety and reliability of the ingredients were the major focus of this development. The company went right back to farmers and carried out training to produce ingredient specifications for all the raw ingredients that were to be used in their restaurants. This is a lesson for other restaurant chains that want to enter the Indian market.

Source: Adapted from ICFAI (2002).

Future trends and developments

We have seen in this chapter, the rapid developments that are happening in the food-service sector in India. The economic growth in the country, which is predicted to grow further, has already meant that the eating habits of urban Indians are moving away from the traditions associated with their cuisine and eating habits. It is predicted that these changes will continue and this, coupled with the expansion of effective food chain systems, will mean that there will be a further explosion of restaurant and contract catering development in the country. New international players will increasingly enter the market and the choices on offer in restaurants will become more varied and international. India can also use their traditional cuisine, however, as the basis of tourism development strategies (Horner and Vinod, 2005).

Learning tasks

1 Research the current food and beverage business of a chosen luxury hotel chain in India. Evaluate the different cuisines that the chain uses and try to assess the importance of the food and beverage operations within the business as a whole.

2 Carry out a small piece of research to investigate the use of Indian food and ingredients as part of holistic treatments and health improvement. How can this knowledge be used to develop new food-service business opportunities?

Discussion questions

1 Discuss the way in which the growth of the middle class in India will fuel the growth of food-service business in India in the future.

2 Discuss the way in which the growth of the fast-food business in India is a reflection of the explosion in economic development and the move to a more global society. Do you expect this early growth to continue?

Mini case study

Nirula's fast-food restaurants India

Nirula's is a fast-food chain that was originally developed in Delhi by Mr L.C. Nirula and and his brother Mr M. Nirula who came from Lahore when the city was still in India. They founded the original restaurant in 1934, which also had a hotel and featured cabaret as part of the offering.

The chain was further developed by the two sons of the founders – Lalit and Deepak Nirula who had studied at the Cornell University School of Hotel Administration in the U.S. They developed a pink and white logo for the restaurant chain which, expanded rapidly under their control. The chain initially developed in Delhi and now has 18 branches in the city. It has also opened restaurants in Uttar Pradesh, Uttaranchal, Haryana and Chandigarh. The family restaurants rely on uniformed employees preparing a wide range of foods including curries, pizzas, tandoori chicken, mutton burgers and sandwiches. The chain is also famous for its elaborate range of ice creams with the favourite flavour being zafrani badaam pista, which contains almonds, pistachio and saffron.

The restaurants have a mixed client group, which ranges from a single person to family groups, who enjoy the relaxed atmosphere and the varied menu. The customers value the hygienic surroundings of the restaurants and recognise that the food is of good value. The arrival of the international fast-food chains in India such as McDonald's, Wimpy and KFC has meant that Nirula's has had to face increasing competition in the fast-food market. They have responded with high-profile campaigns, such as the Nirula's ice cream Olympics that was launched in 2004. Experts predict that Nirula's will continue to attract a loyal customer group who prefer the particular service offering.

Source: Adapted from Dana (1999).

References

Nielsen, A.C. (2006). *Urban Indian Consumers Amongst the Top 10 Most Frequent Eaters of Fast Food Globally*. www.acnielson.co.in.

Daily Telegraph (2006). *Indian Shopper Given Taste of the New*. 4 November.

Dana, L.P. (1999). Nirula's Small Business, *British Food Journal*, **101**(5/6), 500–504.

Horner, S. and Vinod (2005). *Food and Drink as a Tourist Product – The Relevance for India*. Conference paper delivered at the International Food Tourism Conference 17–19 November 2005, Hyderabad, India.

ICFAI (2002). *McDonald's Food Chain*. ICFAI Center.

Jaffrey, M. (1982). *Indian Cookery*. BBC Books.

Reuters India (2006). *Coffee Shop Buzz Draw Out India's Young*. 9 June.

Sen, C.T. (2004). *Food Culture in India*. Westport Connecticut – London, Greenwood Press.

Shurmer-Smith, P. (2000). *India Globalization and Change*. London, Arnold.

The Economic Times, India (2006). *TGI Friday's Buy 25% Stake in Bistro Hospitality*. 30 May.

The Hindu (2005). *Going up the Food Chain*. 17 February.

The Hindu (2005). *Towards a Healthy Food Chain*. 8 October.

Viswanadham, N. (2006). *Can India be the Basket for the World?* Working Paper Series Indian School of Business Hyderabad 500032.

Wickramasinghe, P. and Rajah, C.S. (2003). *A Little Taste of India*. London, Murdoch Books.

World of Food India News (2006). www.worldoffoodindianews.com.

CHAPTER 10

Tourism business – India

Chapter objectives

When you have read this chapter, you will be able to

1 Recognise the nature and the structural characteristics of the tourism sector in India.
2 Chronicle the historical development of the tourism sector in India.
3 Highlight some of the influencing factors on the development of the tourism sector in India.
4 Critically review major issues and operational trends.
5 Discuss the future outlook for the tourism sector in India.

Introduction

A brief introduction to tourism in India was given earlier in the book in Chapter 4. The purpose of this chapter is to give a fuller review of tourism in India and to consider the organisations that provide the infrastructure to allow the tourism business to flourish in the country. There has been a steady growth in tourism arrivals to India over the last decade and the WTO predicts that this will continue to grow up to the year 2020. India has, however, often been accused of neglecting their inbound tourism market at the expense of domestic tourism. The country has an extensive landmass and can offer every type of tourism product ranging from the snowy mountainous areas in the north to the sub-tropical areas in the south. It has a rich heritage and a wide range of religions, customs and cuisines that offer many opportunities for tourism development. This means that the country can offer holiday products ranging from adventure breaks, cultural trips, religious tourism, rural and eco-tourism and Ayurveda and wellness holidays (Mintel, 2003). This chapter will focus on the challenges facing the sector and the different types of opportunity that exist if India is to fully exploit its tourism potential.

The reasons for India having great potential as a tourism destination have been explored by Boniface and Cooper (2005) as follows:

- The country has a very old civilisation that offers many opportunities in terms of tourism development. This includes the different cultures and religions that have been considered in previous parts of the book.
- The country has a population of well over a billion and it has almost 20% of the world's population and over half of the population is under 25 years old so the pressures for economic development including tourism are huge.
- India has retained a democratic government and the country has states and autonomous territories that can determine their tourism development policies.

- India is one of the most rapidly developing economies of the world with the high-tech cities of Bangalore, Hyderabad, Mumbai and Chennai leading the way in terms of business development.
- The country has quite good transport infrastructure compared to other developing countries although there is still a great need for improvements.

Tourism plays a significant role in India and as such the Government of India has taken a significant lead in the development of a suitable strategy to encourage growth. This was highlighted by the Prime Minister of the country – Shri Atal Bihari Vajpayee at a ministerial conference in October 2001.

> Tourism is a major engine of economic growth in most parts of the world. Several countries have transformed the tourism potential to the fullest. Tourism has great capacity to create large scale employment of diverse kind – from the more specialised to the unskilled and all of us know that generations of massive productive employment is what India needs the most.

The Indian government has played a major part so far in the development of tourism in India and the next section considers this involvement within the historical context of tourism development in the country.

The historical development of the Indian tourism sector

The development of the Indian government policy on tourism has already been considered earlier in the book in Chapter 4. The milestones of the development of a coherent government policy are explored in Table 10.1.

It can be seen from Table 10.1 that the Indian government has played a central role in the tourism development policy. One of the critical factors of recent times has been the encouragement of a more robust infrastructure and the development of India as a global brand in international markets. The creation of the "Incredible India" brand has been an important part of this development. Regions of India such as Kerala are now beginning to develop their own regional identity and branding strategy under the umbrella brand of India. One of the most serious challenges facing the development of Indian tourism policy is the improvements that have still to be made to infrastructure and issues of sustainable tourism that will be mentioned later in this chapter.

The Ministry of Tourism and Culture is responsible for the formulation of the tourism policy at Cabinet level in the government. The Ministry is helped by other organisations such as the ITDC, which was set up in 1965 by the Indian government to develop the infrastructure in the areas where private investment was not forthcoming. The ITDC also owns hotels, resorts, restaurants and transport operations. The Tourism Finance Corporation of India was established to help with tourism financing.

Table 10.1 The major milestones in the development of government policy in India

Year	Development/Policy
1982	A national policy on tourism announced.
1988	A comprehensive plan for achieving sustainable growth in tourism formulated by the National Committee on Tourism.
July 1991	Tourism declared a priority sector for foreign investment.
1992	The national strategy for the promotion of tourism formulated.
1996	National strategy for the development of tourism developed.
1997–2002	Ninth plan developed. This focused on the development of basic tourism facilities like hotels, restaurants and recreational facilities, as well as roads, water, sewage, electricity and telecommunications.
2002–2007	Tenth plan attempts to encourage India as a global brand. The tourism sector has received income tax exemptions, interest subsidies and reduced import duties as incentives for private investment.

Source: Adapted from Dhariwal (2005).

The Indian tourism sector

The tourism sector plays an important role in the economic development of India. The infrastructure that supports tourism development is a critical factor. The tourism development strategy not only has to maximise the natural, technological and human resources of India but it also has to make other important linkages. These include links to the airline industry, transport, communication, the retail trade, cottage industries, handicrafts, arts, and of course the hotel industry and restaurants. The Indian handicrafts industry, for example, is a magnet for foreign tourists who love to go shopping for brass work, textiles, leather goods, gems and jewellery. The handicraft industry represents a large part of spend by foreign visitors and provides large numbers of the population with jobs in small- and medium-sized enterprises. The handicraft sector also provides large amounts of jobs for women, young people and tribal populations (Dhariwal, 2005). India also benefits from a long tradition of ancient wellness traditions in the development of specialist tourism offerings. This includes the use of Ayurveda and other healing practices that were considered earlier in the book and the more recent introduction of medical tourism that certain areas of India have already begun to develop.

India has a unique blend of religions, ancient civilisations, spectacular monuments, vibrant cities, wonderful scenery, regional cuisines, mountain resorts and wildlife reserves. All of these allow different kinds of tourism development, which can be summarised as follows:

- **Business tourism**   The growth of the economy and the development of the major urban areas and multinational organisations based in India meant that both domestic and international business travel has grown and will continue to grow.
- **Cultural tourism**   This is often focused on a particular region, such as the "golden triangle tour", and is usually linked to major sights.
- **Beach tourism**   This has developed hand-in-hand with the introduction of package tours to India. Goa and Kerala are examples of areas of India that exploit this type of tourism.
- **Adventure tourism**   This includes trekking, mountain climbing and river running. It is focused on the Himalayan area.
- **Wildlife tourism and eco-tourism**   The first national park in India was established by Jim Corbett during British rule in 1911. There are now 70 national parks and over 300 wildlife sanctuaries, so India is a good place to see wild animals in their natural habitat. The Indian government is trying hard to make sure that this type of tourism is developed along sustainable lines, an example being the "Project Tiger" that tries to protect tigers in India.
- **Health tourism**   The long traditions of health and well-being in India mean that health tourism has flourished. This ranges from luxury spa resorts to hospitals offering medical treatments.
- **Religious tourism**   The long history and the recent resurgence in the global interest in world religions has meant that India can offer many types of religious experience ranging from a visit to a temple to a long religious retreat.

These different types of tourism that India offers come for the natural resources of the country and results in the types of tourist that visit the country. There are also areas of India that are recognised as being of particular interest to the international tourist. These include:

- **Northern India**   This included New Delhi, Agra and the famous Taj Mahal, Jaipur, which is the gateway to Rajasthan and Kashmir in the very north of the country.
- **Eastern India**   This includes Calcutta, Puri, which is a major religious centre for Hindus, and the temple cities in the state of Orissa. The east is also important for the fact that access to the Himalayas is from this area of the country.
- **Southern India**   This includes the beach areas of Kerala. Chennai is an important city and the area also has the temples of Madurai and Kanchipuram.
- **Western India**   This includes the important city of Mumbai with the booming film industry, and Goa which offers fine beaches and was originally attractive to backpackers and hippies. It has now become a package holiday destination.

Many different types of tourist visit these different areas of India and this will be explored in the next section.

The tourist

The balance between domestic and inbound tourism has already been considered in Chapter 4 earlier on in the book. It is interesting to note that there has been a growth in domestic tourism in India due to economic growth and the improvements in the tourism infrastructure, particularly the emergence of the budget airlines. Domestic tourism has seen year-on-year increases during the last 10 years (Euromonitor, 2005). There are estimates of about 15–20% of the population of India in the middle class category which represents a staggering 150 million people who can afford to take domestic holidays in their own country and further away. The domestic tourist has focused on religion in the past, although the interest in beach and mountain resorts has grown in recent years (Boniface and Cooper, 2005). The second type of visitor that comes to India is from abroad as inbound tourists.

The events of 11 September 2001 and the resulting crisis in long-haul traffic coupled with the political unrest with neighbouring Pakistan have both had an effect on the Indian tourist business. The country does offer value for money for the foreign traveller as the rupee has been devalued against foreign currencies. Tourists have continued to visit India in large numbers and the seven leading tourist destinations in 2002 were the UK, USA, Sri Lanka, France, Germany, Canada and Japan. Tourists also arrive in India in large numbers from Bangladesh and Pakistan (Mintel, 2003).

There is a strong focus on the VFR (visiting friends and relatives) market from certain countries with the UK being a good example of this. It is estimated, for example, that 38.8% of arrivals from the UK in 2002 were VFR tourists (Mintel, 2003). This is important because these tourists are less affected by terrorist attacks but they are less likely to spend large amounts of money in the country during their visit. Each international tourist visits on average between two and three states while they are in India. The main states that are visited are Delhi, Maharashtra (Mumbai) and Tamil Nadu (Chennai). New destinations such as Uttar Pradesh, home of the Taj Mahal, and Goa, home of the developing beach-based tourism, have seen particular growth in tourism business over the last decade (Mintel, 2003).

It is interesting to note that the number of male tourists exceeds the number of female tourists which can be largely attributed to the fact that many business tourists are male. India is also a place that young people visit. Tourists from the young adult and early middle-age groups have consistently accounted for about half of all the tourist arrivals to India. It is also interesting to note that the average length of stay for tourists in India is much longer than many other destinations, particularly amongst the long-haul visitors who tend to visit India for periods up to 4–5 weeks. The backpacker from Europe spends longer periods in the country and stays at budget hotels and hostels. This compares with the business traveller who tends to stay at three- and four-star hotels for relatively shorter periods.

The inbound tourist to India visits at particular times of the year and the market is highly seasonal as a result. The peak months for inbound tourism are the winter months from November–January. The lean months for inbound tourism are May–September. This is understandable because of the adverse climatic condition in India during the period from May to

Table 10.2 WTO tourism 2020 vision forecasts of tourist arrival to India by main markets

Origin markets	Actual 1995	Forecasts		Growth rates (% pa) 1995–2020
		2010	2020	
United Kingdom	334,827	821,446	1,471,084	6.1
Bangladesh	318,474	800,017	1,303,144	5.8
United States	203,343	707,016	1,266,161	7.6
Germany	89,040	355,340	767,153	9.0
Canada	63,821	291,848	690,911	10.0
Japan	76,042	289,801	625,658	8.8
Malaysia	50,039	228,824	541,710	10.0
France	82,349	206,863	370,461	6.2
Sri Lanka	114,157	215,691	319,275	4.2
Italy	53,015	86,643	105,617	2.8
Others	738,576	1,085,509	1,438,827	2.7
Total	2,123,683	5,089,000	8,900,000	5.9

Source: WTO (2002).

September with very high temperatures followed by the monsoon season when travel is difficult. It is interesting to consider the sources of inbound tourism to India and the growth that is expected over the next period. The WTO has presented estimates about the likely source of inbound tourists to India up to the year 2020 and these can be seen in Table 10.2.

It can be seen from Table 10.2 that an overall growth in tourism arrivals to India for the period 1995–2020 is predicted. It is estimated that at 5.9% growth this will be marginally below the growth rate for the South Asia area as a whole, which is estimated to show a growth rate over the same period at 6.2%. It is still above that estimate for the global growth rate, which has been estimated at 4.1% (WTO, 2005). The strongest growth rate of inbound tourists will be from the traditional European and North American sources, with the UK still retaining the leading position as a source on inbound tourists. Other areas such as East Asia and the Pacific will also contribute important generating countries and almost 9 million visitors are estimated to visit India by 2020. This growth will mean that the tourism infrastructure will have to develop to support this steady growth in numbers and that the economic contribution of tourism will continue to be an important source of revenue.

It can be suggested that the pattern of purpose of visit that we considered earlier in the book will continue to be seen. This means that the number of inbound business travellers will continue to grow at a fast pace and the number of leisure visitors will continue to grow at a steady pace. The number of inbound visitors who are visiting friends and relatives will probably stay at a fairly static number. The growth in business travellers will mean that the number of three- and four-star hotels will continue to grow and there will be further opportunities for the growth of well-recognised international chains. There will also be further opportunities for airlines to develop services both into and around India.

There is the opportunity for India to focus on new types of tourist as the country develops and new market opportunities arise. For example, India can benefit from a long of ancient wellness customs in the development of specialist tourism offerings. This includes the use of Ayurveda and other healing practices that we considered earlier in the book and the introduction of medical tourism that certain areas of India have already begun to develop. This opportunity is explored in the mini case study.

India is also starting to develop a conference and incentive business with major European companies beginning to consider more exciting and exotic locations for their events. The UK is the largest source of conference and incentive business to India but companies from other European countries such as France and Germany are also starting to organise conference and events in India usually with help from major conference and events organisers. This development, which is explored in more detail in Case 14, illustrates how India is becoming an interesting venue for conference and events when the client base included well-travelled executives who are seeking more exotic destinations for this type of tourism. It also shows how the boundaries between business and leisure tourism are increasingly blurred.

An important factor that influences the development of all the tourism business in India is the development of an effective tourism infrastructure that will now be considered in the next section.

Tourism infrastructure

The Indian government recognised in their national tourism strategy that one of the most important factors that would contribute to their planned growth was the development of an effective infrastructure to support the tourist during their stay in India, whether that was for business or leisure. The first of areas for concentration was the continued development of an effective and efficient transport system to allow tourists to move both to and around the country with ease.

Transport ● ● ●

Most tourists that arrive in India do so by flight because of the difficulties of reaching India, because of the political situation in Afghanistan, the closing of the Khyber Pass and the continued dispute between India and Pakistan on the border. The Indian government has focused attention on the development of the important airports of Delhi, Mumbai, Calcutta and Chennai. It has also allowed foreign charter airlines to fly into resort areas such as Goa to encourage the development of package holidays in the country.

The Indian airlines such as Jet Airways are beginning to offer international flights into Europe and there has been a continued growth of budget airlines in India that offer cheap internal flights between major Indian cities. This has allowed tourists to travel between major areas of India in recent times more easily and has opened up the opportunity of package holidays based on internal flights within India. The growth of these new budget carriers is seen in Case 15.

India also has an extensive rail network that was developed originally by the British when they were in India. Tourists can use the rail network today to get between major conurbations and it is often a very interesting way of getting around the country and seeing the countryside between the major cities. Foreign tourists do, however, have to purchase their tickets in advance (Indrail Pass) to make sure that they have seats in a comfortable carriage and that they are not hassled when they arrive to board the train. Some of the railways in India have become tourist destinations in their own right and the luxury trains, narrow gauge railways and steam locomotives are all promoted as tourist attractions in their own right. Case 16 explores the development of the small railways of India's tourist destinations.

India is also improving the roads in the country and it has a huge network of passable roads that provide access even to remote areas. It is still quite dangerous to drive on roads where accidents are common and driving in the cities can be hair-raising for foreign visitors. It is unusual, therefore, for foreign visitors to hire a car in the country and it is much more common for the tourist to hire a car and driver for anything from a few hours to weeks according to the itinerary. There is a great deal of road improvements happening in the major metros of India. In Delhi and Bangalore, for example, there are major road improvements happening across the cities with plans for flyovers and ring roads. This development will hopefully improve road transport for tourists in the longer term.

Accommodation

The range of accommodation on offer has already been considered earlier on in the book. The development of this accommodation has been encouraged by the policies adopted by the Indian government in recent years. There is now a full range of accommodation on offer from hostels for backpackers to the luxurious five-star hotels and palaces in the large cities and popular tourist destinations such as Agra, Jaipur and Goa. The growth of the accommodation sector in India has largely been due to the Indian owned chains, the Taj Group, Oberoi and the state-owned ITDC. Other interesting types of accommodation include palaces, houseboats, religious institutions and forest lodges.

Major issues facing the Indian tourism sector

The major factors that are facing the Indian tourism sector are numerous and have been summarised by Boniface and Cooper (2005) as follows:

- Inadequate infrastructure with water and power being a particular problem.
- Negative publicity in the Western media, particularly about disease and strife.
- Promotion of the whole of India as one destination when in essence there are a large number of different areas that can be promoted in very different ways.
- The seasonality of the market that creates occupancy problems at certain times of the year.
- The shortage of medium-priced accommodation.
- Other negative factors such as pollution, noise, poor hygiene and harassment by beggars in the main tourist areas.

Source: Adapted from Boniface and Cooper (2005).

It can be seen from the factors outlined above that India has a number of factors that need to be tackled if tourism development is to continue. The worries that individual tourists and tourism companies have about the poor infrastructure in India will continue to be a problem until major improvements are made. This is also coupled with a lack of medium-priced accommodation except perhaps in the major resort locations such as Goa. Foreign tourists also have worries about the pollution noise and poor hygiene factors that they associate with India and which have been well documented in the media. India is a vast country with many different tourism opportunities. The country has started to promote certain areas of India such as Kerala on an individual basis but much more work is necessary to make the most of this promotional activity. The seasonal nature of the market also means that India will have to think of alternative forms of tourism in the quiet periods of the year. It will also be very important to focus on sustainable tourism development so that both the locals and tourists can take full benefit. The education and development of effective tourism management strategies will continue to be a priority for India.

Learning tasks

1 Critically evaluate the importance that the growth of the budget airlines in India will have on tourism development in the country.
2 Evaluate the role of the Indian government in the development of tourism in India.

Discussion questions

1 Discuss the way in which local foods can provide opportunities for tourism development in India.
2 Discuss the ways in which "Bollywood" films and popular Indian literature can provide opportunities for tourism development.

Mini case study

Medical tourism in India

Background India can benefit from a long tradition of health and well-being practices that are embedded in the culture of the country. The country also has developed excellent base in particular medical disciplines such as orthopaedics, non-trauma medical disease treatment, replacement and corrective surgery, urology and dental surgery that can be offered to foreign visitors.

The Indian health system India has invested heavily in hospitals, medical personnel and supporting infrastructure. The Indian hospitals will have to meet global accreditation and standards to compete in the international market but there are signs that this is developing rapidly. Some hospitals in India have already started to develop an international business and it is estimated that around 80,000 non-resident Indians and foreign national already go to India each year to undergo medical treatment and this figure is said to be growing at a rate of 30% per year. An example of a hospital that is offering medical tourism packages is the Apollo group that was founded in Chennai and now has hospitals in India and other areas of South Asia.

Target markets Currently, the patients come mainly from the Middle East and South Asian economies but the group sees potential from the U.S. and Europe. The Indian government and medical facilities have identified further growth potential from the Middle East, North America, the UK and West Asian countries.

Regional offerings Certain areas of India have specialised in the development of medical tourism. This includes Maharashtra in the capital Mumbai, Kerala, Karnataka particularly in Bangalore and Goa. The tour operators are already developing package holidays to target this type of tourism development.

The future There is a need for the development of more medical tourism packages to include travel and tour operators working in tandem with insurance companies, and health care providers. India is poised to develop this new type of tourism and offer these types of packages to a growing number of international visitors.

Source: Mintel (2004).

References

Baggott, K. (2005). *Maharaja Motivation*. Conference and Incentive Travel, July/August, pp. 63–68.

Boniface, B.G. and Cooper, C. (2005). *The Geography of Travel and Tourism*. 4th edition, Oxford, Elsevier Butterworth-Heinemann.

Dhariwal, R. (2005). Tourist Arrivals in India: How Important are Domestic Disorders? *Tourism Economics*, **11**(2), 185–205.

Edensor, T. (1998). *Tourists at the Taj*. London, Routledge.

Euromonitor (2005). *India: Global market factfile*. http//www.gmid.euromonitor.com/CountryProfile.aspx.

Gupta, V. (1999). Sustainable Tourism: Learning From Indian Religious Traditions, *International Journal of Contemporary Hospitality Management*, **11**(2/3), 91–99.

Gupta, S.P., Lal, K. and Bhattacharyya, M. (2002). *Cultural Tourism in India*. New Delhi, D.K. Printworld.

India Travel Planner (2005). New Delhi, Cross Section Publications Pvt. Ltd.

Mintel (2003). *Travel and Tourism India*. Mintel Publications, July.

Mintel (2004). *Health and Wellness Tourism*. Mintel Publications, August, pp. 10–13.

MRM (2002). *Discover Around Mumbai*. Mumbai, MRM Publications.

MRM (2002). *Discover Maharashtra*. Mumbai, MRM Publications.

Noronha, F., (1999). Ten Years Later, Goa Still Uneasy Over the Impact of Tourism, *International Journal of Contemporary Hospitality Management*, **11**(2/3), 100–106.

Outlook Traveller (2005). *The Best of Uttaranchal*. May.

Rao, G. (2005). It's a Smooth Take-off For Budget Carriers, *The Economnic Times*, Friday, 20 May.

Waterstone, R. (2005). *India: The Cultural Companion*. London, Duncan Baird Publishers Ltd.

World Tourism Organisation (1999). *Tourism 2020 Vision*. Madrid.

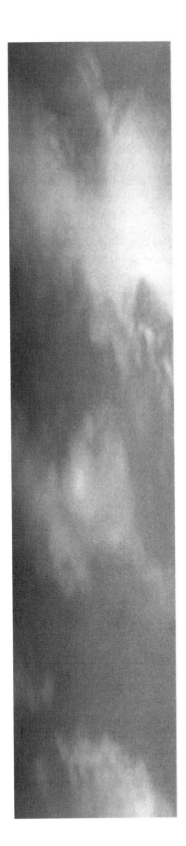

Conclusions

These conclusions come at the end of a text that has dealt with a complex set of issues related to the rapidly developing market for hospitality and tourism products and services in two of the most interesting areas of the world. It is now the intention to bring the contents of the book together and to draw some conclusions. The objectives here are to

1 Identify the main conclusions that have arisen from the previous chapters in the book, highlight the importance of the need for well-educated professionals who will take a leadership role in the rapidly developing business of hospitality and tourism.
2 Make some future predictions about the way in which the sector will develop in the future and assess what this will mean for organisations and their employees.

The authors will start by highlighting some key points that have emerged in the previous chapters of the book.

The first part of the book looked at the importance of China and India in terms of the world economy. It was seen that both countries are in a period of rapid development and as a result both countries have experienced recent periods of expansion in major cities and urban areas. The peoples of both countries are changing, with the rapidly emerging middle classes having a particular effect on the development of both countries. Both countries have very different political systems of government, but it is interesting to note that the government has tried to influence the growth of both the industrial and service sectors of the economy. The Chinese and Indian governments have also had a major influence on the development of the tourism agenda in both countries. Some of the important common features that emerged from the first part of the book include the following:

• The economies of both China and India are in a period of growth.

- The growth in the economy has led to the rapid expansion of major cities, with an emerging service sector to supplement the existing industrial heritage.
- The growth in the economy has led to the emergence of a middle class, who have already begun to demand new products and services.
- The growth in the economy has also led to an increase in both domestic and foreign tourism as the people from both countries have increasingly travelled for both business and leisure, and there has been an influx of foreign tourists, particularly business tourists who have been keen to exploit the opportunities that both economies offer.
- There has been a need in each country for the development of hospitality and tourism infrastructure to underpin this new growth.
- Both countries have many challenges to face in the future ranging from measures to be taken to help the environment and pollution control to policies that are required to alleviate poverty, promote health care for all and clean up the environment.
- Both countries have diverse geographies and very different regional variations, especially as both countries span areas of vastly different climatic conditions.

The first part of the book also highlighted some of the differences between the dragon and tiger economies of China and India. Some of these differences include the following:

- Both countries have a very different history with differing political systems and cultural nuances. This includes distinct differences in terms of cuisines and food choice that has had a major impact on the development of hospitality services.
- The religions of both countries are both diverse and different, and there are tensions and challenges for each country to face as a result of these differences.
- The historical context of both countries is very different and has led to diverse cultural panoramas. These lead to different tourism opportunities in each country.
- The strong link of India to the UK, as a result of the British Empire, provides India with many opportunities in terms of business and tourism development.

The second and third parts of the book have considered the emerging hospitality and tourism sectors in the two countries. The focus was on the market, the industry structure and the business environment in these very different settings. These sections used copious examples and illustrations to try to show the similarities and differences between the two very different settings. Although it was seen that there was some homogeneity between the two countries in certain respects, it was also shown that there is a great deal of heterogeneity. There are trends that are taking place that make the picture more complex and perhaps leading to more homogeneity as time passes. Some of these trends are listed below.

- There are certain market segments that are beginning to focus on standardised hospitality and tourism services as both markets develop. This has led to the growth of international brands in all areas of hospitality and tourism in both countries, and this development is predicted to grow further.
- The growth in business tourism has fuelled the growth in the interest of multinational companies in both countries and the emergence of branded offerings in all areas of hospitality and tourism. There has been a steady growth of international brand names in all areas of hospitality including hotels and fast food, although market restrictions and supply chains has limited some of this growth to date.
- The continuing globalisation of the hospitality and tourism sector is having a major effect on the business in the two countries, although local companies still have a major part to play in the current market.
- The growth of the experienced tourist who demands new cultural experiences has fuelled the growth of special interest tourism in both countries.
- The impact of the international business environment is having a major effect on the hospitality and tourism business in both countries. This has led to technological developments that are global in nature, and organisations in both countries cannot neglect these in the longer term. It is envisaged that this will lead to better food supply chains and more sophisticated distribution systems, for example, amongst many other changes. The international business environment will also lead to political change that will lead to more open markets and increased harmonisation in both countries.
- The growth of more standardised approaches to management education and training and the influence of internally recognised standards of courses and management training will also start to influence the hospitality and tourism sectors in both countries.

The key to the future development of the hospitality and tourism sectors in both China and India seems to rely on the education and training of the professionals who will lead the way in this. There is obviously a need in both countries for the development of educational provision at the higher level to be dovetailed with the management development programmes that already exist in some organisations across the region. Some of these programmes have been highlighted in the book already and are emphasised further in a number of case studies. Hospitality and tourism organisations in China and India will increasingly find themselves in a global industry that requires the development of standardised marketing programmes. This development will require the development and delivery of sophisticated management programmes that will reflect on best practice across the world.

The march of globalisation will mean that Asia will increasingly challenge other areas of the world such as the Americas and Europe that have so far been dominant in terms of global development. The book has shown that organisations in both China and India have the potential for this type of development. It will require leadership and management development so that this potential can be realised in the longer term.

It is interesting to reflect on whether this book has achieved the original objectives of giving the reader an insight into the management challenges that face the hospitality and tourism sectors in China and India. What has emerged as the book has been researched and written is that we have only just begun to scratch the surface of this interesting and varied sector in both countries. There is much scope for further investigations, especially empirical research. The authors thank all the contributors to the book – students, friends and colleagues who have allowed the start of this research process. Our continued return to the two countries and our contacts with practitioners and researchers will allow this journey to continue. Trends that started centuries ago will continue to develop alongside new ideas in the fascinating and never-ending melting pots of China and India.

Case Studies

Full details of any sources used are to be found at the end of earlier chapters.

Case 1

MACAU: THE NEW "LAS VEGAS OF THE FAR EAST"?

Macau has one of the most vibrant economies in China. Until 1999, it was a Portuguese colony that, like Hong Kong, is now a SAR of China. It is situated close to Hong Kong on the Pearl River estuary; the catamaran from Hong Kong to Macau takes less than one hour.

Macau's economy is unusual in that only 2% of its land is cultivated; its main industries are textiles and gambling. Almost 30% of Macau's population is directly employed in gambling, hotels and restaurants. Some believe that over 90% of Macau's employment will derive directly and indirectly from gaming and tourism. Macau's economy has been given a boost by its separation from the Chinese economy (effectively a two-economies policy); a relaxation of the gaming laws, which has produced an upsurge in foreign direct investment; an increase in the number of visitors from the mainland (in part a possible consequence of the "Golden Weeks" and increased leisure time) and the opening of its first international airport in 2006.

Gaming in Macau will be given a further boost as companies that may be found in Las Vegas are now to be found in Macau. The emphasis is on luxurious hotels, luxurious gaming rooms and luxurious surroundings. Between April 2007 and December 2007 no less than eight new "megaresorts" are to be opened. These include the MGM Grand Macau, the Venetian and the Sands Macau. Each of these brands is instantly recognisable as coming from Las Vegas. The attractions of the eight megaresorts other than gambling include restaurants, spas, convention centres, retail plazas, nightclubs, theatres, health clubs, fitness centres and even a "performance" lake!

The eight resorts will add almost 6,000 rooms to Macau's room stock and nearly 3,000 gaming tables. All of this represents a colossal investment that is in the region of HK$43 billion.

This huge investment is a massive upgrade in facilities and is aimed at putting Macau on a par with Las Vegas. However, there are three differences between the two resorts that may prevent this. First, hotel occupancy in Las Vegas is much higher than that of Macau as is the length of stay, can Macau fill 6,000 extra rooms? At present only half of Macau's visitors stay overnight. Second, if the investment is to be worthwhile then expenditure by visitors must be much higher and redistributed; as an example, only 41% of expenditure in Las Vegas is on gambling and Las Vegas's visitors spend ten times more than Macau's visitors on non-gaming items. Many of the facilities of the new megaresorts such as theatres and shopping malls require different spending patterns. Finally, the last imponderable one is that the market that Macau is aimed at is predominantly mainland Chinese; will a *"Las Vegas"* experience be culturally suited to them? What adjustments may be made to accommodate the preferences of this group? Already all eight restaurants at one of the resorts are Chinese and the rooms are priced to suit the middle class Chinese pocket, what other things may be changed?

Case study questions

1 Do you think it advisable to set up a "Chinese Las Vegas"?
2 In your opinion, do the developments as outlined fit with the Chinese culture?
3 What might Macau have to achieve to adjust the spending pattern?

Case 2

GOA: THE RESORT STATE OF INDIA

Background

Goa has become known as India's resort state. Goa has miles of beautiful beaches and the carnivals and quaint Portuguese architecture, cathedrals and seafood cuisine have been a magnet for tourists since the 1960s. The development of the infrastructure alongside the beaches of Goa has fuelled the development of the package holiday for foreign tourists. Many of the foreign tourists who arrive in Goa come on package holidays organised by their local tour operators for modest costs. Many of the package holiday makers are attracted to the all-inclusive type of package where they spend most of their time in the resort and make few, if any, visits to the local sites.

Location

Goa is situated on the southwest coast of India and has a beautiful coastline that has been exploited by the developers who have built the resorts and accompanying infrastructure to support the tourism development. Many package holiday companies offer Goa as a destination and it is particularly attractive to northern Europeans as a place with tropical surroundings at modest prices. It is also accessible to Indian tourists who can fly in using local airline companies such as Indian Airways, Jet Airways and Sahara Airways.

The area is mainly semi-rural with small villages but four major cities have been developed to support the boom in tourism – Margao, Colva, Vasco and the capital city Panjim.

The sights

The main sight of Goa is the wonderful beaches but there are other sights to see such as churches, forts, temples, waterfalls and wildlife sanctuaries. There are also other visitor attractions such as spice plantations, canals, traditional villages and river cruises. The most popular tours from the resort include:

- Sailing in a Chinese junk
- Dolphin watching
- Crocodile watching in the mangrove
- Scuba diving
- Overnight cruises
- Visits to a spice plantation
- Waterfall visit

Eating out

There is a full range of restaurants on offer in Goa. The resorts and hotels all have food and beverage operations in their facilities but there is also a full range of restaurants in the developed area. The speciality of the region is fish curry and rice. Many famous chefs have opened restaurants in Goa to satisfy the growing demand for high quality local food. There is also a full range of pubs and clubs to suit the tastes of the international tourist.

Resorts and hotels

There is a good choice of resorts that have been developed by both Indian and foreign hospitality companies. Some of the most famous resorts are

Deluxe resorts

- Taj Fort Aguada
- The Aguada Hermitage
- The Taj Exotica
- InterContinental The Grand Resort
- The Leela Palace
- Park Hyatt Resort and Spa
- Radisson White Sand Resort
- Cidade De Goa

- Goa Marriott Resort
- Ramada Caravela Beach Resort
- Majorda Beach Resort

Deluxe hotels

- The Taj Holiday Village
- The Heritage Village Club
- Bogmalo Beach Park Plaza Resort
- Holiday Inn Resort
- Dona Sylvia
- The Club Mahindra Beach Resort
- The Kenilworth Beach Resort
- Sun Village

There is also a full range of standard hotels. It can be seen from this list that the major hotel chains have all invested in Goa as a major tourism destination. The resort concept has been a very successful part of this development strategy.

Conclusion

Goa has become a major holiday destination in India. It has relied on the development of an extensive range of resorts and ancillary facilities to help with this growth. There have been some criticisms of the exploitation of the environment but the Goan tourism development has brought substantial revenue to the major companies that have invested in the area.

Case study questions

1 Discuss the role of the resort type complex in the development of beach tourism.
2 Critically analyse the positive and negative effects that the development of a beach resort can have on the local environment of a place such as Goa.

Source: Incredible India (2005).

Case 3

THE OBEROI GROUP INDIA: THE LEARNING ORGANISATION

Introduction

The Oberoi Group, which was founded in 1934, has become a major hospitality company, which has grown up from early beginnings in India. The company owns and manages 30 hotels and five luxury cruisers under the names "Oberoi" and "Trident Hilton". The hotels have become particularly recognised as offering the customer the right blend of service, luxury and quiet efficiency. A distinctive feature of the group is the training that they have undertaken, which has resulted in the high levels of customer service for which they have become recognised.

Nine of the Oberoi hotels are members of the Leading Small Hotels of the World and the company has been active in the development of luxury resorts in India and overseas. The group has also entered into a relationship with Hilton to develop a group of hotels that are particularly aimed at the business traveller. This brand is the Trident Hilton brand. The Group is committed to employing the best environmental and ecological practices and is a contributor to the conservation of natural and cultural heritage. The Group has grown into a major player in the hospitality sector and now owns airline catering, travel and tour services, car rental, and also manages restaurant and airport bars. The Oberoi Group owes its success to the entrepreneurial skills of its founder Rai Bahadur Mohan Singh Oberoi and his son P. R. S. Oberoi.

Key personnel

The Oberoi group was founded by the great entrepreneur – Rai Bahadur Mohan Singh Oberoi (1896–2002). He was born on the 15 August 1896 in the undivided Punjab, which is now Pakistan. He completed his Bachelors degree in Rawalpindi and then went on to study his postgraduate degree in Lahore. After completing his degree he went on to seek his fortune in Shimla, which was the summer capital of British India. He found a job as a front desk clerk at the Cecil Hotel where he impressed the manager of the hotel – Mr Grove.

He then went on to purchase his first property in 1934 – The Clarkes Hotel. Four years later he signed the lease on the Grand Hotel in Calcutta and converted this into a highly profitable business venture. He then purchased shares in Associated Hotels of India (AHI) that owned the Cecil and Corstophans in Shimla, Maidens and Imperial in Delhi, and a hotel in Lahore, Murree, Rawalpindi and Peshawar. Mr Oberoi gained controlling interest of the group in 1943 and as a result became the first Indian to run the country's finest hotel chain. Today the Oberoi group owns the Cecil Hotel after a meteoric rise from these humble beginnings. Other key landmarks in the development of the group by Mr Oberoi include the following:

- He was the first Indian hotelier to enter into an agreement with an international hotel chain to open the first modern five-star hotel in the country. The Oberoi InterContinental, in Delhi, opened in 1965.
- He worked with the Sheraton group to build the 35-storey Oberoi Sheraton in Bombay, which opened in 1973.
- He pioneered the development of an effective management development programme with the establishment of the prestigious Oberoi School of Hotel Management, which opened in 1966.
- He made a major decision to employ women in his hotels.
- He recognised that airline catering would become very important so he founded his own flight catering operations – The Oberoi Flight Services Company.

- He recognised that the hotel and hospitality business relies a great deal on the travel agency business so he founded his own travel agency business – Mercury Travels.
- He recognised that the conversion of historic buildings as hotels would bring particular success. Examples of this type of conversion include the Oberoi Grand in Calcutta, the Mena House in Cairo and the Windsor in Australia.
- The globalisation of the Oberoi group started under his direction and he exported his management expertise to Australia, Egypt, Singapore, and Mauritius. The group has continued to develop internationally after his death in 2002.
- He recognised the growing importance of business hotels and in 1988 he opened his first business hotel under the Trident name that has continued to grow as an important business chain in India.

It is Mr Oberoi's drive and ambition that has led to the position that the group is in today. The development of the premier brand of hotels in India is all due to the vision that Mr Oberoi had in the early years of his life.

P. R. S. Oberoi

The Oberoi group is now controlled by Rai Bahadur M. S. Oberoi's son – P. R. S. Oberoi or "Biki", as he has become affectionately known. He is the current Chairman and CEO of EIH Limited and also the Chairman of Oberoi Hotels. Mr P. R. S. Oberoi has provided leadership to the group after being educated in India, the UK and Switzerland. He has placed India on the international traveller's map by opening luxury hotels in Jaipur, Agra, Udaipur, Ranthambhore and Mashobra in the Himalayas. He has worked hard on the Oberoi brand and has further developed the quality training at the Oberoi Centre of Learning and Development that his father established. He is committed to environmental conservation and has been the driving force behind the WTTC's "India Initiative".

Under his leadership, the Oberoi group has received a number of prestigious awards and in recognition of this achievement he was honoured with the prestigious Lifetime Achievement Award in March 2003 at the sixth International Hotel Investment Forum in Berlin. In January 2004, Mr Oberoi was conferred a Special Award by the Department of Tourism, Government of India, for his outstanding contribution to the tourism sector in India. His work has been recognised as bringing India honour, recognition and visibility across the world and has galvanised the accommodation sector to provide higher levels of customer satisfaction. The hotels of the Oberoi group have received many prestigious awards and accolades as a result of the focus on luxury and customer service.

The Oberoi centre for learning and development

In 1966, there were few hotel schools in India and the late Mr Rai Bahadur Oberoi realised that his company would suffer from a lack of suitably trained staff to manage his expanding group of hotels. He therefore established the Oberoi School of Hotel Management (OSHM) as a corporate University where potential managers could be trained with a mixture of school-based tuition and on-job work experience. This institution was renamed as the Oberoi Centre for Learning and Development in 1996.

The Centre provides potential young managers with a very different experience from the usual work-based training that many hotels operate. The first difference is that the Centre has a physical location at the Maidens Hotel in New Delhi. The second important difference is that the programmes on offer at the Centre are highly structured, fully documented and externally benchmarked. The third difference is that the Centre has developed robust systems for the management, delivery and quality assurance of all the programmes on offer at the Centre. The three two-year post-graduate diplomas that are on offer at the centre are as follows:

- Guest Service Management (GSM)
- Housekeeping Management (HM)
- Kitchen Management (KM)

Potential applicants who apply for the programme come from a diverse range of backgrounds. Some are University graduates from hotel schools, some have been educated abroad, and some are already working in the Oberoi group and want to develop their careers towards a management position in the company. All of the applicants undergo a rigorous selection process and join one of the programmes after being successful in a very competitive interview process. This interview process is focused on Oberoi hotels in New Delhi, Bangalore, Kolkata and Mumbai, so diverse areas of India are covered during the recruitment and selection process.

The programmes are divided into three distinct stages to develop the chosen candidates into the managers of the future. These stages are as follows:

- The Foundation Stage where the objective is to develop a strong and consistent technical base in all the candidates.
- The Intermediate stage where there is still an emphasis on technical skills development but there is also a switch in focus to the quality of relationships with all stakeholders and the need to manage human, physical and financial resources.
- The Executive stage where the focus is on the candidate developing as an individual and as a manager. This involves class-based management subjects as well as the development of individual attributes, motivations and behaviour. The associate will also be encouraged throughout the programme to learn a third language (other than their Indian mother tongue and English).

The establishment and development of the Oberoi Centre for Learning and Development has allowed the Oberoi group to develop a sound human resource strategy that underpins their development of a luxury hotel brand. The group now views itself as a learning organisation due to the culture that has been created over a long period as a result of enlightened leadership. This is what has created the luxury and customer service that guests expect.

Conclusions

The Oberoi group has grown to be a major player in the luxury hotel sector in India as a result of the spirit and commitment of the founder of the company. The company has more recently moved in, the business sector of the hotel market, with the Trident Hilton brand. The expansion outside of India by the company has already begun and it is predicted that the international expansion of the company will continue. The company strategy has been firmly based on the successful exploitation of powerful brands, an effective market segmentation strategy, but most importantly the use of an effective human resource strategy to underpin the luxury service offering that the company has concentrated on. The establishment of the Oberoi Centre for Learning and Development at the Maidens Hotel in New Delhi has underpinned the strong company focus on recruitment, training and development.

Case study discussion points

1 Discuss the ways in which a luxury hotel group can develop an effective management training programme for their junior managers. What will be the key attributes of this training programme?
2 Discuss the importance of a luxury hotel company gaining a series of awards and accolades from a range of sources. Evaluate how these can be used to further market and develop the hotel group.

Case study questions

1 The success of a luxury hotel depends on the development of impeccable service based on an understanding of different consumer's needs and wants. Evaluate the role of training and education of all hotel staff in this process.
2 Critically analyse the effect that the growth of new international entrants into the Indian hotel market will have on companies such as the Oberoi group.

Case 4

EXPANSION OF HOTELS IN BANGALORE, INDIA

Bangalore is a city in India that has experienced rapid economic growth in recent years due to the expansion of the service sector in areas such as banking, call centres and computing. The city reached a crisis point in terms of hotel rooms in recent years with people having to stay in Chennai and travel to Bangalore due to a shortage of hotel rooms in the city. Room rates also escalated as demand outstripped supply. This position is due to change over the next few years as the city undergoes a rapid expansion in hotel development. It was estimated in 2005 that the city had 1,600 rooms and over 3,500 extra rooms will be created over the next four years (Times of India, 2005). Real estate companies are developing properties on behalf of major international players such as Shangri-La, Marriott, Hilton and the Carlson Group. The planned expansion in the city is shown below:

Planned expansion of hotel rooms in Bangalore, India

Developer/Hotel chain	Rooms	Year
Shangri-La Hotels and Resorts and Adarsh Group	1,000	Aug 07–Dec08
Radisson and Prestige Group	350	2007
Hilton and Prestige Group	300	Mid-2007
Marriott and UB Group	250	2007
Chancery Hotels	235	2006 opening
Puravankara and Ibis	80	2006 opening
Puravankara	300	not available
Euroamer Garuda	134	2005
Sterling Mac Hotel	167	2007
Sobha Group	192	2008
Embassy Group	360	2007
Brigade Group	not available	not available
Country Inns and Suites and Sigma Group	104	2007

Source: *Times of India*, 20 May 2005.

The expansion of hotels is also predicted to continue as the numbers of flights that go in and out of the international airport in Bangalore continue to increase. This will include the expansion of five-star hotels but will also mean that three- and four-star properties will also continue to be developed. The location of the hotels will be critical. Some will be developed in close proximity to the airport and others will continue to be developed near to the commercial hub of the city.

Case study discussion points

1 Identify the importance of location and star rating in the development of new hotels in a rapidly expanding city such as Bangalore.
2 Discuss the impact that the influx of international hotel chains will have on the local hotel market of Bangalore.

Case 5

THE HOLIDAY INN RESORT, GOA

The resort is located on the western shores of India on the Arabian Sea in Goa, which is one of the most popular beach destinations in India. The resort is on the beautiful beach in south Goa.

The resort has 170 luxurious rooms and suites.

It is spread over 26 acres on unspoiled tropical landscape gardens.

Guests can get directly on to the beach, which has warm clear waters of the Arabian Sea.

The resort has restaurants, bars, coffee shops, health clubs, tennis courts, a casino, a disco, conference halls, swimming pools and water sports facilities. The resort also offers barbecues and theme parties.

The resort has direct sales offices in Delhi and Mumbai but also takes Internet bookings and accommodates package holiday makers.

Source: Incredible India (2005) and Holiday Inn advertising.

Case study discussion points

1 Discuss the relative importance of the different distribution channels that a resort hotel such as the Holiday Inn Resort, Goa uses to distribute its products and services.
2 Evaluate the importance of the wider infrastructure of Goa on the business development activities of hotels such as the Holiday Inn Resort Goa.

Case 6

THE PARK HOTELS, INDIA

The Park Hotels are part of the Surrendra group, which is a business conglomerate. They are one of the first examples in India of a boutique-style chain that offers luxury service to both corporate and leisure travellers. The hotels are all located in downtown areas and offer trendy original decor and fun food and beverage concepts. This concept appeals to a diverse range of customers. The Park hotels are located in four cities as follows:

The Park, Bangalore

This is a 109-room hotel, which is the first contemporary hotel in India. The design was done by Conran & Partners, UK and is very modern and original. The designer swimming pool is a particular feature of the hotel. The lobby has also been recently redesigned and has a very original decor and original pieces of furniture.

The Park, Chennai

The Park, Chennai was created from the historic premises of the Gemini Film Studios and the original design of the hotel reflects this history. The hotel has 215 rooms and the interior is a haven of interesting lights, surfaces and textures.

The Park, New Delhi

The Park, New Delhi is near to the city centre and all government and commercial sectors. It has 224 rooms and suites that have a contemporary design and a deluxe floor with artworks. The multicultural restaurants are a particular feature of the hotel.

The Park, Calcutta

The Park, Calcutta is characterised by supreme comfort, eloquent design and delicious cuisine. The boutique hotel was opened in 1967 and has a full range of exotic restaurants. It also specialises in banquets and conferences and is close to the commercial centre of the city.

The Park, Vishakapatnam

This deluxe resort hotel is positioned in a 6-acre landscaped tropical garden. The hotel attracts both business and leisure guests. The hotel offers stunning views of the blue sea of the Bay of Bengal and guests can walk down to the beach through the lush gardens.

Source: www.hotels-in-india.com (2006).

Case study discussion points

1 Discuss the relevance of a boutique-style hotel in the rapidly developing urban cities of India.
2 Evaluate the role of original design in the development of the Park Hotel Group in India.

Case 7
ECOTEL® CERTIFICATION PROGRAMME

The ECOTEL® certification programme has not only been developed so that hotels can work towards improving their energy costs but also that they can help the environment and give something back to the community.

The ECOTEL® certification is given to hotels that show a heightened level of environmental responsibility. The scheme is based on five criteria and these are termed globes. The five criteria are – *Employee Education,*

Energy Management, Environmental Commitment, Solid Waste Management and *Water Conservation*. Hotels must achieve at least two of the five globes to qualify as an ECOTEL® hotel. The certificate is awarded for two years and the hotel must submit to regular inspections to keep the certification.

Current ECOTEL® hotels in India include – the Orchid, Mumbai, Uppal's Orchid, New Delhi, Rodas, Mumbai, Lotus Suites, Mumbai and the Raintree, Chennai.

Further hotels are planned in Pune, Lonavala, Jaipur, Hyderabad, Bangalore, and Kolkata.

Source: FHRAI/HVS International (2006).

Case study discussion points

1 Evaluate the role of environmental responsibility in the development of hotels in India.
2 Discuss the ways in which a brand such as ECOTEL® can be used to market a variety of diverse hotels and the lessons that are learned from this initiative.

Case 8

TEA HOUSES IN CHINA AND HONG KONG

Tea is a basic element of life in China and Hong Kong and has had a major influence on the development of Chinese culture. It has traditionally been regarded as one of the fundamental daily necessities along with fuel, oil, soy sauce, vinegar, rice and salt. The art of brewing and drinking tea both at home and in teahouses have long been popular in China. Teahouses in China have been described as being "almost like a pub" (Halsey, 2001) and also as being traditionally quite similar to the cafés of continental Europe (http://en.wikipedia.org/wiki/Tea_house). They are, quite simply, houses or parlours centered around drinking tea rather than alcohol or coffee. They are numerous and can be found just about everywhere in the streets of China. The function and popularity of teahouses, however, variy throughout China. People gather at teahouses to socialise, chat, drink tea, snack and often gamble. Teahouses are also places for people from businesses and organisations to get together to hold trade talks or do business. Some teahouses, such as those in Chengdu, also have theatrical performances, such as storytelling and even opera. Traditionally, teahouses have been largely frequented by older men who wile away their early mornings sipping tea, eating just a few dim sum and reading newspapers. Increasingly, teahouses are becoming brighter and turning into dim sum palaces and today, young people are visiting teahouses for dates and other social activities. The popularity of tea has even led some entrepreneurs in China to develop tea culture tours for tourists visiting tea gardens, tea factories, museums and teahouses. However, are the interest in tea and the existence of teahouses in modern China going to come under threat with the emerging coffee culture (see Sin, 2005), the increase in coffee drinking and as coffee-houses and chains sprout up all over the country?

Sources: Halsey, K. (ed.) (2001). *The Food of China: A Journey for Food Lovers*. London, Murdoch Books.

Sin, L.H. (2005) *At the head of the pack*, Foodservice Europe & Middle East, Trend Edition pp. 46–50.

Web site: http://en.wikipedia.org/wiki/Tea_house

Case study questions

1 What factors are influencing consumer demand for drinking tea in tea-houses?
2 In what ways can teahouses combat any threats from new entrants to the drinking out market?

Case 9

WINTER TOURISM ATTRACTIONS IN CHINA

There are currently approximately 100 ski resorts of different types in China with most of these located in the north of the country, in regions including Heilongjiang, Jilin and Xinjiang. There are also some in the south, for example, in Sichuan and Yunnan. Indoor Skiing can also be found in large cities such as at the indoor ski park in Shenzhen.

Winter tourism has become increasingly popular in China and it was expected that by 2005, 7 million participants would get involved in it while revenue would increase to US $241 million. The market is forecast to expand rapidly aided by increased investment, active support from governments at various levels, promotion campaigns such as that carried out by Heilongjiang province in Beijing. The management of winter tourism has been improved by regulations such as the first Chinese skiing ground quality standards issued by the Heilongjiang government in 2002. The WTTC (2006) considered that regional collaboration and cooperation in winter tourism should strengthen and that diversity was likely and would extend to snow-, water- and grass-skiing and ice sculpture.

Source: China, China Hong Kong SAR and China Macau SAR: The impact of travel and tourism on jobs and the economy, London: World Travel and Tourism Council (2006).

Case study questions

1 Using the SWOT analysis technique and other available data, what are the prospects for winter tourism in China?
2 How can the Beijing Summer Olympics of 2008 be used to boost winter tourism in China?

Case 10

CHINA "BUILDING A WORLD TOURISM POWER AND DEVELOPING A NEW MAINSTAY INDUSTRY" NATIONAL TOURISM ADMINISTRATION OF THE PEOPLE'S REPUBLIC OF CHINA, 2001

Introduction

Three markets and market potential

Inbound, domestic and outbound tourism have all been growing steadily, in terms of numbers and earnings, helping China become firmly established as an emerging travel & tourism economy.

Expansion of tourism and development of the tourism industry

Over the past few years, tourism products and services have rapidly developed and expanded. By the end of 2000, there were 254,300 accommodation establishments/facilities, including 10,500 hotels and 948,200 guestrooms, as well as 8,993 travel agencies. Transport has also been greatly improved with the rapid development of civil aviation, the railways, highways and waterways, and local transport. Tourism services, including restaurants, entertainment and shopping, have also been enhanced in terms of quality and quantity. As the industry has grown, tourism education has followed suit. There are 252 universities and colleges with tourism departments or faculties, 943 vocational schools with tourism programmes and 327,900 students currently following tourism courses.

Tourism product mix

A number of high-quality tourism products/sectors have been successfully established in China during the past few years, and these have proved to be attractive to international and domestic visitors. They include sun-and-beach holidays, skiing, ecotourism products, and the MICE business.

Tourism marketing and promotion

The marketing and promotion of China's tourism at home and abroad has been remarkably successful in recent years. The industry has overcome the negative impact of the Asian financial crisis thanks to increased advertising frequency and spend, and improved promotions and public relations – at tourism fairs and through exposure from its work with international tourism organizations.

Administration and regulation of tourism

The administration of China's tourism industry is being carefully re-examined and restructured so as to improve regulation, management, coordination and services. Building China's Excellent Tourism Cities programme has greatly improved the tourism environment, reinforced urban tourism, and accelerated urban infrastructure development and modernisation.

China's international position in tourism

CNTA and local tourism bureaus have developed bilateral and multilateral cooperation and interchange programmes, thereby expanding their relationships with major tourist generating countries, neighbouring economies and regions. These activities have steadily enhanced the international status of China's tourism industry and reinforced international cooperation.

Seven opportunities for the industry in the 21st century

- Tourism will be a new growth area for the national economy;
- Tourism will act as a catalyst for the industrial realignment of China's economy;
- The development of western China will be a significant opportunity for tourism;
- The legal holiday system (three Golden Weeks) will spur the growth of domestic tourism;
- Entry into the World Trade Organization will optimise and accelerate tourism development;
- The 2008 Olympic Games will internationalise and modernise China's tourism product and improve its image;
- The growth of world tourism will assist China in becoming a world tourism power.

The construction of the world tourism power: Development goals, stages and strategies

Quantitative goals for 2020

- The number of inbound tourist arrivals in China is expected to reach 210–300 million;
- International tourism receipts are projected to total US $58–$82 billion;
- Domestic tourism receipts will reach RMB 2,100—RMB 3,000 billion (US $256–$366 billion);
- Total tourism income is expected to exceed RMB 3,600 billion (US $439 billion), or 11% of GDP;
- Tourism will become the mainstay industry of the Chinese national economy.

Qualitative goals for 2020

Build China into a tourism power, which involves the following ten steps:

- Create, tap and expand tourism consumption;
- Balance inbound, domestic and outbound tourism;
- Develop and improve tourism products;
- Standardise and improve service quality;
- Diversify tourism markets, promotions and products;
- Improve tourism-related information technology;
- Encourage internationally competitive tourism enterprises;
- Establish a market economy-based legal and regulatory regime for tourism;
- Modernise and standardise tourism administration;
- Ensure financial and market efficiency in tourism.

Development stages

The primary stage (2001–05): Laying a Foundation for Building a World Tourism Power

- Breakthrough in policy-making;
- System reform;
- Develop western China;
- Reinforce marketing and promotion.

The Advanced Stage (2006–10): Advancing Tourism Competitiveness

- Optimise policy and the natural and social environment;
- Cultivate the inbound and domestic markets;
- Establish major tourism enterprises;
- Compete effectively on the international stage.

The Consolidation Stage (2011–15): Consolidating International Competitiveness

- Enhance China's competitiveness;
- Seek new development;
- Improve quality;
- Achieve profitable and sustainable development.

The Perfection Stage (2016–20): Shape and Perfect the World Tourism Power

- Optimise tourism output and achieve intensive growth;
- Create world-famous tourism products;
- Promote social development;
- Establish China's image globally.

The development strategy

Tourism is a Momentum Industry: tourism is not only an economic industry, but also a momentum industry in social and economic development.

Quality is Fundamental: the key to building a tourism power is improving the overall level of competitiveness.

Innovation: China's tourism requires innovation in strategy, products, markets, administration, management and professionalism.

Development guidelines

- Under the guidance of Deng Xiaoping's theories and his ideology of the tourism economy, the tourism industry is to be developed, with tourist resources as the "support", tourist products as the "basis", the market as the "guide", and financial benefits as the "core".
- With a view towards opening up the great tourism market, inbound tourism will be vigorously pursued, domestic tourism will be energetically encouraged and outbound tourism will be developed in a moderate fashion.
- While strengthening the government's lead role, people from all walks of life are to be mobilised to vigorously cultivate and develop the new economic growth sector, namely the tourism industry.
- Great importance should be attached to sustainable tourism development.
- Attention should be paid to ensuring both hardware and software development so that professionalism can be enhanced.
- The development strategy will take account of tourism's actual and potential contribution to the national economy – establishing a solid foundation for building "the world's tourism power".

Development policies

- Understanding of tourism development should be enhanced and unified, and the public's enthusiasm for tourism development should be fully awakened.
- All departments and agencies concerned should make joint efforts to promote tourism development under the leadership of the government.
- A detailed development plan should be formulated to guide tourism development.
- Innovation should be encouraged, as well as the creation of imaginative products.
- Regional cooperation is to be strengthened.
- The benefits of tourism should be distributed as equitably as possible across eastern, central and western China.
- Priority should be given to inbound tourism as the sector offering greatest potential for development, followed by domestic tourism.
- Investment in tourism promotion should be increased and improved.

- Tourism administration should to be broadened and its functions improved and modernised.
- Efforts should be made to build a number of powerful tourism destinations within the country to help China become a world tourism power.

Developing inbound tourism

Promotion and marketing should highlight China's wide range of attractions and tourism products.
Cultivating domestic tourism

- Formulate and implement a National Tourism Plan.
- Increase tourism supply, and implement and promote leisure tourism.
- Reform the national system of holiday entitlement to boost tourism consumption.
- Implement a system of paid holidays.
- Develop incentive business (corporate-sponsored leisure travel).
- Enhance the development of domestic tourism products.
- Promote domestic tourism.
- Ensure that domestic tourism is effectively managed.

Outbound tourism

- The moderate development of outbound tourism implies planned, organised and controlled development.
- The administration and management of outbound tourism should be closely linked to that of inbound tourism, ensuring an equitable distribution of trips per destination.
- Different policies should be formulated appropriate to the different purposes of outbound travel – the growth of the sector should be carefully managed.

Tourism product

In addition to developing new products – national and world-class products – existing tourism products should be enhanced. All these should embody national characteristics and highlight specific national attractions, but be developed according to international norms. This requires improved planning, design and innovation.

Perfecting the three major products

Three major types of tourism – sightseeing, stay-put holidays and special interest tourism – should be further improved in quality.

Sightseeing tourism	Holiday tourism
Cultural/historical tourism	Major resorts
Entertainment	Tropical/sub-tropical islands and beaches
Scenic attractions	Mountains, lakes, forests and hot springs
Museums	Urban conurbations
	Timesharing

Special tourism

Festivals, study tourism, adventure tourism, conference and exhibitions, incentives, cruises, ecotourism, skiing, third-age travel, golf tourism, business travel, rail travel.

New products

Attention should be focused on the following eight types of products:

- New archaeological discoveries and natural wonders;
- Theme parks;
- City tourism;
- Agricultural tourism;
- Industrial tourism;
- Science and educational tourism;
- Weddings;
- Health tourism;
- Extreme/adventure travel.

Showcase products

A number of national attractions, such as areas of particular scenic beauty, scenic routes and festivals, should be developed and promoted.

World-class products

World-class products should be created based on the country's natural and cultural heritage, including archaeological and natural wonders.

Joint development of three tourism regions

- Great efforts should be made to promote tourism development in eastern China while, at the same time, placing special emphasis on the development of distinctive products in western China and on stimulating growth in tourism to the central regions.

- Certain destinations in the central and western regions of the country should be developed as test cases in an effort to generate income from tourism, thereby helping to eliminate poverty.
- Ecotourism should be developed in a sustainable manner by planning and constructing a number of national ecotourism resorts.
- Resorts should be developed in line with international resort standards adapted to suit the needs of both domestic and international markets.

Regional tourism development

- Sophisticated tourism developments should be planned for eastern China.
- Larger-scale developments that are based on local natural resources should be earmarked for the creation of unique tourism products in central China.
- Great efforts should be made to ensure that tourism becomes the most profitable industry in the development of western China.

Develop key tourism regions

The different regions of China must cooperate closely in terms of tourism development.

Develop key tourism areas

- The new Asia-Europe mainland bridge;
- The Yangtze River tourism belt;
- The great Beijing-Jiulong tourism belt;
- The tourism belt of the Coastal Superhighway Corridor.

Promote key tourism routes

- The Silk Road tourism route;
- Yangtze River Three Gorges tourism route.

Promote the development of key tourism cities

Develop tourism with science and education on a full scale • • •

More attention should be paid to the use of science and technology in the design, planning and construction of tourism destinations and specific tourism projects.

Develop tourism human resources • • •

Measures should be taken to promote the development of human resources for tourism.

Implement a sustainable development strategy • • •

Promote sustainable tourism development, produce "green tourism" products, popularise "green tourism" management, and construct "green tourism" systems.

Case study questions

1 Evaluate the development goals, strategies and stages for tourism in China contained in "building a world tourism power and developing a mainstay industry".
2 How do the development goals, strategies and stages for tourism in China compare with the approaches planned for tourism in India?

Case 11

HONG KONG DISNEY

The first Disney resort in China was opened in Hong Kong in September 2005. The theme park is built on a 250-hectare plot of reclaimed land at Lantau Island, which was, until the arrival of Disney, more famous for its giant Buddha. The resort is reached quickly and cheaply from Hong Kong by an extension of the Mass Transit Rail system (MTR). The park is small compared to other Disney resorts worldwide. The park is themed around "four lands", which are typical of other Disney resorts. The lands are Main Street, USA; Tomorrowland; Adventureland and Fantasyland. Each of these lands comes with star attractions. However, possibly due to the comparatively small size of Hong Kong Disney some famous attractions such as "Small World" and "Pirates of the Caribbean" are missing.

The resort is the result of collaboration between Disney and the Hong Kong government, which dates back to 1999 or two years after Hong Kong returned to China from Britain. The park was visualised by the Hong Kong government as part of its strategy aimed at revitalising the economy after the Asian financial crisis. Indeed, the Hong Kong government was the biggest investor, investing HK $3.5 billion in the project. Its aim in doing this was to make Hong Kong a focus for tourism in Southeast Asia.

When the park was first mooted cultural fit was not seen as a problem. The reason for this is that Hong Kong has had western ties for over 100 years and was a British colony until 1997. Accepting Mickey and his friends would be natural; Hong Kong would be, and has always been, open to other cultures. Some commentators said that Anaheim, California had been moved to Hong Kong.

Setting up Disney parks outside of America is not new and Disney appears to have remembered the lessons of its French venture, which at one stage was called a "cultural Chernobyl" and has made changes that fit a Chinese culture. The first and most obvious is the food. The cuisine in the theme park and in the Disney hotels is regional, even the burgers are "spicy" pork. Second, although possibly not apparent to the Western eye, is the use of the "lucky" colour red in the park and, in keeping with the lucky theme, the park has been laid out using Feng Shui techniques to ensure its good fortune. Similarly, the unlucky number four is missing. Further, the signage around the park is in Chinese. Next, the "Haunted Mansion" attraction is missing as an attraction that deals with spirits and ghosts could be thought of as disrespectful to families in China. Lastly, the prices are much lower than other Disney attractions worldwide to take in to account the Chinese pocket.

Notwithstanding the changes that have been made, early results for Hong Kong Disney have been disappointing. There are reports that Disney has not made its target of 5.6 million visitors in its first year. The main problems that may have led to this disappointment are first, the cuisine. The cuisine may have been designed to suit the local taste but at least one item of the local cuisine - shark's fin soup had to be withdrawn from Disney hotel wedding menus after agitation and complaints from local environmentalist groups concerned about the fate of the sharks.

Second, the Chinese consumers appear to be confused about Mickey and the history of some of the rides. Customers have complained about the small size of the park and the lack of the "big thrill" rides. Only one ride in the entire park, Space Mountain is considered to be a "big thrill" ride.

Third, Disney employees or "cast members" have complained about pay and conditions. Their complaints mainly concern long hours, lack of breaks, poor treatment by the park's paying guests, low pay compared to other Disney parks and differentials between cast members. Of the 5,000 original employees, 1,000 have left. In the west this would be relatively a low number but is considered high in Hong Kong where the expectation is to stay with an employer. Further, some of the cast members feel over-qualified for the jobs that they are doing. A sign of the employees' misgivings is that the Hong Kong Disney Cast Members' Union has been formed, which is aimed at improving pay and conditions.

Next, Disney was dealt a public relations blow when it was accused of exploitation for the alleged low "sweatshop" wages that are paid to workers who make Disney merchandise. This relates to workers in the Guangdong Province of China who, it is alleged, are paid around $2 per day, which is less than minimum rates and are working excessively long hours. This has led to demonstrations against Disney in Hong Kong. Public relations were dealt a further blow when there were claims of infestations of fleas in resort hotels.

Finally, although it may not have made its target visitors, it miscalculated the impact of the Chinese New Year holiday. It was unable to cope with the demand at Chinese New Year, which is one of the three "golden" holiday weeks. The impact of this was more damage to public relations as some visitors were unable to enter the park and there were reports of the perimeter fences being scaled by unhappy would-be guests.

In summary, Disney's problems have been a combination of cultural misunderstandings, poor public relations and human resource problems. It has not been slow in responding to some of the problems. Disney has plans to increase the size of the park when more land is reclaimed. This will enable it to add more of the "big thrill" rides. It has also set up an educational centre in the park, the aim of which is to educate Chinese consumers about Mickey and the significance of some of its rides such as the tea cups. It is dealing with its other problems as it goes along. How these problems are overcome or otherwise will be important for it when it opens up its next venture in Shanghai. Cultural problems in Shanghai may be more pronounced and the Chinese mainland government may be much wary of the impact of Disney on Chinese culture.

Case study questions

1 Disney made some changes to its operation with regard to culture. What other things should it have considered?
2 Disney is due to open in Shanghai in 2010. What lessons should Disney learn from its Hong Kong operation? What other factors might it take into account?

Case 12
LEISURE TRAVEL IN INDIA
Introduction

Leisure travel in India represents a large amount of the revenue and profitability of hotels in the country. This case study is based on a piece of research that was carried out with hotel managers, travel agents, corporate travel managers and leisure travellers by the Federation of Hotel and Restaurant Association of India (FHRAI) in 2003. The research was completed in 87 hotels, which were members of the FHRAI and had over 50% of their guests coming from the leisure market segment.

Research findings and conclusions

A summary of the research findings is as follows:

- A large proportion of the leisure travellers were travelling with families and women for their holidays. This makes the provision of services for women and children a very important part of the package for leisure travellers as a whole.
- The research found that although there were long-stay guests staying at the hotels the trend amongst domestic travellers was for shorter breaks either mid-week or weekend breaks.
- A large proportion of the hotels in the survey reported that most leisure guests staying in their hotels had booked a package rather than making an independent booking. This meant that the most important form

of promotion for the hotels was via brochures using travel agents as intermediaries.

- The hotels in the survey were found to be spending about 10–20% of their total revenue on sales and marketing activity. Lower star category hotels were found to be spending more on sales and marketing activity compared to the higher star hotels.
- It was found that leisure travellers from Delhi were much more likely to book their holidays directly with the hotel rather than in other cities such as Mumbai and Ahmedabad where booking via a travel agent was much more common. Packages to Goa and Kerala were found to be the most highly developed and often incorporated flights, airport pickup, hotels etc. There were also signs that personalised packages mainly booked on the web were beginning to become popular at the time of the research.
- One of the most important conclusions from the research was the fact that it was considered important for individual destinations in India such as Manila, Udaipur, Kerala, etc. to promote themselves as separate destinations. It was also suggested that these areas should form associations of all stakeholders involved in tourism to act as central focus for tourism development and marketing. Local associations could also be responsible for raising funds for tourism development at a local level. It was also considered important that the destinations developed good Web pages to act as an information and promotional tool for tourism development.
- Travel agents reported that they expected a boom in domestic tourism over the next decade and thought that MICE had a huge potential for growth.
- One of the key factors that had influenced leisure travellers to choose a particular hotel was the brand of the hotel and the perceived quality. Word of mouth recommendation and views of the travel agent were also found to be very influential.
- Hotel guests reported that they were particularly disappointed when the hotel did not have a good travel desk and recommended sightseeing tours etc. They were also sometimes disappointed with the staff quality and language skills. Ongoing renovation of hotels was also seen as a particular problem for certain guests.

A particular success story

The report highlighted particular hotels from the sample, which reported high occupancy levels and tried to consider the strategies that they had adopted to achieve this success. The hotels that were identified and the strategies that they had adopted are shown below:

The best practice hotels identified in the research

Name	City	Average annual occupancy level
Mountain Trail	Nainital	90
The Kenilworth Beach resort	Goa	80
Majorda Beach Resort	Goa	79
Fort Agrada Beach Resort	Goa	75
Hotel Amar	Agra	75
Hotel Siddharth	Mysore	75
Uday Samundra Leisure Beach Hotel	Thiruvanthapuram	70
Dona Archina Resorts	Goa	70
Hotel Ram Regency Honeymoon Inn	Manila	70
Holiday Inn Resort Goa	Goa	70
Amar Yatri Niwas	Agra	70
Gem Continental	Port Blair	70

Source: FHRAI (2004).

Strategies adopted by best practice hotels

- High stress on the quality of services coupled with good pricing policies
- Aggressive and targeted marketing
- Establishment of marketing offices in key Indian cities
- Courteous service with a view to developing repeat customers
- Excellent market assessment supported by quick actions and effective sales networking
- Announcements of yearly tariffs and discounts in advance
- Elaborate brochures and tariffs
- Giving flat commission on all travel agents
- Networking among all sales offices across the country
- Exclusive menu and registration cards and complimentary gifts for children
- Stress on promotions and advertisements in feeder markets
- Participation in all travel trade fairs in different cities
- Evaluation of travel agents
- Friendliness and cooperation with competitors
- Excellent communication between staff and senior management
- Floatation of group packages or incentive programmes with different groups
- Development of combined packages for cities and beach destinations

- In-house facilities particularly in recreation
- International standards of cleanliness
- Professional and well-trained staff

Source: Adapted from FHRIA (2004).

Case study tasks and discussion points

1 Carry out a small piece of research on one Indian hotel to discover their levels of leisure travel business. Consider the different packages, services and loyalty schemes that the hotel currently operates to encourage leisure travellers and suggest ways in which these could be improved.
2 Evaluate the importance of extra services in hotels to meet the needs of the leisure traveller. Consider possible differences in requirements for domestic and international leisure travellers.

Reference

Federation of Hotel and Restaurant Associations in India (2004) *Trends in Domestic Leisure Tourism in India FHRAI*, New Delhi, India.

Case 13

BUSINESS TRAVEL IN INDIA

Introduction

Business travel in India represents a large amount of the revenue and profitability of hotels in the country. More than 50% of the occupancy of the majority of the hotels in India comes from this market segment. This case study is based on a piece of research that was carried out with hotel managers, travel agents, corporate travel managers and business travellers by the Federation of Hotel and Restaurant Association of India (FHRAI) in 2001. The research was completed in 210 hotels in 76 cities and the FHRAI were convinced that the sample was representative of all the hotel industry in India including the five-star category.

Research findings and conclusions

A summary of the research findings is as follows:

- The research showed that business travellers stay in a wide range of hotel accommodation in India. It was found that 70% of all business travellers in the survey stayed in the three-star categories or below and 13% in the five-star categories. There is obviously a difference in these trends depending on whether the business traveller is domestic or international with international business travellers being more likely to stay in the higher star category of hotel.

- It was found in the research that 57% of all hotel guests were business travellers, whereas 43% of all hotel guests are leisure tourists. It was also found that 75% of all guests were Indians showing the importance of the domestic tourist for Indian hotels.
- The report highlighted the fact that the hotels in the sample obtained a higher average room rate (ARR) for business travellers compared to leisure travellers and that this was most marked when the hotel had adopted dollar tariffs for international travellers. Many of the hotels in the sample said that their dealing with corporate clients was particularly important in this market.
- The bookings for business travel were shown to have been made in large parts (60% of bookings) by travel managers, 25% being made by individual managers, and 10% by travel agents. The corporate travel manager was found to be the most influential decision maker in the purchase process and the brand name and the reputation of the hotel were the most important factors when they chose a particular hotel. Other issues such as tariffs and discounts, location and services were also important criteria in purchase decisions.
- Most of the travel companies and company travel managers thought that the prices charged by Indian hotels were expensive compared to other competing areas of the world. Indian hotels were considered to have high rack rates and there is a common policy of discounting and adding on extra services to compensate for these high prices.
- It was found that it is essential for business travellers to be offered good services. This relied on the good training and retention of staff that was found to be excellent in some hotels but much more varied in other hotels.
- The hotels in the sample stated that it was essential to have a good customer retention strategy due to the fact that a large percentage of business travellers are repeat guests. The report recommended that hotels should aim to get at least 50% of their business travellers as repeat customers. Hotels had introduced a wide range of schemes to foster loyal customers and business travellers who were found to have mixed opinions about these schemes depending on the benefits on offer.
- It was found in the research that the hotel web site did not play a large role in the sale but was used more for informational reasons. This position is, however, predicted to change over the next decade.
- The report did try to provide hoteliers with a formula for success but this seemed difficult to identify and it was not clear why certain hotels achieved high occupancy rates, good customer retention and high RevPAR. The one most important feature that was highlighted in the report was the selection, development and training of good staff using professional management training programmes. A powerful brand name or identity was also considered to be a very important feature for success. This finding underlines the importance of sound human resource strategies for Indian hotels.

A particular success story

A wide range of hotels were highlighted in the report as being particularly successful and demonstrating good practice. The hotel that was highlighted as having the highest occupancy rate was the Residency, Chennai, which reported occupancy rates of 92% for the period 2000–01. The hotel reported that it had achieved this figure by having a very central and strategic position in the city. This was coupled with the fact that the hotel management had a philosophy of "the guest is god" and constantly offered new add-on and incentive products and services to enhance the guest experience. The hotel had introduced excellent staff training schemes and encouraged their guests to recommend the hotel to their friends, families and colleagues in "word of mouth" promotion. The hotel as a result had only spent 1% of its revenue on sales promotion in 2000–01.

Case study task and discussion points

1 Carry out a small piece of research on one Indian hotel to discover their levels of business and leisure travel business. Consider the different services and loyalty schemes that the hotel currently operates and suggest ways in which these could be improved.
2 Evaluate the importance of extra services in hotels to meet the needs of the business traveller. Consider possible differences in requirements for domestic and international business travellers.

Reference

Federation of Hotel and Restaurant Associations in India (2002) *Trends in Business Travel in India FHRAI*, New Delhi, India.

Case 14

CONFERENCE AND INCENTIVE BUSINESS IN INDIA

India is becoming an interesting location for conference and incentive business from Europe. The destination is proving to be more interesting for organisations that employ executives that have visited more mundane destinations in the past. Rolls Royce, UK, for example, organised a dealer incentive visit to India in 2005 with the help of their agency Grass Roots Group. The party started in Delhi and then went by private jet to Agra where they were taken by rickshaw to the Taj Mahal and stayed at the Oberoi Amarvilas overlooking the monument. A helicopter took them to see tigers in the national park, they had cookery lessons, and then finally they went to Jaipur where they dined at the royal palace with Jaipur's maharaja in his private quarters.

The large cities such as Delhi, Mumbai and Chennai are becoming increasingly important for conferences and events. The Taj and Oberoi groups are increasingly beginning to develop their business in this area. The best-known Taj property for such events is the Rambargh Palace,

Jaipur that has a suitable colonial charm and wonderful surroundings. Oberoi offers the Rajvilas in Jaipur, which has become an important venue for conference and incentive travel. The Taj offers the Taj View hotel in Agra but the most popular choice is the Oberoi's Amarvilas that has superb views of the Taj Mahal.

The cities of Delhi, Agra and Jaipur provide the venues for most of the conference and events that offered in India.

> Rajasthan alone offers so many amazing experiences, and the itineraries tend to be very similar. First timers to India will always choose Rajasthan. If they have more time they may head down to Goa, but that offers less of an authentic Indian experience. Kerala does offer potential for second-time visitors (PN Nageshwaran (Nagesh) Incent Tours).

Early conference and incentive travel to India has concentrated on Rajasthan but it is likely that this will expand into other areas of India with time and repeat customers.

Source: Baggott (2005).

Case study discussion points

1 Evaluate the positive and negative features of India as a destination for conference and incentive travel.
2 Discuss the ways in which Rajasthan has been at the forefront of the development of conference and incentive travel in India. What lessons can be learned for other areas of India?

Case 15

THE GROWTH OF THE BUDGET AIRLINES IN INDIA

Background   There has been a marked change in the way that tourists travel around India from rail and car to air. This has resulted from the reduction in air fares, a shift from the slow upper class rail carriages to airplanes and a surge in leisure travel, which has been encouraged by the entry of the budget carrier – Air Deccan in 2002. This carrier had 9.3% share of the domestic market in April 2005.

The market   The size of the market in 2004 was estimated at 19 million passengers, which is predicted to grow to 50 million passengers by 2010 according the senior vice president for Asia pacific aviation – Kapil Kaul.

New budget carriers   There has been a growth seen in the budget airlines that are developing their business in the Indian market. The full service carriers which include Jet Airways and Indian Airlines continue to be the biggest players in the domestic airline business but analysts estimate that the budget carriers will continue to grow their market share of the lucrative market to levels of 15–20% by the end of 2006. The new budget carriers include – Air Deccan, Kingfisher and Spicejet.

Air Deccan has grown their fleet size from 18–31 planes and expects to carry 4 million passengers in 2007.

Kingfisher plans to increase their fleet to 12 Airbus 320/319 aircraft.

Spicejet had already introduced seven Boeing 737-700/800 planes in 2005 and has introduced 10 new planes in the later part of 2007.

Conclusion Most of the new players in the budget sector will own 10 or more planes in the next two years. The full service carriers will have to work hard to maintain their market share and may well look to increase their international routes to compensate for lost business at home.

Source: Adapted from Rao (2005).

Case study task and question

Investigate the growth of budget airlines in China.

1 How many budget airlines can you identify and how does the growth compare to that in India?

Case 16

THE RAILWAYS OF INDIA AS TOURIST DESTINATIONS

India offers a number of trains that have become tourist destinations in their own right. These include the following luxury trains:

Palace on Wheels. The Palace on Wheels is an eight-day trip from Delhi taking in Jaipur, Chittaurgarh, Udaipur, Sawai Madhopur, Jaisalmer, Jodphur, Bharatpur and Agra. It is a special tourist train that runs from September to April. The train has 14 air-conditioned carriages and the décor, food and hospitality all exude luxury. There is also a bar, a library and carriages with luxurious bathrooms.

The Royal Orient. The Royal Orient departs from Delhi for an eight-day trip taking in Chittaurgarh, Udaipur, Junagarh, Veraval, Sesangir, Delvada, Palitana, Sarkhei, Ahmedadabad and Jaipur. The train runs between October and March. The train has 13 coaches and saloons. The carriages are all of a deluxe standard and there is a multi-cuisine restaurant.

The Deccan Odyssey. The Deccan Odyssey departs from Mumbai for an eight-day trip visiting Jaigadh, Ganapatipule, Ratnagiri, Sindhudurg, Goa, Pune, Aurangabad, Ajanta and Nashik. The train has 21 coaches and two Presidential suites. There is also a conference hall that transforms into a dance floor at night. Two restaurants serve a range of Indian, Chinese, Continental, Maharashtrian and Goan cuisine. There is also a lounge bar and a spa compartment. A doctor is also available on board.

There are also a number of *toy trains* that operate on narrow gauge tracks as tourist attractions in India. These include:

The Kalka to Shimla line. A variety of trains run on this 96 km track ranging from the Shivalik Express, the Shivalik Palace, and the Shivalik Queen (especially for honeymooners).

The Nilgiri Mountain Railway. This train runs 46 km from Mettupalayam to Ooty over a beautiful twisting track. It offers marvellous views of tea and coffee plantations.

The Darjeeling Hill Railway. Has the narrowest 2-foot gauge. The train is pulled by 100-year old engines and the 86 km route gives unrivalled views of the Himalayan mountain range.

The Matheran Railway. This is an old line that connects Neral to the hill resort of Matteran. The trains run in the day and give lovely views of the surrounding countryside.

The Fairy Queen. This is the oldest running locomotive in the world. The 50-seat train does weekend runs from Delhi to Alwar. The tourists are then transported from Alwar to the tiger sanctuary at Sariska where they stay at the Sariska Palace. Inclusive package fares are available for this trip.

The toy trains can all be booked in Delhi and they have a web page at www.icindia.com/fairy

Source: India Travel Planner (2005).

Case study discussion points

1 Evaluate the importance of history and tradition in the development of tourism business using trains in India.
2 Evaluate the importance of train tourism on the development of India as a tourist destination.

Case 17
PILGRIMAGE SITES IN INDIA

There is a wealth of pilgrimage sites in India and these have been visited over many centuries. The various pilgrimage sites reflect the religious cultures and traditions of India and offer the tourist many spiritual experiences.

The *Hindu* pilgrimage sites are known as tirthas (fords), which are seen to act as a crossing between worldly experiences and divine spheres. A tirtha can be a mountain peak such as Mount Kailasa, the mythical retreat of Shiva, or a river such as the Ganges. There are seven sacred cities in Hindu India that are considered to be the principal pilgrimage centres. These are *Varanasi* and *Hardwar* on the river Ganges, *Ayodhya*, Rama's birthplace, *Mathura*, Krishna's birthplace, *Dwarka*, where Krishna ruled, *Kanchipuram, Tamil Nadu* and *Ujjain*, the site of the Kumbha Mela festival.

The most holy pilgrimage that a Hindu can undertake is to visit the four holy abodes – *Badrinath* in the north, *Puri* in the east, *Rameshwaram* in the south and *Dwarka* in the west.

The Buddhist pilgrimage sites are also important in India and the main sites can be visited in the Buddhist circuit that has been developed to allow the visitor to see the main Buddhist sites and temples. A summary of the tour is as follows:

> *Day 1*   Delhi–Agra
> *Day 2*   Agra–Sankasya–Kanpur–Lucknow
>   Site of temple and sacred place
> *Day 3*   Lucknow–Sravasti
>   Site of various important temples
> *Day 4*   Sravasti–Saunauli Border–Lumbini–Kushinagar
>   Kushinagar is a revered place for Buddhists, with temples and shrines
> *Day 5*   Kushinagar–Kesariya–Vaishali–Patna–Nalanda
>   Site of statues of Buddha
> *Day 6*   Nalanda–Rajgir–Bodhgaya
>   Numerous temples, monasteries and retreats
> *Day 7*   Bodhgava–Sarnath–Varanasi
>   shrines, monasteries and temples

Source: India Travel Planner (2005) and Waterstone (2005).

Case study task and questions

Visit a local travel agent or a travel/tour web site and identify other pilgrimage tours.

1 Who are these aimed at?
2 What type of accommodation and travel arrangements accompany the tours and how much do the tours cost per tourist?
3 Are such tours likely to increase in the future and what is their likely makeup in the future?

Author Index

Subject Index